A QUEER ROMA

It's here and it's queer – popular culture inhabits all our lives, whether it comes in the form of movies or magazines, TV or shopping. *A Queer Romance* brings together critics, writers and artists to debate the possibilities of popular culture for lesbians and gay men.

In a collection that is in-yer-face but never out-to-lunch, the contributors variously visit debates about the gaze to provide a new theory of Queer viewing; discuss texts coded as queer – from lesbian vampires to Hollywood's use of gay codes in mainstream films such as *Top Gun* and *Black Widow*; discover whether Sandra Bernhard is really 'a black man masquerading as a Jewish dominatrix'; consider the sexual and cultural narratives at play in the world of home shopping catalogues; explore the pleasures and perils of gay cultural production, from the radically queer film-making of Monika Treut to the wild world of homocore fanzines, and address the possibilities of texts claiming to be *for* the gay spectator – from pornography 'by women, for women and about women' to 'Out' TV.

The contributors to *A Queer Romance* don't all agree, but, taken together, the collection argues strongly that everyone can have their queer moments.

The editors: **Paul Burston** is the Gay Editor on *Time Out*, Consultant Editor on *Attitude* magazine, and the author of *What Are You Looking At?* (Cassell). Other publications he has written for include the *Guardian*, *Sight and Sound* and *The Modern Review*. **Colin Richardson** is Assistant Editor of *Gay Times*, writes for a number of journals and is the author of the handbook *Equal Opportunities Policy into Practice: Sexuality*. He helped to establish the lesbian and gay film and video distribution company OUT On A Limb Ltd, and is a member of the management committee of GALOP (Gay London Policing).

A QUEER ROMANCE

Lesbians, gay men and popular culture

*Edited by Paul Burston and
Colin Richardson*

London and New York

First published 1995
by Routledge
11 New Fetter Lane, London EC4P 4EE

Simultaneously published in the USA and Canada
by Routledge
29 West 35th Street, New York, NY 10001

Typeset in Times by
Ponting–Green Publishing Services, Chesham, Bucks
Printed in Great Britain by Redwood Books, Trowbridge, Wiltshire

British Library Cataloguing in Publication Data
A catalogue record for this book is available from
the British Library

Library of Congress Cataloging in Publication Data
A queer romance: lesbians, gay men and popular culture/
edited by Paul Burston and Colin Richardson.
p.   cm.
Includes bibliographical references and index.
1. Gays in popular culture.   2. Homosexuality and art.
3. Homosexuality and literature.
4. Homosexuality–Public opinion.
I. Burston, Paul.   II. Richardson, Colin.
HQ76.25.Q38   1994
305.9'0664–dc20   94–10783

ISBN 0–415–09617–0 (hbk)
ISBN 0–415–09618–9 (pbk)

CONTENTS

CONTENTS

Part IV The view from the Other Side

Part V The Mirror Image

LIST OF FIGURES

Every attempt has been made to obtain permission to reproduce copyright material. If any proper acknowledgement has not been made, we would invite copyright holders to inform us of the oversight.

NOTES ON CONTRIBUTORS

Paul Burston is the Gay Editor on *Time Out*, Consultant Editor on *Attitude* magazine, and the author of *What Are You Looking At?* (Cassell). Other publications he has written for include the *Guardian*, *Sight and Sound* and *The Modern Review*.

Steven Drukman has contributed to *The Village Voice, American Theatre*, and *The Advocate* as well as many other journals and periodicals. His interview with Terrence McNally will be in the forthcoming book, *Interviews with American Playwrights* (University of Alabama Press). He teaches and studies at New York University.

Caroline Evans lectures in fashion and cultural studies at Central St Martins College of Art and Design in London. She is co-author of *Women and Fashion: A New Look* (1989) and the author of articles on women and visual culture.

Lorraine Gamman lectures in product and cultural studies at Central St Martins College of Art and Design in London. She is co-editor of *The Female Gaze: Women as Viewers of Popular Culture* (1988) and co-author of *Female Fetishism: A New Look* (1994). She is currently writing *Gone Shopping – the Story of Shirley Pitts, Professional Thief*, to be published by Penguin in 1995, and contributes journalism and reviews to newspapers and journals.

Tanya Krzywinska lectures in film and media studies at the University of North London and Buckinghamshire College, High Wycombe. She is currently working on her Ph.D. thesis, on the subject of hardcore pornography.

Bruce LaBruce is dead and living in Toronto with his pit bull, Cookie.

Z. Isiling Nataf studied Fine Art Film and Film Semiotics at the University of Bridgeport, Connecticut and San Francisco State University. She received a B.A. in Film and Television from the London Institute of Printing and is currently completing an M.A. in Drama: The Process of Production at the University of London, Goldsmiths, where her dissertation topic is 'Producing a Queer Aesthetic in Lesbian Cinema'. In 1986 she made the film *The Mark of Lilith* with Revamp Productions, a short experimental narrative which deconstructs the vampire genre and treats issues of the monstrous feminine and interracial lesbian relationships. She is currently working on a short feature which explores trans-gender subjectivities and experiments with interactive video-disc technology.

Colin Richardson is Assistant Editor of *Gay Times* magazine. He has also contributed articles to *Capital Gay, The Pink Paper, Time Out* and *The New Law Review*. His book, *Equal Opportunities Policy Into Practice: Sexuality* was published by the Independent Theatre Council in 1991. He has made a number of independent videos and one TV programme (*A Plague on You* for BBC Open Space, November 1985). He helped to establish the lesbian and gay film and video distribution company, OUT on a Limb Ltd, and remains a patron of the company. For several years, he has been a member of the management committee of GALOP (Gay London Policing), a project which helps gay people who have been arrested for sexual offences or who have been victims of assault.

Anna Marie Smith is an Assistant Professor in the Department of Govern-ment at Cornell University. A revised version of her Ph.D. thesis, entitled *New Right Discourse on Race and Sexuality, Britain 1968–1990*, will be published by Cambridge University Press in 1994. She is also a former member of OutRage! and Feminists Against Censorship.

Cherry Smyth works in London as a freelance journalist and is the co-curator of the London Lesbian and Gay Film Festival. Her essay on lesbian porn, 'The Pleasure Threshold', was published in *Feminist Review* 34, Spring 1990; and 'Trash Femme', on dykes in queer cinema, in *Sight and Sound*, September 1992. Her book, *Queer Notions*, was published by Scarlett Press in 1992.

Monika Treut is one of Germany's leading independent film-makers. Her first feature film, *Seduction: The Cruel Woman (Verführung: Die Grausame Frau)*, was made in Hamburg in 1984 and released in 1985. Since then, she has released two more features – *Virgin Machine (Die Jungfrauenmaschine)* (1988) and *My Father Is Coming* (1990) – and a collection of documentaries, entitled *Female Misbehaviour* (1992). Her short film, *Taboo Parlour* (1993), was released in 1994 as part of a collection of short films by women film-makers entitled *Erotique*. In 1994, she began the production of her latest feature, *The Virility Factor*, based on the futuristic novel by Robert Merle (*Day of the Dolphin*). Prior to embarking on her film career, Monika Treut studied literature in Marburg/Lahn and wrote her doctoral thesis on the

Marquis de Sade and Leopold von Sacher-Masoch. The thesis has been published in book form as *The Cruel Woman: The Portrayal of Women in de Sade and Sacher-Masoch*. In addition, she has written numerous essays for magazines and books published in Germany, Austria and Holland.

Gregory Woods teaches in the Department of English and Media Studies at Nottingham Trent University. He is the author of *Articulate Flesh: Male Homoeroticism in Modern Poetry* (Yale University Press, 1987) and of a collection of poems, *We Have the Melon* (Carcanet Press, 1992). His essays and reviews on gay culture and on the AIDS epidemic have been published in books and journals in Britain, Italy and the United States. He has been a regular contributor to the gay press in Britain for over a decade, and has also written for the *New Statesman and Society*, the *Times Higher Education Supplement* and the *Times Literary Supplement*.

ACKNOWLEDGEMENTS

Paul Burston and Colin Richardson want to thank the contributors to this book for their enthusiasm and patience; and Rebecca Barden, our long-suffering editor at Routledge, for sticking with us.

Paul Burston would like to thank Gerard Boynton for his keen sense of direction; Caroline Cooper for keeping him on course; William Godwin, Mary and Windsor Stewart for their continued love and support.

Colin Richardson also wants to thank Val Martin for her love and encouragement and for putting up with his moaning; Mark McNestry, Monika Treut, Paul Sigel, Jeremy Clarke, David Smith, Frances Williams, Sandy Andrews, Jenny Wilson and Liz Mansell for the help they gave in so many ways. He also wants to dedicate this book to the memory of his mother, Molly, who died in October, 1992.

INTRODUCTION

Paul Burston and Colin Richardson

'In 1975', wrote Meaghan Morris, 'everything was, oppressively, Political. By 1985, everything has become, obscurely, Cultural.'[1] In 1995, you might be forgiven for thinking that everything is turning suddenly, inexplicably, Queer. Undergraduates are undressing Madonna again, only this time it isn't her feminist credentials they're inspecting, but her attempts to justify her (Queer?) love.

Queer Theory is no more 'about' lesbians and gay men than Women's Studies is 'about' women. Indeed, part of the project of Queer is to attack, as Judith Butler does, the very 'naturalness' of gender and, by extension, the fictions supporting compulsory heterosexuality. By developing a theory of gender as cultural performance, Butler makes the very categories 'heterosexual' and 'homosexual' at least as problematic as feminist theories have made the category 'woman'.[2]

We believe this Queer addition to the tools of critical practice is not only justified, but – dare we say it? – a 'natural' development. In so far as it provides a discipline for exploring the relationships between lesbians, gay men and the culture which surrounds and (for the large part) continues to seek to exclude us, Queer Theory is both 'Political' and 'Cultural': political, because it seeks to expose and problematise the means by which 'sexuality' is reduced to the definitions and relations of gender; cultural, because just about everything we might call Queer Theory concerns itself with the ways in which cultural texts – books, films, television, magazines, etc. – condition understandings of sexuality.

By challenging cultural readings which overlook the dynamic of sexual preference, Queer Theory gives academic credence to something that lesbians and gay men have known all along – that the imagination is, by its very nature, promiscuous; that identification is never simply a matter of believing what you are seeing. By shifting the focus away from the question of what it means to be lesbian or gay within the culture, and onto the various performances of heterosexuality created by the culture, Queer Theory seeks to locate Queerness in places that had previously been thought of as strictly for the straights.

It was with this strategy in mind that we developed the idea for a book of

1

essays exploring how lesbians and gay men might position themselves as spectators of popular culture. Feminist critics have pointed out how Western popular culture is structured as a kind of *Boy's Own Story*. But isn't it time we challenged a theoretical model which privileges gender as the category structuring perspective? Can we identify a specifically 'lesbian' or 'gay' way of looking, and if so, is it the exclusive preserve of people who call themselves 'lesbian' or 'gay'? Equally, can we identify a particular 'lesbian' or 'gay' way of self-representation which is fundamentally different from the ways in which homosexuality and homosexuals are imagined by hetero-sexuals? One double-edged question neatly summarises the themes of this book: to adapt the title of a 'Queer Film and Video Conference' held in New York in 1987, *how do we look?*[3]

In order to answer these (and other) questions, the contributors to this book have deployed a variety of critical approaches which mostly speak for themselves. However, a number of the essays refer to some key areas of theory which, we feel, it would be unwise to assume will be familiar to every reader. So, for the sake of clarity, to provide the reader with an overview of the book's theoretical framework and to minimise repetition, we set out here a short summary of some of the major concepts which underlie much of what is to follow.

> There is a true saying, 'That the spectator oft times sees more than the gamester.'
>
> *(Oxford English Dictionary)*[4]

Psychoanalytical theory has, arguably, been the single most important influence upon the development of critical approaches to popular culture. Given the part that psychoanalysis has played in pathologising homosexuality and homosexuals, it may not seem to have much to offer the lesbian or gay critic. However, as Jeffrey Weeks has argued, Freudianism is open to a wide range of interpretations, not all of them inimical to lesbians and gay men and some positively brimming with potential.[5] Equally, a number of feminist scholars have successfully used Freudian concepts – and particularly the contributions to the development of post-Freudian thinking made by the French philosopher, Jacques Lacan – to challenge many of society's assump-tions about femininity and sexuality.[6]

Psychoanalysis seeks to uncover the unconscious mechanisms by which personality and behaviour are shaped as we move from passive infancy to active adulthood. Freud, the father of psychoanalysis, was the first person to propose a rigorous theory of child development which encompassed biology but which was particularly concerned to discover how *outside* influences impinge upon the developing human child; a theory of *nurture* more than of *nature*. New born infants, Freud argued, are little more than bundles of 'instincts' and 'drives' (including sexual 'drives'), innate, 'natural' feelings which determine their every action. But as they grow, they learn to modify or 'repress' their basic instincts into behaviours which are acceptable to those around them. For example, a hungry infant screams until it is fed; a hungry adult will – usually – find more socially acceptable (and quieter) ways of satisfying its hunger.

But while repression leads to the development of the 'civilised' person – one who can function in society – it also creates within each person an *unconscious*, perhaps best understood as a pool of repressed desires. Freud believed that the unconscious gives itself away in the speech and actions of individuals. Thus, psychoanalysis is to a large extent about revealing and understanding that which is hidden, the main reason why it is such a useful tool for cultural criticism.

Repression begins in earnest as soon as the infant starts to develop a sense of itself as an independent being. Initially, the child is almost inseparable from its mother; she is the key figure in its life, responsible for the basic necessities such as nourishment. Then, as the child becomes less dependent, other figures enter the picture – the father, other adults and children. From these disparate sources, the child learns what is expected of it and what it can expect from life.

Freud theorised the process of the child's break from its mother as the Oedipus complex, a time when the infant's sex and sexuality become central to its sense of self, its subjectivity. It is at this point that girls and boys realise that they are physically different from one another, a realisation which, Freud believed, had profoundly different psychic consequences for the two sexes. In short, it is through the Oedipus complex that biological *sex* is translated into the understandings and performances of *gender*. For the boy comes the discovery that his possession of a penis translates into the possession of social power; though accompanying that knowledge is the fear that his power may be taken away, that he may one day be *castrated* as, he imagines, the girl already has been. The girl, on the other hand, rather than realising she has her own distinctive set of genitals, Freud argued, instead realises that she *does not have* a penis: she has *already* been castrated. The realisation of this loss brings with it a sense of inferiority for which Freud invented the concept of 'penis envy'.[7]

Initially, the child lives through the Oedipus complex in relation to its parents. Girls identify with their mothers and fall in love with (or become sexually attracted to) their fathers. Boys, however, identify with their fathers while simultaneously fearing them as rivals for their mother's affections (or so Freudian theory has it).[8] But as the child grows, it learns to transfer its feelings for its parents on to others; it becomes open to other influences, including popular culture, which allow it to make sense of its experiences and feelings, in part by reliving (and maybe reworking) the Oedipal moment.

Popular culture is important because it allows the individual simply to watch, to spectate without having to participate. Freudian psychoanalysis suggests that merely looking can be a profound experience both for the looker

3

and the looked-at. Three mechanisms first delineated by Freud are of particular relevance here: *ego-identification*, the identification with an image seen (if the image is of oneself, then Freud talked of *narcissistic* identification); *scopophilia*, the derivation of sexual pleasure through looking; and *fetishism*, the investment of material objects, including parts of the body, with sexual properties. All of these mechanisms are triggered by the various forms of popular culture.

Lacan's importance to theories of spectatorship stems largely from his formulation of the *Mirror Phase* as a turning point in the formation of individual subjectivity. This is the stage in a child's development – some time between six and eighteen months – when the infant first becomes aware of itself as a separate and whole entity. Hitherto, Lacan speculated, a baby is unable to differentiate between itself and its mother. Further, it does not have a clear sense of its bodily unity, experiencing life instead as a series of disconnected events and sensations. As Sandy Flitterman-Lewis explains, the child 'perceives itself as a mass of disconnected, fragmentary movements. It has no sense that the fist that moves is connected to the arm and body, and so forth'.[9]

But there comes a point when a child first recognises an image of itself as a unified and discrete being. The child is usually delighted to see itself in this way though at the same time, Lacan argued, it cannot fully reconcile the mirror image with its own fragmentary self-image. To some extent, it views the mirror image as 'other': an ideal image of wholeness up to which it can never quite live. None the less, the child identifies with the image and, as Flitterman-Lewis remarks, 'This process forms the basis for all later identifications, which are imaginary in principle. Simply put, in order for communication to occur at all, we must at some level be able to say to each other, "I know how you feel"' (Allen 1992: 208). The mirror metaphor is thus a particularly suggestive one for cultural critics, the idea being that culture, in one way or another, holds up a mirror to life, reflecting an image we recognise as 'other' yet also somehow connected to us.

The Mirror Phase marks the child's entry into what Lacan called the Symbolic Order (roughly equivalent to Freud's Oedipal moment) which is represented by the figure of the father. As it breaks from the mother, the child leaves behind the world of the Imaginary – where the distinction, 'me/you', is blurred – and begins to work out its relationship with the wider world of societal and familial relations and to develop a sense of itself as 'I'. This process is marked by the acquisition of language, the system of sounds, gestures and symbols which will enable it both to begin to understand what things mean and to make its own meanings. This is essential for the child to become fully human, to be able to participate in the world at large and to understand its place therein – once again, a very different experience for boys and girls.

Laura Mulvey's trail-blazing essay, 'Visual Pleasure and Narrative

Cinema' (1975),[10] was one of the first scholarly attempts to explain how this difference might affect how we look at popular cultural forms. In effect, Mulvey argued that mainstream Hollywood cinema primarily sets out to satisfy the unconscious desires of men. She drew attention to the three 'looks' which, she contended, structure the cinema-goer's response to most films. First, there is the look of the camera itself. Mulvey argued that this was inherently voyeuristic and 'male', especially as most cinematographers and directors are men. Second, there is the relay of looks between the characters within the film. Here Mulvey suggested that films tend to be edited in such a way that the male characters do most of the looking while the female characters are generally looked at, doing little more than reacting to the male gaze. In other words, men are the (active) subjects of most films, women the (passive) objects. Finally, there is the look of the spectator which is directed by the first two looks. Since the spectator can only see what the camera shows, Mulvey concluded that spectators are forced to identify with the male gaze.

In Mulvey's theory, the female spectator must either adopt a 'male' viewing position (by a process she rather unfortunately termed 'transvestism') or she must be assumed to derive no pleasure from going to the cinema. This rather starkly manichean hypothesis has been heavily criticised down the years. Mulvey herself addressed some of the problems in her later essay, 'Afterthoughts on "Visual Pleasure and Narrative Cinema" inspired by *Duel in the Sun*'.[11] None the less, by theorising different and opposed spectator positions – 'male' and 'female' – Mulvey stimulated a wealth of feminist writings concerning the particular meanings of popular culture for women.[12] This book takes that tradition several steps further.

If men and women react differently to popular culture, then, surely, sexual identity – as much a psychic phenomenon as 'maleness' or 'femaleness' – cannot be ignored if we are trying to make sense of popular culture and its likely effects on those who 'consume' it? We do not propose a monolithic lesbian or gay identity, still less a single queer identity. But nor do we propose that lesbians and gay men see things the same way as everyone else. At the very least, belonging to a sexual minority lends one an outsider's viewpoint which, though not entirely predictable in its consequences, does make for different ways of seeing. The contributors to this collection each have their own take on popular culture. They don't all agree with one another but, taken together, their insights represent an expansion of the field of vision.[13]

We begin with three essays which find answers to the question, is there a lesbian or gay gaze? Caroline Evans and Lorraine Gamman are principally concerned in their essay with the question which Laura Mulvey raised, namely do women look at things differently from men and, if so, how? Lorraine Gamman has been here before. In 1988, she co-edited a collection of essays on women and popular culture which is the nearest equivalent to this book.[14] Since then, developments in Queer Theory have prompted her and Caroline Evans to regard theories of the female gaze in a new light. In their essay, 'The Gaze Revisited, or Reviewing Queer Viewing', they start with a comprehensive overview of developments in cultural theory, and conclude that a 'queer gaze' is not limited to those who define themselves as 'queer' or 'lesbian' or 'gay', but that everyone has their 'queer moments'.

Z. Isiling Nataf applies psychoanalytic theory to the cinema to come at the female gaze from another angle. She seeks to make 'whiteness' strange in order to get at the pleasures and problems which mainstream cinema can offer the black lesbian spectator. 'Perhaps', she argues, 'lesbians are such big fans of popular cinema despite its active hostility to homosexuality and its racism and sexism because somewhere the mechanisms of the classic narrative film reflect parallel structures in the construction of lesbian desire.'

Finally, in this first section – our theoretical 'Queer Framework' – Steven Drukman reworks Mulvey's theories of spectatorship to arrive at a theory of the gay male gaze. Where Mulvey talked of 'man as the maker of meaning, woman as the bearer of the look', Drukman suggests that the gay man can be both maker of meaning and bearer of the look. To test out his ideas, he looks at MTV (Music Television), the US station which started as a promotional channel for record companies, playing music videos back-to-back, and which is now something of a worldwide phenomenon. Analysing videos by Madonna and George Michael, he looks at the ways in which pop performers can (more or less) knowingly invite the gay gaze and at how the gay spectator can impose meanings of his own upon even the most unpromising material.

The next section of the book is entitled 'Queer Genres?' We were interested to discover whether there were any particular forms of popular culture which were more open to lesbian and gay readings than others. In her essay, 'La Belle Dame Sans Merci?', Tanya Krzywinska argues convincingly that the female vampire movie does indeed offer much to the lesbian spectator. She uses Lacan's mirror metaphor in a highly original way to analyse the figure of the female vampire, a creature which, according to legend, casts no reflection in the glass. Contrary to many feminist writers, Krzywinska does find the lesbian vampire to be a seductive monster and the vampire film one of the only mainstream cinematic genres to allow the explicit depiction of lesbian desire.

In the 1980s, masculinity and femininity underwent parallel transformations in the cinema but with very different results. *American Gigolo* (Paul Shrader, 1980) was one of the first Hollywood films to feminise the male body (in this case, Richard Gere's) by objectifying it and holding it up to be looked at. The buddy movie, *Top Gun* (Tony Scott, 1986), took this a step further by having men gaze longingly at each other within the film at the same time as offering their bodies for the spectator's gratification. However, Paul Burston argues in 'Just A Gigolo?' that these films are not simply 'for the boys', for as they actively court the gay gaze, so they pointedly disavow it.

The same is not quite true for the tough female films which emerged in the 1980s, triggered by Sigourney Weaver's portrayal of the archetypal phallic mother, Ripley, in *Alien* (Ridley Scott, 1979). Cherry Smyth analyses Bob Rafelson's undervalued 1987 feature, *Black Widow*, in which Teresa Russell's *femme fatale* is pursued by Debra Winger's downbeat, butch gumshoe, to discover the possibilities and the limits of female transgression. Her essay, 'The Transgressive Sexual Subject', deploys psychoanalytic concepts to assess the significance of a movie in which the sexually charged looks exchanged between the two female protagonists threaten to unpick its careful heterosexual underpinnings. Smyth argues that *Black Widow* offers many pleasures to the lesbian spectator, despite its conventional framework.

'Masquerade', the third section of the book, answers the question 'How do we look?' in another way. Dressing-up is central to the outward manifestation of personal identity. Clothes maketh both man and woman. Or, as Gregg Woods puts it in his essay, 'We're Here, We're Queer, and We're Not Going Catalogue Shopping': 'I shop, therefore I am.' Woods looks at how mail order catalogues sell an idea of personal style, arriving early on at the conclusion that: 'It is clear that we must add a new concept to our psychoanalytic lexicon: the phenomenon of catalogophilia.' He examines the strategies by which mail order companies market clothes and other lifestyle accessories and discovers evidence of a 'semiotic panic about homosexuality'. For, as Frank Mort has written, 'Male sexuality is conjured up *through the commodity.*'

The fourth section of the book gives voice to two film-makers who, in different ways, are working out ways of picturing homosexuality. The two chapters grouped together as 'The View from the Other Side' seek to understand the weight of expectations upon lesbian and gay artists. It's all very well criticising the images produced by the cultural mainstream but at some point we have to get our hands dirty and have a go ourselves.

Monika Treut is arguably the foremost lesbian film-maker in the world. A German with a creative fascination for the US, her films play from Taipei to Sydney, Hong Kong to Helsinki. They can even be seen in the UK. In 'An Outlaw at Home', an interview with Colin Richardson, she talks about her work, the expectations upon her and her own means of resistance and survival.

Bruce LaBruce is Canada's leading underground film-maker, a not entirely enviable position as he explains in 'The Wild, Wild World of Fanzines: Notes from a Reluctant Pornographer'. Self-proclaimed founder of 'queercore' – a mixture of punk attitude with gay style – he is now being criticised for selling the movement out, simply for making films which have achieved a degree of commercial success.

The last two chapters of the book, grouped together under the heading, 'The Mirror Image', are, in a sense, a response to the previous two. What is the lesbian or gay spectator to make of work produced by other lesbians and gay men, especially when it explicitly claims to be *for* her or him?

In '"By Women, for Women and about Women" Rules OK? The Impossibility of Visual Soliloquy', Anna Marie Smith argues that evidence of lesbian cultural production is not sufficient to make a piece of work acceptable to a lesbian spectator. She looks at the new pornography that is taking shape – pornography 'by women, for women and about women' – to consider whether this makes sense as a guarantee 'that nothing which is not "womanly" is involved in the production/consumption process'. And she looks closely at Madonna's *Justify My Love* video, itself a mini porn scenario, to find out whether the absence of such a guarantee actually matters.

Out on Tuesday was billed as the world's first television series by and for lesbians and gay men. Since it first went on air in Britain in 1989, it appears to have set a standard by which other lesbian or gay programmes are judged. Yet, in 'TVOD – The Never-Bending Story', Colin Richardson argues that *Out* (as it became after two series) was only *for* us in that it saw its mission as the presentation of the acceptable face of homosexuality to the world at large. In this way, it was more concerned with telling comforting stories than with making good or challenging television.

A final thought: the popular form which dominates this collection – and which in turn hogs most of the limelight in the field of cultural theory – is cinema. However, we hope that this book encourages other writers to apply the insights Queer Theory has to offer to more neglected forms: children's books, women's magazines, detective fiction, romantic novels, the sex-and-shopping 'bonkbusters' so (perversely) popular in Thatcher's Britain, TV soap operas, children's TV, sex education videos, game shows, theatre, stand-up comedy, to name but a few.

But first, read on . . .

NOTES

1 Meaghan Morris, *The Pirate's Fiancée: Feminism Reading Postmodernism*, Verso, London, 1988, p. 177.
2 Judith Butler, *Gender Trouble*, Routledge, London 1990. Similar points have been made by a number of other writers, for example Eve Kosofsky Sedgwick in *The Epistemology of the Closet*, University of California Press, Berkley, 1990.
3 See Bad Object-Choices (ed.), *How Do I Look?*, Bay Press, Seattle 1991.
4 The date of this saying is given by the *OED* as 1645. However, a very similar phrase can be found in *Of Followers and Friends* by Francis Bacon (1561–1626): 'Lookers-on many times see more than gamesters.' Whether Bacon himself made the saying up or was simply the first to record it is not a matter we can settle.
5 Jeffrey Weeks, *Sexuality and its Discontents*, Routledge, London, 1985, notably chapter 6, 'Sexuality and the Unconscious'.
6 See, for example, Juliet Mitchell, *Psychoanalysis and Feminism*, Penguin, Harmondsworth, 1975.
7 Thus demonstrating why orthodox Freudianism poses such problems for feminists. For what the theory of the Oedipus complex does, among other things, is to suggest that the secondary social status of women is somehow natural or inevitable and that a healthy female psychology requires an acceptance of that fact.
8 Thus demonstrating why Freudianism is just as problematic for lesbians and gay men, for despite his belief in the innate bisexuality of human beings, Freud also

saw homosexuality in adults as a kind of neurosis. This is the constant tension in Freud's writings – between the radical possibilities in his ideas of infant (poly) sexuality and his capitulation, as an analyst treating real patients, to society's norms. He understood, on the one hand, that bisexuality was 'natural'; but on the other, when he sought to treat adult homosexuals, he began to talk of their 'immature' adjustment, mistaking the ideology of compulsory heterosexuality for a 'natural' or 'normal' human trait. None the less, though Freud himself took the easy way out, his ideas can be developed in other directions.

9 Sandy Flitterman-Lewis, 'Psychoanalysis, Film and Television' in Robert C. Allen (ed.), *Channels of Discourse, Reassembled*, Routledge, London, 1992, p. 208.

10 Reprinted in Laura Mulvey, *The Sexual Subject: A Screen Reader in Sexuality*, Routledge, London, 1992.

11 Reprinted in Laura Mulvey, *Visual and Other Pleasures*, Macmillan, Basingstoke, 1989.

12 See, for example, Lorraine Gamman and Margaret Marshment (eds), *The Female Gaze*, The Women's Press, London, 1988.

13 Vision, of course, is not the only sense. Sound, in particular, is a crucial element of many popular cultural forms yet its impact and influence remain under-theorised. This is perhaps because, as Elizabeth Grosz notes,

> Of all the senses, vision remains the one which most readily confirms the separation of subject from object. Vision performs a distancing function, leaving the looker unimplicated in or uncontaminated by its object. With all of the other senses, there is a contiguity between subject and object, if not an internalisation and incorporation by the subject. The tactile, for example, keeps the toucher in direct contact with the object touched; taste further implicates the subject, for the object must be ingested, internalised in order for it to be accessible to taste. As Sartre recognised, the look is the domain of domination; it provides access to its object without necessarily being in contact with it. Moreover, the visual is the most amenable of the senses to spatialisation. . . . The tactile, auditory, and olfactory sense organs depend on some spatial representation, which, in our culture if not in all civilizations, is hierarchically subordinate to the primacy of sight.
>
> (Grosz 1990: 38)

14 Gamman and Marshment, op. cit.

REFERENCES

Allen, Robert C. (ed.) (1992) *Channels of Discourse Reassembled – Television and Contemporary Criticism*, London: Routledge.

Grosz, Elizabeth (1990) *Jacques Lacan – A Feminist Introduction*, London: Routledge.

Part I

A
QUEER
FRAMEWORK

1

THE GAZE REVISITED, OR REVIEWING QUEER VIEWING

Caroline Evans and Lorraine Gamman

INTRODUCTION

Over the last ten years or so many critical reflections on what has been called 'the gaze' have been published and we are not the only writers who have grappled with the complexity of the theory.[1] Many debates about the gaze have been dogged by factionalism, theoretical impasse, and a kind of orthodoxy which this article hopes to review and challenge. It is our feeling that many writers have demanded too much of the gaze, and that it has almost become a cliché. Often when individuals use the term the 'male gaze' they mean nothing more complex than the way men look at women or, worse, they refer to the male gaze as a metaphor for 'patriarchy'. For example, in Figure 1, the graffiti

1 Playboy graffiti (Séan O'Mara)

13

slogan 'resist the male gaze' is coupled with a playboy motif. We liked the graffiti but we felt the ideas underlying it were a troubling sign of something else. Such usage undermines complex argument and produces crass and essentialist models of social relationships. Primary texts about the gaze were originally much more sophisticated. But even they have proved inadequate as a tool for analysing the complex ways in which individuals look at, and identify with a range of contemporary images, beyond cinema, from art to ads, fashion mags to pop promos.

In this article we want to shift the course of the debate about the gaze by engaging with what Constantine Giannaris has described as 'genderfuck'.[2] By importing some queer notions into the world of critical theory it may be possible to begin to acknowledge many perverse but enjoyable relations of looking. Our reasoning is not only that today's complex visual iconography requires the sort of theory that can comprehend it, but that previous models of the gaze have produced some very one-dimensional accounts of viewing relations.

This article is therefore written in two sections. The first section reviews gaze theory, including important work which has addressed gay and lesbian spectators, but argues that even this work is flawed by the essentialism of the terms that frame the debate. The second section explains why 'adding on' or including the experiences of gay and lesbian spectators is not enough. Instead, we should be problematising the very categories of identity themselves. We go on to locate ideas about queer looks with reference to an anti-essentialist model of gender (and other) identifications.

The first section implicitly draws on the work of two theorists often thought incompatible, Michel Foucault and Jacques Lacan. Instead of making a choice between the two we have opted to act like smash and grab artists and help ourselves to concepts from both. In the second section we have also helped ourselves to the ideas of Roland Barthes. Rather than trying to negotiate a monogamous relationship between Foucault and Lacan, we thought instead a *ménage à trois* might be productive and that promiscuous relations, even group sex, with Barthes might show the way forward. It is not that this orgy of theory produces any single cohesive model but that none of the models are adequate on their own. We see the only position to take theoretically is to oscillate between all the theories, to be eclectic and make the best of the recognition that the new grand narratives are no better than the old ones in explaining everything.

GAZE THEORY REVISITED

The gaze: two models, some preliminary observations

'The gaze' has been theorised primarily in two ways and to some extent both models deal with questions raised about objectification. First, Michel

Foucault has discussed the 'panopticon', the perfect prison, where the controlling gaze is used at all times as surveillance. This model posits a relationship between power and knowledge.[3] Second, film theorists have used psychoanalysis to formulate a cinematic gaze in terms of gender which functions on the level of representation, rather than in terms of other types of cultural practice.[4] Here, film theorists have raised questions about the viewer's identificatory experiences in relation to what is seen/read. They argue the viewer's identificatory experiences are constituted exclusively by the visual text in question. One of the things this section tries to do is to challenge this 'exclusivity' of definition by the visual text through looking at context (although in the second section we do return to issues about the way texts produce meanings).

Cinematic theories have been applied to many types of visual representation, from high art to popular culture, even though Laura Mulvey's influential writing on the gaze never claimed to explain more than spectatorship of 'classic narrative cinema'.[5]

In this convergence the distinction was lost between cultural activities (such as cruising, cottaging and even market place shopping) which may involve a reciprocal exchange of looks, and cinematic viewing which does not. Most of the theory conceptualises the gaze in relation to representations of people and not inanimate or 'natural' things. Hence it is posited as constitutive of social or psychic relations. Neither model (the Foucauldian or the film theorists') posits the gaze as a mutual one. Of course the cinematic image is an object and therefore cannot look back, so obviously we need to distinguish questions of representation from other cultural practices. But in some writing this distinction has been elided. When individuals cruise each other on the street, or in clubs, the mutual exchange of glances is sexualised and often reciprocal; of course this mutuality is not the case with cinematic viewing.

Our reasons for writing this article stem from mutual discussions about gaze theory and its relevance in teaching critical theory and visual culture to art students. We both found that these ideas about the gaze didn't help us very much to think about the complex ways images resonate in contemporary culture. This is because when people use the term the 'male gaze' they often mean nothing more complex than the way men look at women, and notions about the ubiquitous male gaze often go unquestioned and unspecified.[6] Student essays frequently use the term 'the male gaze' as shorthand both for the voyeurism implicit in spectatorship (for example, when looking at paintings) and for the idea that women are objectified in Western culture (advertising and porn are often used as examples). It seems as if these ideas about the gaze have entered academic language without students necessarily having read the primary texts which engendered the terms. Also most students seem unable to comprehend from their reading the distinction between looking and gazing. This is not surprising, because the theoretical material on the 'gaze' also fails frequently to distinguish between the look (associated with the eye) and the gaze (associated with the phallus). Indeed, there is much conflation in discussion about 'the look' and 'the gaze'. To clarify the differences between the terms, requires a 'return to Lacan'. Lacan posits the gaze as a transcendental ideal – omniscient and omnipresent – whereas he suggests the eye (and the look) can never achieve this status (although it may aspire to do so).[7] Indeed, Carol J. Clover argues that 'the best the look can hope for is to pass itself off as the gaze, and to judge from film theory's concern with the "male gaze" . . . it sometimes succeeds'.[8] Elizabeth Grosz has argued:

> Many feminists . . . have conflated the look with the gaze, mistaking a perceptual mode with a mode of desire. When they state baldly that "vision" is male, the look is masculine, or the visual is a phallocentric mode of perception, these feminists confuse a perceptual facility open to both sexes . . . with sexually coded positions of desire within visual (or any other perceptual) functions . . . vision is not, cannot be, masculine . . . rather, certain ways of using vision (for example, to objectify) may confirm and help produce patriarchal power relations.[9]

One of the reasons students may be confused is because gaze theory is so difficult and it has been applied differently by different academic writers. Therefore we felt it necessary, in the next few sections, to go back and review those texts which have been influential, directly or indirectly, in conceptualising the gaze, starting with the male gaze.

Both in and out of college the phrase 'the objectifying male gaze' has become a cliché used to identify the way men look at women, almost as a metaphor of patriarchal relations. Within such clichés there is no space to conceptualise queer relations of looking, or to explain changes in some contexts where women's experience is not completely defined by patriarchal discourse. Nor is there any space to talk about the implications of a fashion system which encourages women to take pleasure from images of other women, or an advertising system which uses eroticised images of men to sell products to both sexes.

But advertising cannot be construed simply as a 'determining' discourse because there is always resistance to consumer marketing. At the time of writing this article graffiti appeared all over a British advertising campaign for Vauxhall Corsa cars in which supermodels were photographed, supposedly with irony, draped glamorously over cars in the classic 'woman-as-object' pose. At the same time a piece of spray-canned graffiti appeared on the wall opposite the London college in which we work which said 'resist the male gaze' over a Bunny Club/Playboy motif (see Figure 1). Whether this graffiti was 'real' or a spoof slogan was unclear. Certainly, in a college where young female students often say 'I'm not a feminist but . . .' it was heartening to read a feminist slogan imprinted on the masonry. Yet there is a negative implication to this graffiti if it means, as we suspect it does, that ill-formed ideas about 'the male gaze' have simply replaced the radical feminist model of 'patriarchy'.[10]

Woman as object – feminist critiques

The most familiar article which refers to ideas about 'the male gaze' is without question Laura Mulvey's 'Visual Pleasure and Narrative Cinema' (1975).[11] But even before she wrote it, many similar ideas about the way women are objectified in Western culture had been raised by feminist critics. Simone de Beauvoir in *The Second Sex*[12] is perhaps the first feminist writer to use the idea of woman as 'other'.[13] De Beauvoir describes at length how she learned to appraise her adolescent self through male eyes during the processes of adornment. As Jane Gaines has pointed out, in de Beauvoir's writings on this subject 'there is a premonition of the theory of female representation as directed towards the male surveyor-owner.'[14] Later texts from the second wave Women's Movement, such as Betty Friedan's *The Feminine Mystique* (1963),[15] Sheila Rowbotham's *Woman's Consciousness, Man's World* (1973)[16] and the anthology of feminist writings from the 1970s edited by Robin Morgan, *Sisterhood is Powerful*,[17] all in some way make the association between women's appearance via fashion, cosmetics and body shape and women's social inequality and oppression. These books have in common not only an anti-consumer strategy but also the notion that there is some place outside the fashion system for women   a point many subsequent feminist critics have rejected.[18] However, the vast majority of feminists do hold on to the idea that women are objectified and this is connected with the experience of being looked at.

John Berger

John Berger's collaborative book and four TV programmes, *Ways of Seeing*, which appeared in 1972, were very influential in introducing similar ideas about women's oppression through objectification to the debate.[19] Although Berger does not use the phrase 'the male gaze' or psychoanalytic concepts, his analysis has much in common with Laura Mulvey's subsequent attempt to raise questions about the objectification of women. We start with him because in *Ways of Seeing* he was strongly influenced by feminism in his discussion of women's objectification through *representation*. Berger, like Mulvey, cites representation as a basis for political struggle and cultural intervention and suggests that the perspective of cultural forms like art are not free of social ideologies.

In *Ways of Seeing* Berger argues that oil paintings in the European tradition privilege unequal relations of looking. By introducing the terms 'surveyor' and 'surveyed'[20] to explain the way oil paintings position those who survey them as active, Berger begins to discuss the way women are objectified in the representations of Western culture.

Berger's thesis about who owns perspective is based on a reading of the way capital influences everything, even viewing relations. He says, 'It reduced everything to the equality of objects. Everything became exchangeable because everything became a commodity.'[21] Whereas Marx had argued that the commodity form produced fetishised relations between men, Berger extends his argument to explain how commodity fetishism has impacted upon relations of looking. He also suggests that relations of class, colonisation and gender become codified in the image-making process. Edward Said has subsequently made similar observations about the impact of colonial relations on visual and other discourses about the Orient.[22]

In *Orientalism* (1978) Said shows how Europeans and Americans have seen Eastern and Arab culture, not as it is, but 'through their own eyes'.[23] Said argues that Westerners are 'spectators' who see the Orient from a privileged point of view, one which allows them to construct representations of the Orient as a mysterious, occulted, fragile and static place. By mobilising Foucault's ideas about discourse,[24] Said has raised questions about the power relations underlying various representations – in literature, architecture, fine art and film – of the Orient. Hence, Berger and Said have in common the desire to make visible the invisible power relations in art and other cultural forms. Both Berger and Said find 'unequal' relations of looking reproduced everywhere.

Unlike Said, however, Berger has no model of 'discourse' to explain power relations. Instead his account is limited by a rather crude Marxist reading which places social values above aesthetic values.[25] Nevertheless, despite its analytical shortcomings,[26] Berger's account is particularly clear in explaining how images, and the codes and conventions which govern them, feature unequal gender relations of looking. And he is also clear about how these relations affect personal, as well as cultural, definitions of masculinity and femininity. In 1972 Berger could argue: 'Men look at women. Women watch themselves being looked at.'[27] He went on to explain that in our culture the spectator is 'usually assumed to be male' because:

> to be born a woman is to be born, within an allotted and confined space, into the keeping of men. The social presence of women has developed as a result of their ingenuity in living under such tutelage within such a limited space. But this has been at the cost of a woman's self being split into two. A woman must continually watch herself. She is almost continually accompanied by her own image of herself. Whilst she is walking across a room or whilst she is weeping at the death of her father, she can scarcely avoid envisaging herself walking or weeping. From earliest childhood she has been taught and persuaded to survey herself continually.[28]

Berger explains how power inequalities, deriving chiefly from the economic and ideological effect of capital, operate to impact on relations between the sexes and position women as objects and men as subjects. He argues that gender relations and relations of looking are constructed by the commodity form. Further, he asserts that the 'ideal' spectator is always assumed to be male and the image of woman is designed to flatter him'.[29]

What Berger does not do is use the word 'gaze' (although, as mentioned already, he does use the word 'spectator'), nor does he have a concrete model of how these visual relations work upon the unconscious, except as an act of power, an overall effect of processes of commodification. It is Laura Mulvey who formally introduces ideas about the 'gaze' and the 'unconscious' to the debate some three years later, although clearly Berger's work has been formative upon feminist thinking.

Michel Foucault

Berger's work does implicitly contain a model of 'power' which is connected to ideas about consumer fetishism and the operations of capital, but it is a Marxist model of power 'from above'. Foucault's model is somewhat different in that it is diffused throughout all social classes and it is not purely economic. Foucault aligns knowledge with power. Yet when referring to the 'male spectator' Berger does seem to be implicitly addressing similar ideas about 'discourse', which Catherine Belsey defines as follows:

> A *discourse* is a domain of language-use, a particular way of talking (and writing and thinking). A discourse involves certain shared assumptions which appear in the formulations that characterise it. This discourse of common sense is quite distinct, for instance, from the discourse of modern physics, and some of the formulations of the one may be expected to conflict with the formulations of the other. Ideology is *inscribed in* discourse in the sense that it is literally written or spoken *in it*; it is not a separate element which exists independently in some free-floating realm of 'ideas' and is subsequently embodied in words, but a way of thinking, speaking, experiencing.[30]

Foucault has suggested that such discourses regulate power/knowledge/perspectives and produce:

> An inspecting gaze, a gaze which each individual under its weight will end by interiorising to the point that he (sic) is his own overseer; each individual thus exercising the surveillance over, and against, himself. A superb formula, power exercised continuously.'[31]

Foucault's discussion also refers to the panopticon, where prisoners learn to internalise their supervisors' inspecting gaze. The discussion about the way discourses of power culminate in effect to assure 'internalisation' of specific values by individuals, relates to the experiences of more than just prisoners. There are similarities between Foucault's analysis of the public spectacle of the body[32] and Guy Debord's reading of the way consumer society relies on spectacle to graft social relations and social values onto things.[33] But Foucault's reading goes further and explains the internalisation of the idea of spectacle in terms of discipline imposed on docile bodies.[34] Foucault suggests that we all internalise this control as, for example, when we agree to submit to work to timetables or when soldiers engage in military drilling and parading. Frantz Fanon has made similar observations about internalisation, in particular the way self-hatred via racism is taken on through definitions which negatively frame experience.[35] The same point could be made about the internalisation of homophobia by some gay men and lesbian women as well as the way oppression is internalised by other groups.

Foucault's discussion of the way prisoners learn to internalise oppressive discourses, and may be appellated[36] by such discourses, is also appropriate to describe the experience of many women. In particular the processes that inform the subjectivity of women who experience themselves as more visible (like the prisoner being watched), and learn to appraise themselves through male eyes, seem comparable to us. This is because women in Western culture continue to experience more social 'surveillance' and objectification than men. This point about the oppressive way women often survey themselves is made specifically by Sandra Lee Bartky, who applied this Foucauldian model to the female experience of being looked at. She argues that 'a panoptical male connoisseur resides within the consciousness of most women'.[37] This point about self-appraisal and objectification is also increasingly experienced by gay men, who have used the term 'body fascism'. It seems that the gay fashion for bare torsos and body building puts men on display in ways that can be experienced as oppressive.

In brief, Foucault gives us a model with which we can talk about the objectification of both women and men without drawing on psychoanalysis. This theoretical writing is very useful but offers an inadequate account of desire underlying sexualised looking. Although we are critical of some of the applications of psychoanalysis in Laura Mulvey's approach we nevertheless feel psychoanalysis does give us a way of talking about desire and fantasy. Perhaps it is not enough to say that the social subject is merely an effect of discourse because most individuals feel they are agents of their own desire and have feelings that are unique. While we recognise that all subjects are constructed, we also feel that fantasy has a relationship to 'the real'. Such feelings of desire could be explained with reference to what Judith Butler has described as 'constitutive discourses'.[38] However, it is only psychoanalysis that provides a model to formulate questions about agency and desire at all. It is within this psychoanalytic framework that one can talk about emotional situations or social contexts which produce instabilities which may disturb many things, including gender performance and gender identifications.

Laura Mulvey

Foucault's central thesis is that power lies at the root of the gaze. A psychoanalytic perspective shifts the emphasis onto the idea of gendered power relations (specifically 'phallic power'). The principal contribution of accounts of the gaze which incorporate psychoanalytic theory, primarily since Laura Mulvey applied the ideas of Freud and Lacan, has been to introduce consideration of the gendered 'unconscious' to the debate in relation to the Oedipus complex. In 'Visual Pleasure and Narrative Cinema'[39] Mulvey suggests that unequal gendered relations of looking are a universal effect of the way men acquire sexual identities and resolve castration anxiety.

Published at a time when women's objectification by men was a crucial issue for many feminists, her analysis of cinematic codes drew on psychoanalysis as a feminist strategem and a way of theorising how sexual difference is culturally, but not merely sociologically, constructed. Implicit in Mulvey's model of the gaze, therefore, are questions of gendered identity, as well as 'sexual looking', although it must be noted her model was only originally intended to explain classic Hollywood narrative cinema. Like Berger, she is concerned with the idea of 'woman as spectacle' for the pleasure of men. But if there is a notion of power implicit in Mulvey's account of spectatorship it is the cultural power of men over women and the film text over the spectator. Other relations of power are not dealt with, because they literally cannot be 'seen' if a psychoanalytic framework is central to the analysis.

At the heart of Mulvey's essay is the idea that a cinematic narrative can be more influential in structuring the spectator's viewing experience than the discourses the spectator brings to the text. While Mulvey is only talking about cinematic spectatorship, other writers have extended this theory beyond the cinema to other viewing situations. Within film theory:

> [Mulvey's] initial insights have led to a number of different feminist responses . . . contesting and modifying Mulvey's one-to-one correlation between masculinity and voyeurism and femininity and exhibitionism.[40]

Before Mulvey, Christian Metz in his book *The Imaginary Signifier*[41] uses Lacan's idea of the 'mirror stage'[42] to explain cinematic identification. For Metz the 'imaginary signifier' of the mirror image is reproduced wholesale in the cinema where star images created by the camera offer 'ego ideals' to the audience who often identify with them and thus 'misrecognise' themselves. Metz is the originator of the model of spectatorship based on identification rather than power. He argues that the imaginary union provided by film images has a comparable relationship to the way the mirror constitutes us as subjects.

Laura Mulvey takes the work of Metz as the starting point of her argument when she points out: 'Important for this article is the fact that it is an image that constitutes the matrix of the imaginary, of recognition/misrecognition and identification . . .'[43] Like Metz, Mulvey suggests that the spectator's relationship to visual texts may accommodate 'narcissistic' identifications. This occurs in the darkened arena of the cinema when images are bigger than ourselves and so idealised they inspire us to identify with characters and even imagine that we are the characters we see before us, who are so much larger than life. But Mulvey also suggests that relations of looking which articulate classic narrative cinema are voyeuristic, to the extent that the spectator's look stands in for the look of the camera. Mulvey discusses three types of looking in the cinema:

- the look of the camera as it records the filmic event;
- the look of the audience as it watches the final film product;
- the look of the characters at each other in the visual images of the screen illusion.

She says these looks are linked to the issue of gender because many relations of looking in the cinema are informed and disrupted by sexual desire and the erotic contemplation of the female form:

> In a world ordered by sexual imbalance, pleasure in looking has been split between active/male and passive/female. The determining male gaze projects its fantasy onto the female figure which is styled accordingly. In their traditional exhibitionist role women are simultaneously looked at and displayed, with their appearance coded for strong visual and erotic impact so they can be said to connote *to-be-looked-at-ness*. Woman displayed as sexual object is the *leitmotif* of erotic spectacle. . . . The presence of woman is an indispensable element of spectacle in normal narrative film, yet her visual presence tends to work against the development of a story-line, to freeze the flow of action in moments of erotic contemplation.[44]

In explaining the male gaze, Mulvey argues that certain 'erotic' scenes in films do not move the actual plot along, so much as provide 'many pure examples of fetishistic scopophilia'.[45] Mulvey explains this phenomenon of woman as erotic spectacle in psychoanalytic terms when she argues:

> the female figure poses a deeper problem. She also connotes something that the look continually circles around but disavows; her lack of a penis, implying a threat of castration and hence unpleasure.[46]

Thus Mulvey suggests the reason why women in film always looks so perfect – so glamorous, through the way their clothes, make-up and hair are styled, the way the camera lingers upon them – is linked to male castration anxiety and the way it is resolved. She suggests:

> woman in representation can signify castration and activate voyeuristic or fetishistic mechanisms to circumvent the threat.[47]

That is, the visual image of the woman is 'fetishised', although she does not specify the type of fetishism she is discussing.[48]

The question of how women look in the cinema was subsequently addressed by Mulvey in a later article.[49] Her first article formulated the gaze as gendered and discussed the pleasure of the male spectator. The second article, while adhering to the idea of the gaze as gendered (i.e. male), nevertheless asks whether or not something different happens when women, in contrast to men, look at classic narrative cinema. This is partly because she acknowledges the pleasure she and other women experience in relation to Hollywood movies. Her explanation of the female spectator, however, remains connected to ideas about the male gaze. She argues for female spectatorship as masculinisation and consequently makes the case for 'visual transvestism':

'for women (from childhood onwards) transsex identification is a *habit*, that very easily becomes *second nature*. However, this Nature does not sit easily and shifts restlessly in its borrowed transvestite clothes.[50]

This psychosexual model of cross-gender identifications does not, how ever, explain autonomous lesbian or gay desire, except in the heterosexual terms of psychoanalytic discourse. As Hearn and Melechi have identified, there are two problems with her conceptualisation of the male gaze: first, the heterocentrism of its 'repressive hypothesis' (citing Foucault) 'which ap- proaches homosexual desire as the barred subtext of the image'; second, its maintenance of a dichotomy between homosexuality and heterosexuality as mutually exclusive.[51] Other writers – Green, for instance – challenge Mulvey's contention that spectators are always forced into a masculine subject position, citing narratives in which men are encouraged to identify with female characters and to objectify male characters without a homosexual 'threat' emerging.[52] All these criticisms suggest the possibility of multiple identifications and a less rigid spectatorial position. They move towards a more post-structuralist analysis, as do we in the second section.

The masquerading gaze

Mary Ann Doane tries to take Laura Mulvey's work one step further to theorise female spectatorship. She retains Mulvey's explanation of the gaze but brings in Joan Riviere's account of the masquerade in order to substantiate why the 'masculinisation of female spectatorship' results in psychic trans- vestism. Doane suggests: 'The transvestite wears clothes which signify a different sexuality, a sexuality which, for the woman, allows a mastery over the image and the very possibility of attaching the gaze to desire.'[53] Her point is that women are far more transvestite:

Thus, while the male is locked into sexual identity, the female can at least pretend that she is other – in fact, sexual mobility would seem to be a distinguishing feature of femininity in its cultural construction.[54]

She argues that it is understandable for woman to want to be men, but their masquerade as 'womanly' women is a 'reaction formation against the woman's transsex identification, her transvestism'.[55] Doane therefore employs the idea of femininity as masquerade in relationship to identification because she says 'the female look demands a becoming'[56] to explain not the sexual desire of women in the audience for women on the screen, but female agency in spectatorship through fluidity of identification:

> The masquerade, in flaunting femininity, holds it at a distance. Womanliness is a mask which can be worn or removed. . . . To masquerade is to manufacture a lack in the form of a certain distance between oneself and one's image.[57]

In brief, Doane is implying that because women know how to put identity on, they also know how to take it off (although this point is contested by Judith Butler)[58] and thus offers an explanation of fluid female identifications in the cinema.

Despite an interesting discussion of Riviere, we feel Doane's explanation of how women look is inappropriate. She connects arguments about masquerade (essential to explanation of identity) to arguments about spectatorship, which she herself admits in a subsequent article does not work.[59] We agree that masquerade is an inappropriate concept with which to discuss female spectatorship. The pleasures from performance of identity are very different from cinematic identifications (which are mainly vicarious in terms of the pleasures they offer). Furthermore, it is arguable that men can 'masquerade' as well as women, although Lacan accounts for this phenomenon as 'phallic parade' rather than 'masquerade'. In his account women masquerade as the phallus because they don't have it – although it has been argued that men don't have the phallus either, only the inadequate penis.[60]

Black representations – reviewing black looks

Who is viewing, as well as the context of viewing, raises questions about the spectator/viewer her/himself. One of the biggest criticisms of the psychoanalytic framework is that it privileges gender inequalities over all other forms of inequality, including that of race. It has no model of ethnicity in relation to the sexualised looking of the male gaze, nor can it address the *social context* of the spectator's experience.

This point about contextual issues being dominant in terms of the way images are read has been made by many cultural studies writers, who have been critical of the somewhat universal application of psychoanalytic concepts. Some critics have looked at the social context of viewers and readers (as well as spectators of the cinema) and suggest that contextual issues require further analysis than is allowed by gaze theory. It should be noted, however, that much of this cultural studies work which has applied gaze theory to the study of forms and processes of popular culture uses the terms 'Spectator' (deriving from psychoanlytic film theory) and 'Audience' (deriving from a more sociological or cultural studies approach to the media) as if they were interchangeable. As Annette Kuhn has pointed out, there is a distinction between the two terms and they are not simply interchangeable, because:

> 'Spectator' is a term associated with a mode of analysis focusing on the subject positions constructed by the film and belongs to psycho-analytic film theory. 'Audience', on the other hand, refers to the actual people in the cinema and is associated with a more sociological or cultural studies approach to the visual media, especially television and video.[61]

Several points about cultural difference are raised by the study of context. These concern not only the cross-cultural differences between spectators and viewers but also the fact that different media produce different responses. Obviously, watching a video in your own home when the image is smaller, and you may not be confined to your seat, is quite different to the more formal atmosphere of cinematic viewing when images are larger than life.[62] In order to challenge ideas about the determining gaze these contextual differences of viewing have been highlighted by 'media effects research' to argue for (a) active viewing and (b) differences between viewers.[63] Such research also indicates that individual identities, in the sense of ethnicity or class differences, for example, are often relevant to the way people view things.

Looking at the diversity of viewers watching television programmes *EastEnders* and *Crimewatch*, and also the mainstream film *The Accused*, media effects researchers in *Women Viewing Violence* argue that 'ethnicity proved to be a strong differentiating factor between different groups of women viewers'.[64] Evidently, many black women viewers felt alienated because of the 'perceived irrelevance of some of the images to them'. Researchers observed that 'Ethnicity, therefore, played a crucial role in two quite distinct ways: it was an indicator of alienation among Afro-Caribbean women and a way of affirming difference amongst Asian women.'[65]

In regard to the film *The Accused*, which provoked a strong identificatory response from many women interviewed, black women's experience of viewing was found to be somewhat different. Researchers argue that ethnic identity functioned to limit the measure of identification they had with the rape victim.

Despite the limitations of media effects research,[66] it does show that ethnicity is an issue to be taken seriously in regard to the context of spectators/ audiences. Nevertheless, Laura Mulvey's framework cannot conceptualise ethnicity in relation to the gaze. In the film *Some Like It Hot* (Billy Wilder, 1959), where Marilyn Monroe walks to the train as the focus of a voyeuristic male gaze, the black train guard she passes might as well be invisible. He is seen by the camera but he is not constructed by either of the two other gazes identified by Mulvey (see p. 22). (See Figures 2, 3, 4 and 5.)

The train guard's gaze on the screen has no potency or power; he is symbolically castrated by his subordinate social position. Despite the erotic spectacle provided by Monroe, the blankness of the black train guard's gaze perhaps creates some level of anxiety for certain spectators. This raises the question of whether narrative pleasure from the film text can only be achieved by identifying as a *white* man. Such a reading would suggest that classic narrative cinema does exclude black looks. Obviously, being black doesn't stop individuals enjoying the film, but one might question the nature of the pleasure on offer to black men and women. There is no straightforward answer, but Kobena Mercer's ideas about 'contradictory identifications' may help us think through those issues.

Kobena Mercer has written about the question of ethnicity in relation to spectatorship, and has raised questions about 'sexual ambivalence' in relation to viewing. As a gay black man he was originally surprised by his own contradictory responses to Mapplethorpe's collection of nude photographs (*Black Males*, 1982). He wanted to review his previous criticism of the book,[67] and to look at the contradictory feelings he first experienced when viewing the photographs. He says:

> On the one hand, I emphasised objectification because I felt identified with the black males in the field of vision, an identification with the other that might be described in Fanon's terms as a feeling that 'I am laid bare. . . . I am a slave not of the "idea" that others have of me but of my own appearance. I am being dissected under white eyes. I am *fixed*. . . . Look, it's a Negro.' But on the other hand, and more difficult to disclose, I was also implicated in the fantasy scenario as a gay subject. That is to say, I was identified with the author in so far as the objectified black male was also an image of the object chosen by my own fantasies and erotic investments. Thus sharing the same desire to look as the author-agent of the gaze, I would actually occupy the position that I said was that of the 'white male subject'. . . . Taking the two elements together, I would say that my ambivalent positioning as black gay male reader stemmed from the way in which I inhabited two contradictory identifications at one and the same time.[68]

The focus on gender rather than ethnicity in relation to voyeurism and identification in the cinema, taken up by many cultural studies writers in the last ten years, mirrors some early feminist debates which virtually ignored the issue of race.[69] Pratibha Parmar and Valerie Amos in 'Many Voices One Chant'[70] berated British socialist feminists, among others, for their ethnocentrism. Similarly, it could be argued that psychoanalytic gaze theory is an ethnocentric discursive practice. Indeed, psychoanalysis has had many limitations and misuses. Lola Young has discussed the possible dangers of transcultural and ahistorical uses of psychoanalytic theory.[71] She notes such dangers occur when explaining 'the psychic processes involved in racism and racist ideologies' but nevertheless goes on to argue that psychoanalysis can be helpful in understanding how blackness is constructed as a category in white fantasy, in a particular context where

> white is a non category. . . . White is the norm against which everything else is measured and it has no need for self-definition.[72]

Yet gaze theory is notorious for ignoring contextual issues, particularly significant when explaining the experience of black people, because the context of viewing film in Western culture posits whiteness as the norm and blackness as other. Indeed, gaze theory's universal focus on questions of gender has been applied wholesale to the extent that it cannot begin to address or explain how other dynamics of identity, in addition to gender – such as race, class, and generation, and the complex ways these categories intersect – may influence representations.

Female spectators and the female gaze

Questions about ethnicity are not the only ones absent from gaze theory. Even on the issue of gender the psychoanalytic framework is not completely adequate in so far as it aligns the masculine position with active looking and the feminine with passivity. Various writers have taken up Mulvey's arguments,[73] and tried to include the female spectator in more detail within the original framework of the gaze.[74] Many of these writers, as well as the fifty feminist film critics and theorists who contributed to the journal *Camera Obscura* on female spectatorship in 1989,[75] have argued that women spectators are *active* in the cinema.

Overall, most feminist writers remain loyal to the psychoanalytic foundations of gaze theory, and indeed have tried to adapt it to explain the agency of female spectators, as well as the 'female gaze' on the screen. Laura Mulvey's original argument about the male gaze suggests there is no space for women within mainstream narrative cinema. She suggests only the avant-garde can accommodate feminist narratives and that 'women . . . cannot view the decline of traditional film form with anything much more than sentimental regret'.[76] This position is not shared by many subsequent feminist critics. They see the mainstream as a site of possible 'feminist intervention' for film makers as a way of taking feminist messages into mainstream cinema, particularly as elsewhere in popular culture 'strong' women performers and actresses seem to have had some success with introducing feminist meanings into the popular arena.[77]

Gamman and Marshment (1988) argue that overall, during the 1980s, there were moments in popular culture, as well as the cinema in films from *Black Widow* (1987) to *Aliens* 2 and 3 (1986 and 1992) where feminism had

2–5 (from top to bottom) The absent black gaze (*Some Like It Hot*, Billy Wilder, 1959; stills by Séan O'Mara)

permeated certain genres and the female gaze could be seen to 'interrupt' patriarchal discourse, to the extent of disrupting the objectifying erotic gaze at women. Here the female gaze is argued to 'be able to literally throw itself within the frame to whoever is clever enough to catch it.[78] This often means that in order to get the jokes both men and women in the audience are required in some way to identify with the female point of view (of course point of view is not the same thing as spectatorship). This use of mockery and irony to subvert the subordinate female position is a common and by now familiar sit-com strategy, found in TV programmes from *The Golden Girls* to *Absolutely Fabulous*. Many female comedians now present a discourse that does seem to indicate an autonomous space for women within popular culture – a space that may resist objectification and accommodate feminism.

The male body as erotic spectacle – women and sexual looking

Mulvey bases many of her arguments on the assumption that 'the male figure cannot bear the burden of sexual objectification'.[79] It is true that when she wrote this in the 1970s there were fewer eroticised images of men in circulation, although Steve Neale has pointed out instances of covert male objectification in mainstream cinema, specifically in Hollywood epics involving gladiators and cowboys.[80]

In 'Don't Look Now: The Male Pin-Up' Richard Dyer looks at the circumstances in which the eroticisation of the male body is sanctioned, and the conditions under which women are permitted to look. He argues for the instability of the male pin-up, first, because the pin-up denies he is the object of the female gaze by the direction of his look. Second, the pin-up denies his passivity as an object for the gaze by being active. Third, the pin-up wants to be the phallus but can't; his flaccid penis can never match the mystique and power of the phallus. 'Hence the excessive, even hysterical, quality of so much male imagery. The clenched fists, the bulging muscles, the hardened jaws. . .'[81]

Whereas Richard Dyer's article considers the heterosexual eroticisation of the male body, Steve Neale's article looks at the homoerotic component of the male gaze and, while agreeing with many of Mulvey's premises, he argues that mainstream cinema has to deny the possibility of an erotic relationship between the male spectator and the protagonist. This argument about the disavowal of the explicitly homoerotic in representation has also been made by Michael Hatt and D. A. Miller.[82] Yet Miller, unlike Neale, argues that the gay male cult of developed musculature is an 'explicit aim . . . to make the male body visible to desire'.[83] Miller differentiates

the macho straight male body and the so-called gym-body of gay male culture. The first deploys its heft as a *tool* (for work, for its potential and actual intimidation of other, weaker men or of women) – as both an armoured body and a body wholly given over to utility. . . . The second displays its muscle primarily in terms of an *image* openly appealing to, and deliberately courting the possibility of being shivered by, someone else's desire.[84]

Many writers, among them Andy Medhurst and Yvonne Tasker, have argued that the degree of objectification of men in cinema has become more overt than ever before.[85] Male stars such as Rudolf Valentino and Cary Grant had always achieved the status of sex objects but over the last twenty years, from Richard Gere to Mel Gibson, the naked male body has been increasingly displayed and sexualised.

This objectification of the male body is not only confined to cinema. Throughout the 1980s and 1990s mens' bodies were increasingly featured in advertising and fashion imagery. Examples include: the first Calvin Klein advertising campaign; Nick Kamen in the Levi's ad; fashion spreads in magazines such as *i-D* and *The Face*; the work of photographer Bruce Weber and stylist Ray Petri, and fashion designers such as Jean-Paul Gaultier. Frank Mort describes how, in the 1980s, young men were sold advertising images in which they were 'stimulated to look at themselves – and other men – as objects of consumer desires . . . getting pleasures previously branded taboo or feminine'.[86]

By the 1990s 'porn' magazines for women, such as *For Women* and *Women Only*, founded in 1992 and 1993 respectively, were utilising codes about male objectification previously only found in gay magazines aimed at homosexual men. These women's magazines created eroticised images of men specifically for women to consume, perhaps for masturbatory purposes. Their founding editor, Isabel Koprowski, says that even though they

> can't show an erection . . . we found that many women do want to see the Chippendale type, very muscular, oiled bodies. They also want to see men who look as though they've got personality: men who perhaps aren't as well developed: and they want, you know, dark men, fair men, red-headed men – all kinds of men. The thing that really impressed me was that for a men's magazine you could fill it with busty blondes and with very little editorial and men would buy it. You cannot do that with women. . .[87]

Despite the appearance of male sex objects in the early 1980s, some feminist critics continued to argue that men cannot bear the burden of sexual objectification and that the male gaze cannot be simply inverted to produce a straightforward female gaze. Mary Ann Doane, for example, in her first essay on female spectatorship, suggested that when a woman looks at male striptease her first reaction is to associate this body with a female role and to imagine a woman stripping. This is because, she argues, the male striptease, the gigolo – both inevitably signify the mechanism of reversal itself, constituting themselves as aberrations whose acknowledgement simply reinforces the dominant system of aligning sexual difference with a subject/object dichotomy'.[88]

Suzanne Moore, in 'Here's Looking at You, Kid',[89] was among the first critics to differ from Mary Ann Doane and to draw attention to the voyeuristic heterosexual female gaze as well as to shifts, in the last ten years, in representations of men and masculinity. Moore points out that gay porn had always eroticised the male body. She argues that the codes and conventions associated with gay porn, taken up by photographers like Bruce Weber (whose work was regularly featured in magazines in the 1980s) created a different space for women (as well as men) as active voyeurs of erotic male spectacle.

The British style magazines of the 1980s (*The Face, i-D, Blitz*) were the first magazines that were marketed to both sexes and recognised that pictures of pop stars and fashion models were 'polysemic'. They could speak, for example, both to a gay man and a straight woman at the same time (see Figure 6). (Lynda Williams has discussed pornography which is targeted equally at gay men and straight women in the USA.)[90] More and more images in contemporary culture make many forms of address to more than one audience, and allow the possibility of multiple identifications by the spectator. Of course, images have always been capable of speaking differently to different spectators, but the new style magazines of the 1980s were more knowing. They gave readers 'permission' to be promiscuous with images, and they permitted images to function ambiguously, and thereby to speak to a range of different subject positions. Indeed in the 1980s advertisers used images of 'new men' to promote products to men – who were now discovered to be shopping – as well as to women, whom they recognised would also enjoy them, because traditionally women were found to make 85 per cent of consumer purchases.[91] While Moore did not overtly make the case for a ubiquitous female gaze, she argued that 'homoerotic representations, far from excluding the (voyeuristic) female gaze, may actually invite it'.[92]

Lesbian/gay spectators and lesbian representations

Many lesbian and gay critics have argued that gay and lesbian representations and gay and lesbian desire pose a challenge to the Mulveyian framework.[93] All have utilised psychoanalytic models to some extent, either using Freud, Lacan or debates informed by psychoanalysis from film theory. Two main themes emerge throughout this work. The first concerns the dynamics of sexual desire of the audience in relation to images. The second concerns the way in which individuals narcissistically identify with images of people in

6 Buffalo Boy (© *The Face*, March 1985, p.86; photograph by Jamie Morgan; stylist Ray Petri)

all sorts of ways, including people not of the same sex. (For instance, Richard Dyer has discussed the way some gay men identify with Judy Garland.)[94] These questions often get conflated and below we discuss Jackie Stacey's paper on the lesbian spectator to illustrate how such conflation is problematic.

Jackie Stacey's analysis of two mainstream Hollywood films from different periods, *All About Eve* (1950) and *Desperately Seeking Susan* (1985),[95] reviews the psychoanalytic framework of film. This project, for virtually the first time, includes the lesbian spectator in the debate and looks at sexual desire in relationship to sexual 'similarity' as opposed to sexual difference. Her approach is different from that of Richard Dyer, who writes about identification. Although Stacey does ask how lesbian women identify with male protagonists she suggests this approach can be too narrow:

one of the limits of this approach may be that a more detailed analysis of the lesbian audience would reveal a diversity of readings and pleasures or displeasures in relation to mainstream cinema. . . . There is likely to be a whole set of desires and identifications with different configurations at stake which cannot necessarily be fixed according to the conscious sexual identities of the cinematic spectator.[96]

Stacey goes on to argue that 'the rigid distinction between *either* desire *or* identification, so characteristic of psychoanalytic film theory, fails to address the construction of desires which involve a specific interplay of both processes'.[97] So Stacey's approach frames lesbian desires partly in relationship to similarities between women on the screen and the possibilities for identification this creates for women in the audience. She stresses that lesbian spectatorship, like all spectatorship, is often a 'contradictory' experience. Teresa de Lauretis is one of several writers who criticise Stacey's account. She argues that Stacey has 'desexualised' the lesbian spectator, and instead made the case for female narcissism, rather than erotic contemplation of women by women.[98]

Nevertheless, Stacey's article highlights the psychoanalytic point that all forms of looking are sexually charged because of the scopic drive. As Jacqueline Rose argues:

> there can be no work on the image, no challenge to its power of illusion and address which does not simultaneously challenge the fact of sexual difference. . . . Hence one of the chief drives of an art which addresses the presence of the sexual in representation – to expose the fixed nature of sexual identity as a phantasy and, in the same gesture, to trouble, break up, or rupture the visual field before our eyes.[99]

Furthermore, Stacey relies on the specifically Lacanian point that looking itself is split between sexual objectification and narcissistic identification. Obviously in sexual relationships there may be elements of narcissism co-existing with voyeuristic objectification. Stacey, like Metz and Mulvey, suggests a connection between the mirror and the cinema screen and the capacity individuals have to identify with objects (the mirror image or the cinematic image). Her model of spectatorship returns to Lacan's point that the mirror image of the mirror stage is both an adversary (a specular opposite) and an identical image.[100] Lacan argues that identification is partly made through aggression and rivalry – hence objectification and identification may be closely meshed and not opposites.

Additionally some feminist critics have found Stacey's paper on lesbian spectatorship limited. The equation of complexity and fluidity specifically with the lesbian spectator is thought to be a problem, not least because all spectators may be both complex and fluid in their identificatory processes. Judith Mayne has argued that no adequate model of lesbian spectatorship has

34

yet been found. Lesbian desire may disrupt the psychoanalytic model but, she says:

> Quite honestly, I have some ambivalance about a theory of lesbian spectatorship. The models of female spectatorship that have been elaborated in feminist film theory disturb me on two counts. First, female spectatorship becomes the process of displacement itself: contradiction, oscillation, mobility. Though I'm as interested in contradiction as the next person, there is too great a tendency to valorise contradiction for its own sake. So, second, the female spectator becomes the site at which contradiction itself is embodied and it begins to appear that the female spectator functions very much like the Woman in classical cinema – as the figure upon whom are projected all the messy, troublesome, complicated things that don't fit elsewhere. I would rather start from the assumption that all spectatorship is potentially contradictory, so contradiction doesn't have to carry this utopian burden as proof of some kind of resistant force.[101]

We would take Mayne's arguments about lesbian spectatorship further and suggest that no adequate model of spectatorship has been posited for any individual or social group. But certainly it seems far too simplistic to argue that who you sleep with may determine how you identify with cinematic images.

However, while there may be no such thing as an essentially 'lesbian' gaze, there is certainly lesbian imagery in circulation.[102] As Suzie Bright has observed,[103] lesbian porn videos featuring butch/femme relationships (women without bouffant hair and long fingernails, enthusiastically performing sex) are experiencing a consumer boom in the USA. Evidently, many lesbians enjoy these videos which eroticise women for women. Some would argue that this is because there is a different gaze at work within them. We would argue, however, that there is no essential 'lesbian gaze' at work here, but that lesbian film-makers and lesbian audiences bring diffent cultural competences[104] to bear on the production and consumption of lesbian imagery. This is why, as Bright points out,[105] mainstream porn producers don't seem to be able to get it right; they don't know lesbian subcultural codes and fail adequately to address the lesbian market.

We would also argue that the 'cultural competence' of the lesbian spectator (and lack of such competence in other viewers) may influence the way representations are viewed and understood by some women. Using Foucault's model of discourse we would argue against any essentialist model of the lesbian gaze and instead suggest that lesbian viewers may bring certain subcultural experiences and knowledge to the reading of specific texts. This may give these women a different perspective on the erotic images in question.

The point we are making is that there are many visual clues and 'cultural competences' which generate interpellation, identification and voyeurism in the cinema. And these visual signs need more analysis and investigation, rather than relying on ideas about 'authentic' sexual aims.

On looking at the photographs of British-based photographer Della Grace in her book *Lovebites* Reina Lewis has commented:

> There is an element of being looked at in this collection that does not simply relate to the stereotypical gaze of the (male) voyeur . . . [it] forces us to theorise a lesbian gaze. . .[106]

But when we looked at this overtly 'lesbian' collection we, like Reina Lewis, found it impossible to pin the photographs down to any fixed reading. Although Grace may deliberately be celebrating lesbian imagery, Lewis makes the point that it is not only lesbians, or straight women, who may find the images erotic. Indeed, there is no controlling, single ubiquitous female gaze that excludes heterosexuals but a range of possibilities for spectatorship offered by the photographs. Similarly, lesbian films from *Lianna* (1982) to *Desert Hearts* (1984) appear to invite a multiplicity of spectator positions, including lesbian spectatorship, and certainly do not simply equate with popular notions about the male gaze or any simple 'inversion' of it.

With regard to Della Grace's photographs it is possible that the spectator may not necessarily 'understand' the relationship of particular 'signs', specific haircuts, footwear and clothing, that have subcultural meaning in some lesbian communities (see Figure 7). What we are arguing, then, is that some codes associated with visual images of women (which are often overt in lesbian representation but perhaps require subcultural knowledge in order to recognise or even eroticise them) may be central to constructing lesbian subjectivity.

The s/m scenarios and subcultural fashion codes of Della Grace's work may interpellate 'lesbian spectators' as well as other knowing viewers (be they heterosexual, bisexual, lesbian or homosexual in their 'real' lives) and so address and form the spectator because of the spectator's relationship to knowledge about specific objects and products. These items, as a consequence of activities and histories associated with contemporary sexual subcultures, carry heavy symbolic meanings and connotations, not least because they have been used by gay men and lesbian women to carve out more fluid gender identities for themselves.[107]

AFTERTHOUGHTS: REVIEWING QUEER VIEWING

In the first section we reviewed and criticised gaze theory for its treatment of the visual text as being the sole determinant of viewing experience. We emphasised the importance of context as much as text. In this section we want to reinstate the text in order to ask questions about how, and to what extent,

7 Robyn (Della Grace, 1989)

representations position us as spectators. But first we want to deal with the ontological assumptions of gaze theory, the assumption that we know what the categories of 'male' and 'female' mean without question (and, by extension, other categories of identity such as gay and lesbian). Even before we look at theories of the gaze we want to question some assumptions about what representations signify and who spectators really are. If you talk about women as 'objects' of the male gaze it presupposes that you know what a man is, and what a subject is. These categories obviously are not challenged in everyday life, but in feminist practice the ontological category of 'woman', for example, is frequently challenged in order to reveal the stereotypes underlying constructions of 'natural' sexuality as well as 'natural' gender.[108]

Identity politics and gaze theory

Laura Mulvey's influential writing on the gaze was about the spectatorship of 'classic narrative cinema'. Subsequent writers developed and critiqued her theme of how cinematic representations constructed spectatorial positions for gendered subjects. Their emphasis on 'essential' identities, particularly of groups that gaze theory has *missed out*, has proved productive but also problematic. Such a model serves to fix identity rather than to understand how promiscuous and contradictory the processes of identity formation may be. Somewhere along the way a theory of cinematic representation bumped into identity politics. Questions about gendered spectatorship and the cultural construction of identity converged.

Given that questions of identity – i.e. gay, straight, male, female identities, etc. – have been raised in relation to film theory about gendered spectatorship, for better or worse, it is necessary to consider the relationship between the gaze and 'identity politics'. Quite simply a collision has occurred and assumptions have been made in various approaches to film and we can't go backwards. Even the best of those texts, such as writing by Richard Dyer,[109] have sought to define identities – sexual or otherwise – as social constructs which are articulated, even formed, through cinema. Here, identities have been posited straightforwardly as gay, female, black, say, as if there were no intersection between them, and also as if there were no significant differences between people in specific groups.[110]

It is here that queer politics may help us; for as Alan McKee argues, 'queer politics is, explicitly, no longer the identity politics of [the] 1970s . . . where a transcendental and essential "gay identity" stabilised homosexual subjects'.[111] Certainly throughout the 1970s and 1980s some people who were gay, female, black, or whatever, needed to articulate a group identity (even if an illusory one) in order to organise. Without the illusion of cohesive group identity group resistance would be impossible. McKee cites Gayatri Spivak's idea of 'operational essentialism', which she describes as 'a false ontology of women as a universal in order to advance a feminist political programme';

likewise he cites Stuart Marshall's 'necessary fiction', as a way of understanding how individuals are often involved in 'accepting what is known to
be untrue in order to facilitate action'.[112] And of course imaginary fictions
also frame the way we understand unified categories of gender and sexual
orientation.

A homosexual identity or a homosexual identification, as Foucault pointed
out, are very different from a homosexual act[113]. Nowadays, one might
identify politically, and with pride, as gay, lesbian, female or black, but in
reality the sense of unity and sameness on which such identification is
predicated might be illusory. Alan McKee states: 'Queer politics has come
with the realisation that, to quote Derek Jarman, "There never was a
[homosexual] community, in fact."'[114] Perhaps the differences between us
are as great as the similarities.

In homophobic society, the necessary fiction of a cohesive identity must
be spoken in order for political communities to maintain any sort of
presence. But there are obviously problems with the articulation of any sort
of fixed identity. Judith Butler has argued that even within the field of gay
and lesbian studies there are problems with essentialism. This is because a
kind of discourse of sexual identities emerges and 'identity categories tend
to be instruments of regulatory regimes, whether as the normalising categories of oppressive structures or as the rallying points for a libratory
contestation of that very oppression.' But she adds: 'This is not to say that
I will not appear at political occasions under the sign of lesbian, but that I
would like to have it permanently unclear what precisely that sign signifies.'[115] Indeed, this deconstructive mode, which may produce ambiguity,
can itself be a political strategy:

> it is no longer clear that feminist theory ought to try to settle the
> questions of primary identity in order to get on with the task of politics.
> Instead, we ought to ask, what political possibilities are the con-
> sequence of a radical critique of the categories of identity?[116]

If one formulates identity as a more fluid category, one might then be able
simultaneously to talk of queer identifications and to acknowledge the
complexity and variety of different subjectivities. The impact of these ideas
on gaze theory is that, because identity itself is not fixed, it is inappropriate
to posit any single identification with images.

If we deconstruct the subject we must by implication also deconstruct the
subject's reading/viewing position and, therefore, the text also:

> because subject-positions are mutiple, shifting and changeable, readers
> can occupy several 'I-slots' *at the same time* . . . there is no 'natural'
> way to read a text; ways of reading are historically specific and
> culturally variable, and reading positions are always constructed. . . .
> Readers, like texts, are constructed. . . . If we read from multiple

subject-positions the very act of reading becomes a force for dislocating our belief in stable subjects and essential meanings.[117]

Such an approach might sound like heresy in a collection where many writers for political reasons are concerned to establish the idea that gay and lesbian spectatorship has a material reality (not adequately conceptualised by critical theorists to date), and where other writers are arguing that specific relations of looking are produced by visual texts they suggest constitute evidence of a 'gay gaze'. Our reasoning in aligning ourselves with a sort of Judith Butler mode of analysis is that anti-essentialist discussion of identificatory processes actually challenges the fixity of notions about gay, lesbian or straight identities. It also challenges essentialist ideas that relations of looking are determined by the biological sex of the individual/s you choose to fornicate with, more than any other social relations (such as those associated with ethnic or class subjectivities). We would argue that the heterosexual subject position is equally as unnatural, and more importantly, as *fluid*, in terms of gender identifications, as homosexual or lesbian subjectivities. This collection is politically important because it looks at gaze theory from a gay and lesbian perspective. But our inclusion reveals the anti-essentialist nature of the project and recognises that we too might be queer, if not personally then theoretically. Our political stance here is that all sexuality is a construct and sexual categories and definitions impinge on us all. Rethinking gaze theory to include lesbian and gay perspectives means rethinking heterosexual perspectives too, not least because the responsibility for radical sexual politics should be a heterosexual as well as a homosexual imperative. As the 'closet' heterosexuals of this collection, we feel gaze theory as it stands cannot explain all our experiences of viewing. We are probably as perverse in our looking habits as many 'essentially' gay or lesbian spectators, and only by introducing some queer notions can we begin to explain our experiences beyond the dogma of ideas associated with the meaning of specific sexual orientations.

Further, we recognise that most women dress up as 'women' every day and yet, like us, frequently feel they are in drag. As Judith Williamson has written:

> often I have wished I could . . . appear simultaneously in every possible outfit, just to say, how dare you think any one of these is *me*. But also, see I can be all of them.[118]

If we have such a strong sense of our identity as being constructed through appearances, even though we are biologically as well as culturally defined as women, how therefore can we identify in any straightforward or 'authentic' way with images of women? Queer theory, perhaps, gives us the space to start to rethink difficulties with cohesion of identity or identification through viewing, and to look for greater fluidity in terms of explanation. It also raises

40

critical questions about cross-gender identifications. Kobena Mercer has talked about inhabiting 'two contradictory identifications at one and the same time' and this idea of multiple and simultaneous identification, we would argue, has always been part of the female experience of viewing.[119] This idea of ourselves as split subjects can also be extended into the metaphor of genderfuck where the free floating signifier, biological sex, is detached or cut loose from its signified, cultural gender.

Genderfuck

Della Grace's images of 'lesbian boys' (see Figures 8a, 8b and 8c) cause gender trouble, not least because often her images of lesbian women look so much like gay men that they have attracted a large gay male following. Evidently, in one gay bar when the lesbian 'object of desire' was revealed not to be a biological man the picture was removed from the wall: genderfuck was not to be allowed in this bar.[120] Conversely, in the 1990s some gay men have adopted the opposite strategy, and have celebrated finding images of lesbian women whom they mistake for 'boys' as perversely attractive. Here, then, 'genderfuck' or 'gender trouble' is created not only by the image but by the subjectivity of the viewer, who likes playing games with political hierarchies as well as those of gender.

June L. Reich has suggested that genderfuck is

the effect of unstable signifying practices in a libidinal economy of multiple sexualities. . . . This process is the destabilisation of gender as an analytical category, though it is not, necessarily, the signal of the end of gender. . . . The play of masculine and feminine on the body . . . subverts the possibility of possessing a unified subject position.[121]

She aligns the notion of genderfuck with the end of identity politics and makes the case for a politics of performance (exemplified for her in butch/femme role-playing). She goes on to argue:

We are defined not by who we are but by what we do. This is effectively a politics of performance. It neither fixes nor denies specific sexual and gendered identifications but accomplishes something else. . . . Genderfuck . . . 'deconstructs' the psychoanalytic concept of difference without subscribing to any heterosexist or anatomical truths about the relations of sex to gender. . . . Instead, genderfuck structures meaning in a symbol-performance matrix that crosses through sex and gender and destabilises the boundaries of our recognition, of sex, gender, and sexual practice.[122]

Queer viewing . . . queer texts?

These ideas about 'fluidity' of gender identifications may be accommodated by two things. First, that we are at a specific moment in history in which

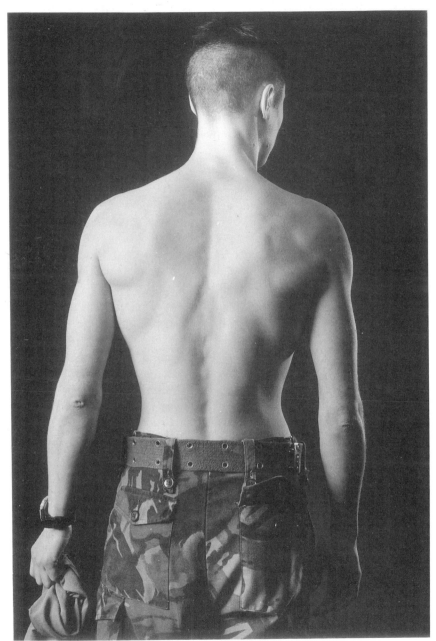

8a Jack's back I (Della Grace, 1994)

8b Jackie II (Della Grace, 1994)

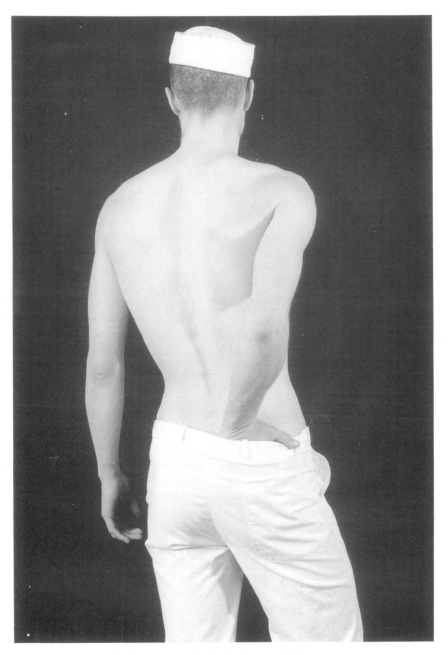

8c Jack's back II (Della Grace, 1994)

television images have copulated wildly with film and other visual texts. Today ideas about the interrelationship or intertextuality of visual images are generally accepted. Second, new generations of gays and lesbians have articulated their experiences differently from before, and what is being called 'queer cinema' and the 'queer gaze' has come into being as a consequence of that experience.[123] Although we would argue against the idea of an essentially gay or lesbian gaze, we do not want to make the case for the 'queer gaze' either. Rather, we want to make the case for identifications which are multiple, contradictory, shifting, oscillating, inconsistent and fluid. But does the queer gaze always reconstitute the visual text as queer? Or do some images encourage polymorphous identifications more than others? As we argued in the first section of this paper, context is important, but the text also is a structuring discourse. Cultural meanings are actively generated through representation,[124] and as Michèle Barrett has argued, 'Cultural politics are crucially important . . . because they involve struggles over *meaning*.'[125]

The visual text alone cannot exclusively construct spectator positions or identities and in the first section we criticised the fixity of Mulvey's analysis as opposed to the notions we raise here about spectatorial fluidity. There we shifted the focus from filmic text to spectatorial context, minimising the determining power of the texts and therefore by implication questioning the political usefulness of a Mulveyesque analysis, one committed to a structural analysis of the ideological character of the filmic or other text.

In this section we criticise the essentialism of the subject implied in gaze theory, in order to suggest a 'queerer' or more fluid model of identifications, and consequently of the text. If we accept that visual texts do produce meanings to some extent, regardless of arguments about viewing competences and contexts, we need to decide whether these texts encode dominant meanings (which then allow for the possibility of reading against the grain) or whether all texts can be read anyhow, that is, 'queerly'.[126] Media effects research, as well as some of the theoretical writings associated with Stuart Hall, has discussed the way that some texts present material in order to construct a 'preferred reading'.[127] Despite examination of how the cultural codes that frame representation achieve this, most cultural studies critics are rarely able to identify causal mechanisms. This is perhaps because structuralist methodology never sought to explain why things existed but instead focused on the way codes were arranged.

So Roland Barthes on codes is helpful in thinking through whether a textual code is a system of signs governed by rules agreed explicitly or implicitly, or whether these codes are unstable and open to different interpretations. Barthes's early work focuses on cultural codes, which he describes as dominant or conventional ways of reading the signs in the text, whereas his later work moved towards the idea of reading as a 'writerly' process 'because it can involve the production of plural texts, with different meanings'.[128] Despite the apparent rigidities of semiotic analysis, with its suggestion of a universal language of codes, Barthes's model gives us a way of thinking through the ambiguities as well as the clarity of visual texts. For while there might be consensus on the denoted meaning, there is always ambiguity in the realm of connotation.[129] For example, in texts with a homosexual subtext D. A. Miller has argued that the love that dares not speak its name, except ambiguously, is relegated by virtue of its very ambiguity to a system of connotation. He argues that even in Barthes's writing homosexuality is nowhere proclaimed but everywhere inflected as 'a gay voice'.[130] Elsewhere he argues that the trouble with connotation is that homosexuality simply disappears, becomes invisible.[131] In Hitchcock's *Rope* (1948), for example, homosexuality is consigned to connotation . . . to a kind of secondary meaning. . . . Connotation will always manifest a certain semiotic insufficiency. . . . It suffers from an abiding deniability' because you can refuse a connoted meaning, just by saying, '"but isn't it just. . . ?" before retorting the denotation'.[132] In *Rope* homosexual meaning is elided at the same time as it is being elaborated. Miller goes on to say that connotation is the signifying process of homophobia, denying homosexuality even as it re-iterates it, although we would not necessarily agree that this process amounts to homophobia *per se*.

But this suggests ambiguity which is 'coded' in the text, which is different from reconceptualising the reader as 'queer' in his/her identifications. We have said above that some images encourage polymorphous identifications and perhaps it could be implied that any text can become an object of a queer gaze. However, this suggests (by semantic implication) that some texts do *not* encourage such identifications. Again we are back to asking questions about the definition of particular texts, how they are structured and what kinds of spectatorial positions they authorise or elicit. What exactly does it mean for a text to encourage 'polymorphous identifications' and how do we recognise the characteristics of such a text? Do some texts discourage queer viewing?

In short, because we are arguing that identification is fluid in terms of gender identification, we recognise that we are virtually saying that all texts can be viewed queerly. Some texts do seem to 'encourage' queer viewing (e.g. Madonna's 'Justify Your Love' pop promo) because the sexualised images are so ambiguous. But even texts which have overt heterosexual narratives can come over time to be seen as queer. This is because such re-readings are not ahistorical but the product of a queer cultural moment in which images have been subject to so much renegotiation (including subcultural renegotiation) that the preferred heterosexual reading has been destabilised.

So our point is that some representations, what we call 'queer' representations, seem to share in common the capacity to disturb stable definitions. As Judith Butler points out, many such representations cause 'gender trouble'. What she means is that such images mobilise 'subversive confusion and proliferation of precisely those constitutive categories that seek to keep gender in its place'.[133]

These new images from queer cinema shatter and fragment images of 'normative' gender, and 'essential' gender. For example, in the film *Paris is Burning* (1990)[134] the act of 'passing' as a particular gender or profession is not an index of authenticity. The term 'realness' is used simply to mean 'convincing' image rather than 'real' image. The implications of this categorisation system are that gender is constantly changed and remade in and through the process of performance and representation.[135] This is because representation is an arena in which meanings about gender can be and are contested and constantly renegotiated. Queer representations are important not least because they offer wider opportunities for viewing/identification than those associated with the more stereotypical cinematic representations, even though we note some lesbian film critics like Pratibha Parmar have argued that queer film usually means homosexual (rather than lesbian) film in terms of the funding of such productions.[136]

But what do we mean by a queer representation? In cinema, the term has come to mean a representation that is not necessarily right on. Queer representations may not always be positive; they are frequently ambiguous, slippery, and in total don't add up to a coherent whole. They often leave the spectator/viewer questioning.

This type of imagery crops up in advertising and fashion photography too. What do we make of advertisements which use a heterosexual couple who look like lesbians (to one of us) and gay men (to another), to sell jeans (see Figure 9)? What viewing position is the male or female spectator supposed to take when Thierry Mugler uses drag queens to model women's clothes on the Paris catwalk and when Naomi Campbell says she would kill for RuPaul's legs? Or when Bette Midler on stage pretends to be a type of woman based on her viewing of gay men in drag? Or in the film *The Crying Game* (1992) when the 'female' lead turns out to be a biological man acting as a transsexual complete with male genitalia? Perhaps the answer is that we enter some sort of 'drag' when viewing, but what sort of drag is it?

Carole-Anne Tyler argues that the transvestite look of Mulvey's theory may be an option for men too. She argues that the concept of the phallic woman, embodied by a drag queen with an erection, is a queer concept, citing the scene in *Pink Flamingoes* (1972) where a 'beautiful woman' lifts up her skirt to reveal a penis.[137] The question raised here is one of authenticity. If anti-essentialist notions of the self construct identities as fictions,[138] then what's the difference between a lesbian boy and a gay man in terms of the transvestism of the spectator? Is there a difference between a woman with a dildo and a man with an erection, or a drag queen and May West? Or between mimicry and masquerade? None of the examples is authentic. As Tyler says, 'Style is the wo/man: there is no authentic, "real" self beyond or before the process of social construction.'[139] If all identities are alienated and fictional how can we differentiate parody, mimicry, camp, imitation and masquerade? Yet words like 'masquerade' or 'parody' both imply there is an opposite, i.e.

9 Women's fashion ad.: Joseph (*Arena*, no. 1, Winter 1986)

a 'real', and posit a binary opposition between May West and a drag queen. As Diana Fuss has usefully pointed out, anti-essentialism is in a dependent relationship to essentialism, so the two positions are not opposites but mutually dependent:

> what is *essential* to social constructionism is precisely this notion of 'where I stand', of what has come to be called appropriately enough, 'subject positions'.[140]

But genderfuck is about play and performance which destabilise subject positions. In playing with binary opposition it moves towards a model of gender as a simulacrum (without an original). These questions about essential identities cannot be answered within the confines of this paper. Nevertheless, by raising them we recognise that we are invariably challenging the essential categories that frame models of gendered spectatorship. Ultimately, such questions bring us back to two familiar debates. First, the idea that the underlying model of human sexuality is 'polymorphously perverse'. Second, that debates about identification in the cinema necessarily raise questions about gender, masquerade and identity – questions unanswered by film theorists to date.

NOTES

1 See bibliography in Linda Williams, 'Film Theory', and Elizabeth Grosz, 'Voyeurism/Exhibitionism/the Gaze', in Elizabeth Wright (ed.), *Feminism and Psychoanalysis: A Critical Dictionary*, Blackwell, Oxford, 1992, pp.118–26 and pp.447–50.
2 Constantine Giannaris, 'The New Queer Cinema', *Sight and Sound*, September 1992, p.35.
3 Michel Foucault, *Discipline and Punish: The Birth of the Prison*, trans. Alan Sheridan, Harmondsworth, Peregrine Books, 1979. See Foucault's discussion of the panopticon in Colin Gordon (ed.) *Power/Knowledge: Selected Interviews and Other Writings 1972–77 by M. Foucault*, Harvester, Brighton, 1980.
4 Christian Metz, *The Imaginary Signifier: Psychoanalysis and the Cinema*, Indiana University Press, Bloomington, 1975. Laura Mulvey, 'Visual Pleasure and Narrative Cinema' (first published in *Screen*, vol.16, no.3, Autumn 1975), and 'Afterthoughts on "Visual Pleasure and Narrative Cinema" inspired by King Vidor's *Duel in the Sun* (1946)' (first published in *Framework*, vol.6, nos 15–17, Summer 1981), both reprinted in Laura Mulvey, *Visual and Other Pleasures*, Macmillan, Basingstoke, 1989, pp.14–26 and pp.29–38. See too bibliographies on 'Film Theory' and 'Voyeurism/Exhibitionism/The Gaze' in Wright, (ed.) op. cit., pp.118–26 and pp.447–50.
5 Mulvey, op. cit., pp.15–16.
6 Andrea Dworkin, *Intercourse*, Martin Secker & Warburg, London, 1987.
7 See Kaja Silverman 'Fassbinder and Lacan: A Reconsideration of Gaze, Look and Image', *Camera Obscura*, no.19, January 1984, pp.54–84.
8 Carol J. Clover, *Women, Men and Chainsaws*, BFI Publishing, London, 1992, p.210.
9 In Wright (ed.), op. cit., p.449.

10 So eloquently criticised in terms of their political shortcomings by Lynne Segal, *Is the Future Female: Some Troubled Thoughts on Contemporary Feminism*, Virago, London, 1987 and Meaghan Morris, *The Pirate's Fiancée*, Verso, London, 1988.

11 Mulvey, op. cit.

12 Simone de Beauvoir, *The Second Sex*, Penguin, Harmondsworth, 1989 (first published in 1949, in France).

13 ibid, ch.1.

14 Jane Gaines, 'Introduction: Fabricating the Female Body', in Jane Gaines and Charlotte Herzog (eds), *Fabrications, Costume and the Female Body*, Routledge, New York and London, 1990, p.3.

15 Betty Friedan, *The Feminine Mystique*, Gollancz, London, 1963.

16 Sheila Rowbotham, *Woman's Consciousness, Man's World*, Penguin, Harmondsworth, 1973, reprinted 1981.

17 Robin Morgan, *Sisterhood is Powerful*, Doubleday, New York, 1984.

18 Caroline Evans and Minna Thornton, *Women and Fashion: A New Look*, Quartet Books, London, 1989, ch.1.

19 John Berger, *Ways of Seeing*, BBC Publications & Penguin Books, Harmondsworth, 1972.

20 ibid., p.46.

21 ibid., p.87.

22 Edward W. Said, *Orientalism: Western Conceptions of the Orient*, Penguin Books, Harmondsworth, 1991 (first published 1978). Said has pointed to the political effects of European and American definitions of the Orient. We would call Western discourse about the Orient 'ethnocentric' in its bias (although in some instances 'racist' seems like a more appropriate definition). Furthermore, we would argue that the 'ethnocentric gaze' can be found in many visual representations which privilege the Eurocentric viewpoint above those of other cultures, and affect the way many individuals see themselves.

23 ibid.

24 For Said on discourse, see ibid., pp.22–3 and p.94.

25 See Lorraine Gamman and Merja Makinen, *Female Fetishism: A New Look*, Lawrence & Wishart, London, 1994, ch.6.

26 Geoff Dyer, *Ways of Telling: The Work of John Berger*, Pluto, London, 1986, p. 97.

27 Berger, op. cit., p. 47. See Marcia Pointon's critique of the sweeping nature of this assertion in *Naked Authority: The Body in Western Painting 1830–1908*, Cambridge University Press, New York, Cambridge and Sydney, 1990, p.4.

28 Berger, op. cit., p.46.

29 ibid., p.64.

30 Catherine Belsey, *Critical Practice*, Methuen, London, 1980, p.5.

31 Gordon (ed.), op. cit., p.156.

32 Foucault, op. cit., part 1, ch.1: 'The Body of the Condemned'.

33 Guy Debord, *Society of the Spectacle*, trans. Malcolm Imrie, Verso, London, 1988 (first published in 1967).

34 Foucault, op. cit., part 3, ch.1: 'Docile Bodies'.

35 Frantz Fanon, *Black Skins, White Masks*, Paladin, London, 1970.

36 Judith Williamson, *Decoding Advertisments: Ideology and Meaning in Advertising*, Marion Boyars, London, 1978, defines interpellation in relation to appellation thus: 'All ideology hails or interpellates concrete individuals as concrete subjects'; e.g. 'people like you are changing to number six'. She defines appellation thus: 'A transaction between the people in it and the product; but since

we ourselves are a part of this meaning, we can decide if we will be "appellated"; e.g. "I am a number six man myself . . .".'

37 Sandra Lee Bartky, 'Foucault, Femininity and the Modernization of Patriarchal Power', in Irene Diamond and Lee Quinby (eds), *Feminism and Foucault: Reflections on Resistance*, Northeastern University Press, Boston, 1989, pp.61–86.
38 Judith Butler, *Bodies That Matter: On the Discursive Limits of 'Sex'*, Routledge, New York and London, 1993.
39 Mulvey, op. cit.
40 In Wright (ed.), op. cit., p.448.
41 Metz, op. cit.
42 Jacqueline Rose, 'Introduction II', in Juliet Mitchell and Jacqueline Rose (eds), *Feminine Sexuality: Jacques Lacan and the Ecole Freudienne*, Macmillan Press, Basingstoke and London, 1982, p.53, cites Lacan (1949):

> The mirror stage . . . took the child's mirror image as the model and basis for its future identifications. This image is a fiction because it conceals, or freezes, the infant's lack of motor co-ordination and the fragmentation of its drives, but it is salutary for the child, since it gives it the first sense of a coherent identity in which it can recognise itself. For Lacan, however, this is already a fantasy – the very image which places the child divides its identity into two. Furthermore, that moment only has meaning in relation to the presence and the look of the mother who guarantees its reality for the child. The mother does not (as in D. W. Winnicott's account) mirror the child to itself; she grants an image *to* the child, which her presence instantly deflects. Holding the child is therefore, to be understood, not only as a containing, but as a process of referring, which fractures the unity it seems to offer. The mirror image is central to Lacan's account of subjectivity, because its apparent smoothness and totality is a myth. The image in which we first recognise ourselves, is a *misrecognition*. Lacan is careful to stress, however, that his point is not restricted to the field of the visible alone; 'the idea of the mirror should be understood as an object which reflects – not just the visible, but also what is heard, touched, and willed by the child'.

Toril Moi in *Sexual/Textual Politics*, Methuen, London and New York, 1985, p.100, defines the mirror stage as follows:

> The Imaginary is for Lacan, inaugurated by the child's entry into the Mirror Stage. Lacan . . . postulates that the child's earliest experience of itself is one of fragmentation . . . between the ages of 6 to 8 months the baby enters the Mirror Stage. The principal function of the Mirror Stage is to endow the baby with a unitary body image. This 'body ego', however, is a profoundly alienated entity. The child, when looking at itself in the mirror – or at itself on its mother's arm, or simply at another child – only perceives another human being with whom it merges and identifies. In the Imaginary, there is then, no sense of a separate self, since the 'self' is always alienated in the Other.

43 Mulvey, op. cit., p.18.
44 ibid., p.19.
45 ibid., p.22.
46 ibid., p.21.
47 ibid., p.25.
48 Gamman and Makinen, op. cit., p.179:

> Furthermore, it seems to us that Mulvey tends to conflate the terms voyeurism and scopophilia with fetishism, and that these terms, at times, appear to be used

interchangeably. Mulvey suggests that 'scopophilic' pleasure arises principally from using another person as an object of sexual stimulation through sight. Voyeurism and scopophilia for most cinematic viewers rarely replace other forms of sexual stimulation, nor are they preferred to sex itself. Thus these forms of pleasure cannot be encompassed within our definition of fetishism.

49 See 'Afterthoughts on "Visual Pleasure and Narrative Cinema" inspired by King Vidor's *Duel in the Sun* (1946)' in Mulvey, op. cit., pp.29–38.
50 ibid., p.33.
51 Jeff Hearn and Antonio Melechi, 'The Transatlantic Gaze: Masculinities, Youth and the American Imaginary', in Steve Craig (ed.), *Men, Masculinities and the Media*, Sage Publications, California, London, New Delhi, 1992, p.215.
52 Ian Green, 'Malefunction: A Contribution to the Debate on Masculinity in the Cinema', *Screen*, vol.25, nos 4–5, 1984, pp.36–48.
53 p. 81, Mary Ann Doane, 'Film and the Masquerade: Theorising the Female Spectator', *Screen*, vol. 23, nos 3–4, September–October 1982, pp.74–87.
54 ibid., p.81.
55 ibid.
56 ibid., p.78.
57 ibid., pp.81–2.
58 Butler, op. cit., p.x and p.230.
59 Mary Ann Doane, 'Masquerade Reconsidered: Further Thoughts on the Female Spectator', *Discourse*, 11, Fall/Winter 1988/89, pp.42–54.
60 Richard Dyer, 'Don't Look Now: The Male Pin-Up', in Screen Editorial Collective (ed.), *The Sexual Subject: A Screen Reader in Sexuality*, Routledge, London and New York, 1992, pp.265–76; Mark Simpson, *Male Impersonators: Men Performing Masculinity*, Cassell, London and New York, 1994.
61 Annette Kuhn (ed.), with Suzannah Radstone, *The Women's Companion to International Film*, Virago, London, 1990, p.25.
62 John Ellis, *Visible Fictions*, Routledge, Chapman & Hall, New York, 1983, p.137.
63 Media effects research on viewing is diverse but perhaps the most central texts include: Stuart Hall *et al.* (eds), *Culture, Media, Language*, Hutchinson, London, 1980; David Morley, *Family Television: Cultural Power and Domestic Leisure*, Comedia, London, 1986; Sean Cubbitt, *Timeshift: On Video Culture*, Comedia for Routledge, London, 1991; Lisa A. Lewis (ed.), *The Adoring Audience: Fan Culture and Popular Media*, Routledge, London, 1992.
64 Philip Schlesbinger *et al.* (eds), *Women Viewing Violence*, BFI Publishing, London, 1992.
65 ibid.
66 For the strengths and weaknesses of 'media effects research' see Tim O'Sullivan *et al.* (eds), *Key Concepts in Communication*, Methuen, London and New York, 1983.
67 Kobena Mercer, 'Skin Head Sex Thing: Racial Difference and the Homoerotic Imaginary', in Bad Object-Choices (ed.), *How Do I Look? Queer Film and Video*, Bay Press, Seattle, 1991, pp.169–210; Robert Mapplethorpe, *Black Males*, Introduction by Edmund White, Gallerie Jurka, Amsterdam, 1982, and *The Black Book*, Foreword by Ntozake Shange, St Martin's Press, New York, 1986.
68 Mercer, op. cit., pp.179–80.
69 Stuart Hall, 'New Ethnicities', ICA Document 7, *Black Film/British Cinema*, ICA/BFI, London, 1988, p. 28; Jane Gaines, 'White Privilege and Looking Relations: Race and Gender in Feminist Film Theory', *Screen*, vol.29, no.4, Autumn 1988, pp.12–27; bell hooks, *Black Looks: Race and Representation*, Turnaround, London, 1992.

70 Pratibha Parmar and Valerie Amos, 'Many Voices One Chant: Black Feminist Perspectives', *Feminist Review*, 17, Autumn 1984.

71 Lola Young, 'A Nasty Piece of Work – A Psychoanalytic Study of Sexual and Racial Difference in *Mona Lisa*', in Jonathan Rutherford (ed.), *Identity, Community, Culture, Difference*, Lawrence & Wishart, London, 1990.

72 ibid., p.194.

73 Although it should be again noted that Mulvey's original model only applied to the cinema and other critics have extended it to explain other forms of popular culture.

74 Doane, op. cit., 1982 and 1988/89. See also Teresa de Lauretis, *Alice Doesn't: Feminism, Semiotics, Cinema*, Macmillan, Basingstoke, 1984; Kaja Silverman, *The Acoustic Mirror: The Female Voice in Psychoanalysis and Cinema*, Indiana University Press, Bloomington and Indianapolis, 1989; Deidre Pribham (ed.), *Female Spectators*, Verso, London, 1988; Lorraine Gamman and Margaret Marshment (eds), *The Female Gaze: Women as Viewers of Popular Culture*, The Women's Press, London, 1988. All these books attempt to reconceptualise the female gaze/spectator.

75 *Camera Obscura*, no. 19, January 1989.

76 Mulvey, op. cit., p.26.

77 Gamman and Marshment (eds), op. cit., p.17.

78 Lorraine Gamman, 'Watching the Detectives: The Enigma of the Female Gaze', in Gamman and Marshment (eds), op. cit., p.16.

79 Mulvey, op. cit., p.20.

80 Steve Neale, 'Masculinity as Spectacle: Reflections on Men and Mainstream Cinema', in Screen Editorial Collective (ed.), op. cit., pp.277–87 (first published 1983).

81 Dyer, op. cit., p.270 (first published 1982).

82 Michael Hatt, 'The Body in Another Frame', *Journal of Philosophy and the Visual Arts* ('The Body' issue, ed. Andrew Benjamin, Academy, 1993); D. A. Miller, 'Anal Rope', in Diana Fuss, (ed.), *Inside/Out: Lesbian Theories, Gay Theories*, Routledge, New York and London, 1991; D. A. Miller, *Bringing Out Roland Barthes*, University of California Press, Berkeley, Los Angeles, London, 1992.

83 Miller, op. cit., 1992, p.30.

84 ibid., p.31.

85 Andy Medhurst, 'Can Chaps Be Pin-Ups?', *Ten 8*, vol.8, no.17, 1985; Yvonne Tasker, *Spectacular Bodies: Gender, Genre and the Action Cinema*, Comedia by Routledge, London and New York, 1993.

86 Frank Mort, 'Boys Own? Masculinity, Style and Popular Culture', in Rowena Chapman and Jonathan Rutherford (eds), *Male Order: Unwrapping Masculinity*, Lawrence & Wishart, London, 1988.

87 Isabel Koprowski, unpublished interview with Lorraine Gamman, 1992, available in Central St Martins College of Art & Design Library.

88 Doane, op. cit., 1982, p.77.

89 See Gamman and Marshment (eds), op. cit., pp.44–59.

90 At 'On/scenities: Looking at Pornography: A Conference at the NFT', Summer 1993.

91 Rosemary Scott, *The Female Consumer*, Associated Business, London, 1986.

92 Gamman and Marshment (eds), op. cit., p.55.

93 Teresa de Lauretis, op. cit., 1984; Dyer, op. cit., 1984; Doane, op. cit., 1982 and 1988/89. See also Mark Finch, 'Sex and Address in *Dynasty*', *Screen*, vol. 23, nos 3/4, September–October 1982; Mandy Merck, 'Difference and its Discontents', *Screen*, vol. 28, no.1, Winter 1987; Jackie Stacey, in Gamman and Marshment, (eds), op. cit.; Teresa de Lauretis, 'Sexual Indifference and Lesbian Representations', *Theatre Journal*, vol.40, no.2, May 1988.

94 See Richard Dyer on Judy Garland in *Heavenly Bodies*, St Martins Press, New York, 1987.
95 Jackie Stacey, 'Desperately Seeking Difference', in Gamman and Marshment (eds), op. cit. (first published 1987).
96 ibid.
97 ibid.
98 Teresa de Lauretis, 'Film and the Visible', in Bad Object-Choices (ed.), op. cit., pp.223–64.
99 Jacqueline Rose, *Sexuality in the Field of Vision*, Verso, London, 1986, pp.226–7.
100 Jane Gallop, *Reading Lacan*, Cornell University Press, New York and London, 1985, pp.59–61.
101 Judith Mayne, 'Lesbian Looks: Dorothy Arzner and Female Authorship' and subsequent 'Discussion', in Bad Object-Choices (ed.), op. cit., p.136.
102 In Tessa Boffin and Jean Frazer (eds), *Stolen Glances: Lesbians Take Photographs*, Pandora, London, 1991, lesbian critics and photographers offer a variety of approaches to explaining the meaning of overtly lesbian representations. But none offer an adequate model of lesbian spectatorship or significantly move beyond the contribution Jackie Stacey has made.
103 In *Every Conceivable Position*, Clare Bevan (Director), Mandy Merck (Producer), roughcut never broadcast by the BBC, London, 1991.
104 Elizabeth Ellsworth, in 'Illicit Pleasures: Feminist Spectators and *Personal Best*', *Wide Angle*, vol.8, no.2, 1986, pp.45–56, discusses 'interpretive communities' in terms of the cultural competences brought to a viewing situation. See also Alan McKee, 'Review', *Screen*, vol.34, no.1, Spring 1993, p.91.
105 In Claire Bevan (Director), Mandy Merck (Producer), op. cit.
106 Reina Lewis, 'Dis-Graceful Images: Della Grace and Lesbian Sado-Masochism', *Feminist Review*, no.46, Spring 1994, pp.76–91; Della Grace, *Lovebites*, Aubrey Walters, London, 1991.
107 For historical accounts of butch/femme codes see Joan Nestle, *A Restricted Country* Sheba Feminist, London, 1988 and Lillian Faderman, *Odd Girls and Twightlight Lovers: a History of Lesbian Life in Twentieth-Century America*, Penguin, Harmondsworth, 1992. For a discussion of the way gay men and lesbian women use clothing to carve out identities see 'Chic Thrills', in Elizabeth Wilson, *Hallucinations: Life in the Postmodern City*, Hutchinson Radius, London, 1988.
108 See Diana Fuss, *Essentially Speaking: Feminism, Nature and Difference*, Routledge, New York and London, 1989.
109 Richard Dyer, *Gays and Film*, Zoetrope, New York, 1984.
110 This issue is discussed by Kobena Mercer, op. cit., pp.169–222. See in particular p.193 where Mercer criticises 'the mantra of "race, class, gender" (and all the other intervening variables) which does not deal with 'the complexity of what actually happens "between" the contingent spaces where each variable intersects with the others'. See also pp.215–17.
111 McKee, op. cit., p.89.
112 ibid., p.90.
113 Michel Foucault, *The History of Sexuality. Volume I: An Introduction*, trans. Robert Hurley, Penguin, Harmondsworth, 1981, p.43 (first published 1976).
       At a *Marxism Today* conference, in June 1992, Suzanne Moore described a gay New York journalist who had an affair with a military cadet. The military cadet said he wasn't 'gay', he just enjoyed homosexual sex (which is not surprising given the penalties for being gay in the army). The point of her argument was that the sussed-out New York journalist said that in relation to the military cadet he felt 'straight' too. . .

114 McKee, op. cit., p.89.
115 Judith Butler, 'Imitation and Gender Insubordination', in Henry Abelove, Michele Aina Barala, David M. Halperin (eds), *The Lesbian and Gay Studies Reader*, Routledge, New York and London, 1993, p.308, reprinted from Fuss (ed.), op. cit., 1991.
116 Judith Butler, *Gender Trouble: Feminism and the Subversion of Identity*, Routledge, New York and London, 1990, p.ix.
117 Fuss, op. cit., 1989, p.35.
118 Judith Williamson, 'A Piece of the Action: Images of "woman" in the photography of Cindy Sherman', *Consuming Passions*, Marion Boyars, London and New York, 1986, p.91.
119 Mercer, op. cit., p.180.
120 Reina Lewis, op. cit., p.89.
121 June L. Reich, 'Genderfuck: The Law of the Dildo', in Cheryl Kader and Thomas Piontek (eds), *Discourse*, vol.15, no.1, Fall 1992, p.125.
122 ibid., p.113.
123 See Cherry Smyth, *Queer Notions*, Scarlet Press, London, 1992.
124 This point was made in response to this paper by Gavin Butt who lectures in fine art and teaches a course on 'Homovisibilities' at Central St Martins College of Art and Design. He also argued 'that what is lost in the shift from determining text, to determining context, is an analysis of the way images structurally encode power relationships, which of course was the strength of Mulvey'. The reason why he took such an analysis to be important is because it enables us to comprehend how, for instance, homophobic representations consistently encode and disavow 'queer pleasure'. He went on to argue that in homophobic culture the queer look is still largely an illegitimate one, relying on D. A. Miller's notion that in many representations homosexuality is disavowed in so far as it is 'pushed' into the shadowy realm of connotation. (See D. A. Miller, op. cit., 1991 and 1992.) In this context Gavin Butt also cited the arguments of Michael Hatt, op. cit. Hatt argues that the homosocial and the homosexual must be kept apart in cultural representations in order for the erotic to be disavowed in the homosocial so that it can be contained by the homosexual.
125 Michèle Barrett, 'Feminism and the Definition of Cultural Politics', in Rosalind Brunt and Caroline Rowan (eds), *Feminism, Culture and Politics*, Lawrence & Wishart, London, 1982, p.37.
126 See Alexander Doty, *Making Things Perfectly Queer: Interpreting Mass Culture*, University of Minnesota Press, Minneapolis, 1993.
127 There has been so much media effects research that discusses ideas about 'preferred readings'. This debate has been summarised by Tim O'Sullivan *et al.* (eds), *Key Concepts in Communication*, op. cit., as follows:

> **preferred reading** . . . a **text** is open to a number of potential readings, but normally 'prefers' one (or, occasionally more). Analysing the internal structure of the text can identify this preference.
>
> Texts according to Eco (*The Role of the Reader*, Hutchinson, London, 1981), can be open or closed. A *closed* text has one reading strongly preferred over others; an *open text* requires a number of readings to be made simultaneously for its full 'richness' or 'texture' to be appreciated (to use literary critical terms). Open texts tend to be highbrow, high culture, whereas closed texts tend to the more popular, mass culture. Most mass media texts are closed in so far as they prefer a particular reading.
>
> Alternative readings to the preferred one usually derive from differences between the social positions and/or the cultural experience of the **author**

and the **reader**, or between *reader* and *reader*. Eco uses the theory of **aberrant decoding** to account for this but Hall and Morley produce subtler and more sophisticated accounts based on Parkin's theory of **meaning systems**. Hall *et al*. (S. Hall, D. Hobson, D. A. Lowe, P. Willis (eds), *Culture, Media, Language*, Hutchinson, London, 1980) propose three main types of decodings or readings of tv texts which correspond to the reader's response to his/her social condition, not to the structure of the text. These are:

(1) *The dominant-hegemonic* which accepts the text 'full and straight' according to the assumptions of the encoder. This is the preferred reading, and corresponds to F. Parkin's (*Class Inequality and Political Order*, Paladin, St Albans, 1972) dominant meaning system.

(2) *The negotiated reading* which acknowledges the legitimacy of the dominant codes, but adapts the reading to the specific social condition of the reader. This corresponds to Parkin's subordinate meaning system.

(3) *The oppositional reading* which produces a radical decoding that is radically opposed to the preferred reading, because it derives from an alternative, oppositional meaning system. (Radical meaning system in Parkin's terminology.)

128 Diana Saco, 'Masculinity as Signs: Poststructuralist Feminist Approaches to the Study of Gender', in Steve Craig (ed.), *Men, Masculinity and the Media*, Sage Publications, California, London, New Delhi, 1992, p.31.

129 Miller, op. cit., 1991 and 1992.

130 Miller, op. cit., 1992, pp.24–5.

131 Miller, op. cit., 1991, p.123.

132 Miller, 1991, ibid., pp.123–4.

133 Butler, op. cit., 1990, pp.33–4.

134 *Paris Is Burning*, Jenny Livingstone, 1990.

135 Teresa de Lauretis, *Technologies of Gender*, University of Indiana Press, Bloomington and Indianapolis, 1987, p.3, argues that:

gender is (a) representation – which is not to say that it does not have concrete or real implications, both social and subjective, for the material life of individuals. On the contrary . . . the representation of gender *is* its construction – and in the simplest sense it can be said that all of Western Art and high culture is the engraving of the history of that construction.

Janet Wolff, *Feminine Sentences*, Polity Press, Oxford, 1990, p.1:

culture is central to gender formation. Art, literature, and film do not simply represent given gender identities, or reproduce already existing ideologies of femininity. Rather they participate in the very construction *of* those identities. Second (and consequently), culture is a crucial arena for the contestation of the social arrangements of gender.

136 This is not to say that there haven't always been transvestite effects in theatre and cinema. For a wide-ranging survey see Marjorie Garber, *Vested Interests: Cross-Dressing and Cultural Anxiety*, Routledge, New York and London, 1992.

137 Carole-Anne Tyler, 'Boys will be Girls: The Politics of Gay Drag', in Fuss, op. cit., 1991, pp.32–70.

138 See Butler, op. cit., 1990 and 1993, and Fuss, op. cit., 1989.

139 Tyler, op. cit., p.53.

140 Fuss, op. cit., 1989, p.29.

2

BLACK LESBIAN SPECTATORSHIP AND PLEASURE IN POPULAR CINEMA

Z. Isiling Nataf

INTRODUCTION

What I'm interested in drawing out and discussing in this chapter are new forms of pleasure that black lesbian spectators write for themselves against the grain of popular cinema, which I take to include Hollywood films as well as so-called cult and subcultural alternatives on mainstream release. I want to start by raising the possibility of pleasure as political and fantasy as progressive, even transgressive, in its potential to subvert the status quo and to propose other ways of being that fall outside or exceed the boundaries of naturalised ideological positions.

Pleasure in the place of erasure, invisibility, misrepresentation and othering is already progress. Pleasure that empowers and transforms certainly gives a political role and function to the active reading of the text as well as the forms of representation. So what kind of pleasure am I actually talking about? Who are these spectators? And how do they engage in the text in order to bring about a positive, meaningful and beneficial result?

Though spectatorship is a dynamic process of negotiation or exchange, the author and audience members are not in direct communication and each of their goals may be different or opposing. That does not stop meaning being made, subjectivities being formed or reinforced, even from an oppositional stance, and representations evolving. Thus positive images are only one strategy for transforming authors, texts, representations and audiences politically. Indeed, I believe that it is in fact those strange and threatening narratives and images, with their resultant feelings and understandings, that really point to deep and effective exchanges.

DEVIANT READINGS, RESISTING SPECTATORS

The black lesbian spectator has a schizophrenic response to mainstream, popular film. That is because her experience with the mass media is that it has rarely reflected or represented anything that resembles her life, doing so

57

only in ways that are stereotypical and marginal, or monstrous, fetishising and othering. The function of such representations is often to find a site for redemption, punishment or annihilation of all that the dominant society feels is threatening in its own psyche and wants to repress or destroy.

So when there is a moment which reflects black lesbian lives – however inadequately – the black lesbian spectator's desire and need for it to be there is often so strong that the negative part of the experience is ignored and what is of use is engaged with and received.

The model of encoding/decoding developed by Stuart Hall and colleagues working at the University of Birmingham Centre for Contemporary Cultural Studies is useful in understanding how this takes place. The model is concerned with understanding the operation of the communication process in a specific social and cultural context and is drawn from the political sociological work of Frank Parkin. In his 'theory of meaning systems', Parkin 'delineated three potential responses to a media message: dominant, negotiated or oppositional'.[1] I would add a fourth term – deviant – as an active reconstructive response that might follow logically from the distancing and deconstructive oppositional reading. That is because readings reflect spectators' goals as well as their social positions and this fourth term may allow for a subversive reading as well as a critique. It is also, of course, another form of oppositional reading.

A dominant reading of the text is the solicited or preferred reading which accepts without question the 'content of the cultural product'.

> A negotiated reading [may] question parts of the content of the text but does not question the dominant ideology which underlies the production of the text. An oppositional response to a cultural product is one in which the recipient of the text understands that the system that produced the text is one with which she/he is fundamentally at odds

and may in fact be actively hostile to her/him. 'The viewer of the film (reader of the text) brings to the moment of engagement with the work a knowledge of the world', her/his history, 'whether social, cultural, economic, racial, or sexual' and 'a knowledge of other texts, or media products'.

'An audience member from a marginalised group has an oppositional stance as they participate in mainstream media' and may have a clear subcultural identification outside mainstream society. Jacqueline Bobo explains that

> the motivation for this counter-reception is that we understand that mainstream media has never rendered our segment of the population faithfully. We have as evidence our years of watching film and television programmes and reading plays and books. Out of habit, as readers of mainstream texts, we have learned to ferret out the beneficial and put up blinders against the rest.[2]

From this wary viewing standpoint, a subversive reading of a text can occur. The viewer is distanced by something in the film that does not seem quite right from the knowledge and viewpoint this spectator brings to bear on the work (which lays bare its operations). Something appears strange or amiss such that the film's authority, truth and accuracy are challenged. Its ideological system shows through and disrupts identification and the natural flow of the narrative.

These spectators are simultaneously hailed to engage with the film and are distanced by it. From this position of wary detachment, the spectator can read against the grain or intentions of the film-maker and identify with the villains in the narrative, for example, because they are shown disrupting the social order. At least, that is, until they get stopped and punished or recuperated at the end of the film.

Another type of reading opened up by this distance is seeing other things in the film than the film-maker had intended and radically misreading the text. 'These films are transformed by the subcultural viewer's active and deliberate misreading into something of peculiar significance to those involved in the group.' These films have a subtext which allows them to be appropriated by the subculture and 'to be read in an originally unintended way'.[3]

'Camp is perhaps the best documented example of this phenomenon. Camp transforms a classic Hollywood film, through a sense of ironic humour, into an object with totally different significance,'[4] especially for gay audiences.

I would like to suggest that queer may be the next register of distancing, of radical or camp misreading, in that it can be applied to cult and subculturally produced lesbian texts as well.

A queer reading as a deviant reading is also a writerly one in two directions. A film is queer for a general audience when it makes heterosexuality strange. It is queer for a queer audience and a lesbian audience in that it subverts the lesbian subject's position within lesbian identity, transforming her point of identification in relation to the text as camp might transform the point of identification within a classic cultural product from Hollywood, making what might otherwise be a heterosexist text into something pleasurable and identifiable with.

For the queer spectator this reading causes a crisis of categories and identification and offers a 'thrill' which, as Laura Mulvey has suggested, 'comes from leaving the past behind . . . transcending outworn or oppressive forms, or daring to break with normal pleasurable expectations in order to conceive a new language of desire'.[5]

A 'category crisis' 'threatens the established class, race and gender norms'.[6] The transgressive image or juxtaposition in the film-text becomes a disruptive element that involves not just a category crisis of, say, lesbianism or what it is to be a woman, but the 'crisis of the category itself'. In this way it is a critique or commentary on our own stereotypes. It is an interdiscursive articulation with the text in a new mode, a way of describing the space of possibilities opened up by the queer thrill or shock that gives a glimpse beyond the borders as we know them and allows these borders to be crossed.

The pleasure is in the liberation from what was possible before and its fixed limits and the proliferation of subject positions, a jouissance.[7] Equally the threat is in the danger of dissolution into disorder when borders between certain categories become permeable.

The queer engagement with mainstream texts is similar to the subcultural subject's relation to the cult text. The cult film is specifically intended to give the spectator that experience of transgression.

The cult film experience 'represents a "supertext"' and can be described in terms of boundary crossing.

> If that crossing evokes a kind of loving experience, it is because we thereby sense something special in the cult film: that we are part of this text, our embrace necessary for its very identity. In this experience, we celebrate a most pleasurable transgression, as we vicariously cross over into taboo territory – the self's terra incognita – and then emerge to tell of it.[8]

In a similar kind of interpellation, in the queer encounter with a mainstream text, the 'transgressive thrust helps us see beyond, trace our own limits and even feel a momentary power over them. Of course, eventually the film ends, and then we return to that world and its boundaries . . .' But the experience 'leaves us feeling better about ourselves and our world, better because we have seen and spoken our desires'.[9]

But the other side of the coin of transgressive pleasures is danger. In her discussion of 'frontier fears: butches, transsexuals, and terror',[10] Gayle Rubin describes how the boundaries between the categories of butch and transsexual are permeable. Female-to-male transsexuals are therefore dangerous and present a challenge to lesbian gender categories as that category excludes men. Lesbians are forced by certain images to self-consciously examine their own common sense assumptions and ask questions like: what is at the root of my desire? What are lesbians? What are men?

The result of a queer shock of gender-bending identification or a 'transsexual narrative' may linger long after the spectator's engagement with them on the screen, continuing 'to disturb and threaten with collapse our age-old distinction between the Same and the Other'.[11]

The same of course occurs with categories of race. Jean Baudrillard, describing Michael Jackson's 'androgynous and Frankensteinian appeal', points to the artifices used by the singer which allow him to slip into the interstitial spaces these open at the borders of the categories of gender and race. He has both 'surgically and semio-urgically' mixed a hybrid cocktail of gender and race signifiers on his own body. Race for him seems to become another prosthesis.

Consider Michael Jackson. . . . Michael Jackson is a solitary mutant, a precursor of a hybridisation that is perfect because it is universal – the race to end all races. Today's young people have no problem with a miscegenated society: they already inhabit such a universe, and Michael Jackson foreshadows what they see as an ideal future. Add to this the fact that Michael has had his face lifted, his hair straightened, his skin lightened – in short, he has been reconstructed with the greatest attention to detail. This is what makes him such an innocent and pure child – the artificial hermaphrodite of the fable, better able even than Christ to reign over the world and reconcile its contradictions; better than a child-god because he is a child-prosthesis, an embryo of all those dreamt-of mutations that will deliver us from race and from sex.[12]

I do believe Michael Jackson when he says he is proud to be African-American;[13] but that does not contradict the drive to transgress if not transcend the limits and limitations of race as category.

With his whitened skin he is not so much erasing his blackness as giving race a clean slate, a *tabula rasa* upon which new potentials can play and mix in impossible and seductive combinations. His excess of a race signifier which is beyond existing races, through artifice, is in Baudrillard's terms a simulacrum. It is also a way of representing race which does not chain it to existing stereotypes and myths but opens it up to a universalism which says we are all raced and all human, so why should one race have a more dominant position than another and why should people suffer or be victimised by this sign of race. It also clearly points to the fact that the boundaries between races are permeable and the ever-increasing mixing of the races makes it difficult to keep these categories distinct.

This hermaphrodite image of Michael Jackson and his mask of new-races-to-come addresses bisexual desire in the spectators of his music videos. And 'it makes no difference if you're black or white' as the lyrics to one of his songs says, you are free to identify with him. The transgressive signs in the text give spectators a thrill and a queer feeling, addressing the transsexual and racially amorphous position of all spectators whether or not they ever realised that that space could open in them.

TEXT POSITIONING ADDRESS

In Laura Mulvey's application of Freudian/Lacanian psychoanalytic theory as a 'radical feminist weapon' in the analysis of classic Hollywood cinema texts,[14] she examines how cinematic looking, the representation of women and narrative structure speaks to the imaginary of the spectator, hailing repressed material of primal memories.

The black lesbian spectator, as a resisting spectator, has a schizophrenic relationship with the cinema interdiscourse. On the one hand if she responds to the beckoning of the text, her subjectivity is engaged at the level of the imaginary; but this is simultaneous with a critical or resisting distance which opens the possibility of a deviant reading in order to draw moments of pleasure and empowerment from a text that is otherwise replaying the fears, obsessions and pre-occupations of the patriarchal order in its striving to maintain the status quo.

The classic Hollywood text may try to construct a feminine position for her in which she is a misfit and an outlaw. The positions for the female spectator that Laura Mulvey identifies are explainable in Freudian terms because our society is caught in the patriarchal order in such a way that no issues of the female unconscious can be fully articulated as long as it is formed within the social formations and language of the patriarchy.

It becomes necessary, then, to create a subject position against the grain of the grammar of phallocentric language and interpretive strategies which result in impossible meanings within the patriarchal order. One of these kinds of relations is butch-femme which is different from the masculine and feminine positions within Freud's hetero-male libidinal economy in which spectator positions can only be similar to or opposite to the masculine.

Pleasure is thus to be found in the 'radical feminine misbehaviour',[15] the blatant breaking of codes and rules, ignoring the law, discrediting the value and guaranteed possession of the phallus, unfixing the point of identification to allow the subject to shift between multiple, even contradictory, points of identification; and in transgressing not only gender role but the boundaries of the body, to precipitate the disorder and final collapse of the centrality of the dominant phallocentric discourse into 'heterotopias'.[16]

The refusal to 'achieve a stable sexual identity' as the 'correct' feminine position in patriarchy gives the lesbian spectator more room to play, just as the deconstruction of stereotypes in colonial discourse does for black women spectators. The black lesbian spectator, destined to be an outlaw, already on the frontiers, can see a greater terrain of possibilities from this vantage point.

Mulvey explains how the 'logic of the narrative grammar' of classical fiction film triggers a transsex identification of the female spectator with the hero/star (ego-ideal). This is in fact a familiar habit for most female spectators given the cultural (social and symbolic) content of the patriarchal order present in most texts, and is a usual way for women spectators to gain access to and achieve some pleasure. This transsex identification becomes a habit early in life and becomes second nature, according to Mulvey. However, she goes on, 'This Nature does not sit easily and shifts restlessly in its borrowed transvestite clothes.'[17]

Although external to the spectator, the text imposes a grammar that engages her and she responds co-operatively because, Mulvey says, the masculine identification reactivates a fantasy or nostalgia for a pre-Oedipal stage in which she was not only capable of 'action' but was herself phallic.[18] These memories or fantasies, when personified on the screen, are said to 'represent an internal oscillation of desire, which lies dormant, waiting to be "pleasured"'.

Mulvey argues that it is a limitation of Freud's phallocentric language that the only possible signifier for a woman's expression of action is through a metaphor of masculinity. Society 'straitjackets' any attempts to represent the feminine and female desire within the patriarchal order.

According to Freud's formulations these recurring irruptions of the female phallic phase later in life are regressive and neurotic because they point to an unsatisfactory resolution of the Oedipal phase and assumption of the 'correct' feminine position. Any persistence of this fantasy of an 'illusory organ'[19] can only lead to tragedy.

Although Mulvey notes that the returning masculinity 'conforms more closely with women's actual empirical conscious experience', she seems almost to agree with Freud's position that the oscillation of sexual identity, the inability to achieve 'stable sexual identity' must somehow be at cross-purposes with a woman's goals. Perhaps this is due to her assessment that 'important issues for the female unconscious' cannot be articulated or even conceived because they are of no relevance to phallocentric theory and cannot be achieved using the language of patriarchy, even though the unconscious is structured by this dominant order and this language.

From a transgressive and queer perspective, however, it is this refusal of a stable identity and this oscillation and play which could have radical consequences for the pleasure of the resisting subject and her interpretations of the texts. To see how this might be so, I want to look at four very different films, each directed by a man, but each yielding surprising pleasures for the black lesbian spectator.

MONA LISA

Mona Lisa (1986), an independent British feature directed by Neil Jordan, is a contemporary, self-conscious thriller/*film noir*. Cathy Tyson plays Simone, the film's *femme fatale* and central enigma. Unlike the classic Hollywood *film noir* there is no clear crime to be solved in parallel to the solving of the Freudian question, 'What do women want?' There are, however, parallel investigations.

When the film opens Simone is operating as a prostitute without a pimp. George (Bob Hoskins) is just out of prison and has been thrown out of home by his wife and daughter. Simone's former pimp assigns him the task of getting her back, but things don't go according to plan. Instead, Simone persuades George to help her find her friend, Cathy. Simone had lived with Cathy and their pimp in a kind of family, until she escaped.

The pleasure for black lesbian spectators in this text is precisely in identifying with Simone when she is seen in moments of phallic narcissism, with hints of masculinity and top-femme sadism.[20]

There is a real charge in the scenes when George and Simone are driving slowly through the streets of King's Cross in his Jaguar, looking for Cathy. This is partly because the gaze being directed at the young prostitutes on the street is clearly Simone's; and the acknowledgement of her presence by the prostitutes, and their direct flirtation with her, connects them in a complicity that is at the same time sisterly and erotic. One girl says, 'Oooh, isn't she pretty?' Another giggles and says to a friend, 'Maybe it's for her.'

The drive through the night-time streets of King's Cross is like a descent into another world, not so much an underworld as a past world. The tunnels under the railway bridges, smoke-filled from open fires which have been lit to keep the street people warm, are reminiscent of a past time, Victorian, Dickensian. So the mood is one of nostalgia.

The camera's framing of Simone in these scenes seems to dislocate and isolate her. A close-up of her reflection in the rear-view mirror, where we have previously seen her looking at herself, appears to be floating and superimposed over the shadowy night streets. The calls from the girls in the street become more distant, the tense but mournful pace of the film pointing at desire but seeming also to anticipate that something is amiss.

Simone's beautiful reflection in the mirror, the build-up of desire and the erotic teasing of the girls, would understandably seduce black lesbians in the audience. The hints at Simone's 'masculinity' or gender instability are equally seductive, notably in the scenes where she gives George money to - buy clothes and in the men's clothes store.

The large bank roll Simone slips into George's pocket, makes her seem sexy and powerful – and despite his verbal resistance, he receives it passively. If the possession of the Jaguar is a reminder of who has the penis in these scenes, then the exhibition of the bank roll is a reminder of who has the balls. It is Simone's power and desire that is driving the events of the narrative forward.

In the men's shop we see Simone for the first time out of her fetish clothing, her prostitution masquerade, and dressed in trousers. When George asks her in a low voice, 'Do you like men's clothes?', and she whispers back 'Sometimes', their tones are conspiratorial. Her fascinated, sensual caressing of the herringbone fabric of a suit jacket and the cashmere of an overcoat leads her to an erotic, breathy exclamation of 'It's lovely'. Her transvestite fetishising of the clothes – symbolically her purchasing power – leads George to believe for a moment that she is a cross-dresser and is intending to buy the garments for herself.

Finally, her sadistic treatment of men, who represent the power of the social order, is a vicarious pleasure. Being a bitch or being bad is unavoidable in transgressing the feminine constraints of the social order. To see a black woman do so on the screen is very pleasurable.

The scene where Simone sprays mace in the face of the pesky hotel manager, causing George to worry that she doesn't need him to protect her after all, is likely to get laughs. But a woman being violent is still extremely taboo, and the blood-thirsty, castrating, frenzied, rageful woman is as monstrous and repressed in feminism as she is by the phallocracy. So the pleasure in seeing her beat up George and blow away the patriarchal bad guys is perhaps ambivalent and certainly a queer pleasure which black lesbians might allow themselves. Violence feeds into transgressive fantasies we don't always want to admit even to ourselves.

Judith Butler, in her essay, 'The Force of Fantasy: Feminism, Mapplethorpe and Discursive Excess', 'attempts to disentangle the threads of repression, fantasy, absence and presence that weave through lesbian imagery, arguing that fantasy and political discourse are deeply contradictory, and yet inextricable. Isolated from each other, they are like twin sisters separated at birth, who end up echoing each others' lives'. She writes: 'The effort to enforce a limit on fantasy can only and always fail; in part because limits are, in a sense, what fantasy loves most, what it incessantly thematises and subordinates to its own aims. . . . Prohibitions of the erotic are always at the same time, and despite themselves, the eroticisation of prohibition.'[21]

As Butler and a handful of other writers and practitioners have begun to acknowledge, 'a flat and literal stance on sexual representation no longer serves us well. Madonna's success is built on this knowledge: that hets fantasise queerness, dykes fantasise about boys, and being bad is what we all wish, from time to time, we could be.' Butler calls it 'gender trouble': 'It may well be more frightening to acknowledge an identification with the one who debases than with the one who is debased, or perhaps no longer to have a clear sense of the gender position of either.'[22] Yet it is this sort of opening up of fantasy and morality, she argues, which will encourage a further proliferation of lesbian texts and images.

The complexity and contradictions of emotion, desires and power dynamics are played out in a scene where Simone responds to George's underlying masochism and identifies herself with the sadistic bastards who might be exploiting and terrorising Cathy.

George has found a sex video featuring Simone and her old pimp, Anderson. He asks himself, and Simone: 'Why am I doing this?' She responds: 'Because you like me, you fancy me. But having me is nothing George. Any prick can have me . . .' In an effort to stop her revealing any more sordid details about her activities with the fat old men that she screws, he gives her a back hand slap across the face. At this point she freaks out and hits him back.

She then picks up her black leather whip and hits him hard around the head and face, shouting: 'Don't hit me, George, nobody hits me. They can have me but they can't hit me. That fucker did, every day, every hour, whenever he had a spare minute.'

She then stops and holds George. He has tears in his eyes. They hold each other. She says, 'You don't understand, do you?' He asks, 'What don't I understand?'

Simone says, still holding up the whip, 'There are people out there who like this kind of thing and pay him to get it for them. If he has Cathy anyone can have her for whatever they want.' George: 'I thought that was the idea.' Simone: 'I mean anyone, any sadistic bastard that likes little girls, George.'

The male sadist actively negates the mother, punishing her and subsequently all women for their guilt in provoking his castration anxiety. And he over-inflates the power of the father.[23] Simone's sadism transgresses the Oedipal order, disrupting, destabilising and decentring the paternal phallus. By the mobility of the phallus in the text, freed from all fixed references (maternal as well as paternal) Simone harnesses, plays with and eludes its power, allowing the spectator to recognise that no one has the phallus.[24]

SWEET SWEETBACK'S BAADASSSSS SONG

Sweet Sweetback's Baadasssss Song (1971), is an American low budget thriller directed by Melvin Van Peebles. In the opening scene of this film, after the title sequence, there is a strange, almost extra-narrative episode. In a carnivalesque hilarity of democratisation, with more audience participation than at the usual striptease or sex show, a mutual identification of equality of status is acknowledged between black whores, dykes, faggots, studs and white negrophiles. All are outlaws from dominant mainstream white America and the collective common sense belief system which unites them gets played out in a burlesque pantomime staged in the living room of a brothel. It is a mocking parody of society's fears and obsessions. Van Peebles refers to this scene in his shooting script as a freak show and the 'Brothel Circus Scene'. It is like a morality play from the Middle Ages.

It serves as a prologue for the events which follow, arming the cinema audience with the critical tools of distance and irony with which to examine the events of the story and what their significance might be for themselves, their group, predominantly black and working class, as addressed by the film and society at large.

In this sequence a black man with a cane picks up a black girl on a park bench. It takes a while before it becomes clear, when he takes off his suit, that this dildo-packing drag-king is a lesbian.

> They walk in the park. The lesbian persuades the girl to go up to her room and they make love. The exhausted girl finally falls asleep, and the lesbian rolls away from her. She kneels on the dingy carpet, she folds her hands and begins to pray. The lights go off in the living room. Some of the women spectators squeal. Then something appears in the centre of the stage spotted with a flashlight. It sports an outlandish costume, a white frilly dress, perhaps from some long-ago ball or wedding, a garland of plastic flowers on its head, cardboard wings and a Fouth of July sparkler as a wand. It turns full circle and announces: 'I'm the Good Dyke Fairy Godmother. Why, didn't you know that all

good dykes have fairy godmothers? And I'm here to answer this prayer of a good dyke. Zap, child.'

The fairy godmother touches the lesbian with the wand. She then takes off her false beard, her falsies and bra, and her strap-on to become, magically, with the assistance of cinematic dissolves, and as if in answer to her own prayers, a mustachioed stud with a big dick.

'The ex-lesbian awakens the girl. The girl is overjoyed at the transformation and they make love once again.'[25] Signs of femininity and masculinity seem to play across the same eroticised black body. Desire surprises us and mystifies gender positions. A lesbian does have the penis through the power of her desire.

The crowd laughs and screeches and the GDFGM concludes by offering 'as a special added attraction, if one of you young ladies would like to step up and try this gentleman . . .' And when a young white woman jumps up to have a go, the GDFGM, knowing that two white police detectives are lurking at the door, watching, discreetly dissuades her with: 'But, ah, that is to say, however, this offer is only open to, ah, sisters.' At which, the crowd knowingly laughs.

This pageant play presents four myths in circulation about race, gender and sexuality. First, that all black men have big penises and are accomplished lovers; second that, given half a chance, most white women would jump at the chance of being bedded by a black man with a big dick. Third, black lesbians are imitation men whose deepest wish is to have a big black penis; and last, femme lesbians are heterosexual women lost and gone astray and, given the opportunity, they too would wander off to be bedded by a black man with a big dick.

The fascination with the big black penis is hilarious when so grotesquely overdetermined in the brothel mime. But there is a thin line between this parody of obsession and the reality of the destructive force with which the white American psyche has distorted this simple member into a satanic symbol which they equate with their own annihilation. The last two myths are of significance for the black lesbian spectator's reading of this scene.

Heteropatriarchal ideology confuses sexuality and gender. The assumption that there can only be, in binary opposition, one gender/sex male and the other gender/sex not-male mistakenly conflates them into the same phenomenon and construes them as 'natural'. And for feminism, clearly based on the same assumption about the natural distinctness of sex, even if gender is socially constructive, polarised sexes are key in determining who is defined as oppressed and who as the oppressor.

A reading of this scene in the first instance results in the myth that lesbians want to be men, that butch lesbians are proof of that and that femme lesbians are not really lesbians.

A feminist reading of this scene might suggest that butch/femme roles imitate and reinforce male/female polarisations because feminism conflates the butch role with the male sex, linking that in turn with oppression, and the femme role with female and victim of oppression. This persists from early feminism. Seventies feminism sought to eradicate butch-femme behaviour, dress codes and lifestyles from the lesbian community in order to change lesbians into lesbian feminists.

Strangely, for these feminists femmes were also seen not to be real lesbians but 'lost heterosexuals who damage birthright lesbians by forcing them to play the butch role'.[26] Sue-Ellen Case quotes Del Martin and Phyllis Lyons who asserted in their book *Lesbian/Woman* that 'most femmes are divorced heterosexual women who only know how to relate to men and thus force their butches to play the man's role'. And that 'the minority of lesbians who still cling to the traditional male–female or husband–wife patterns in their partnerships are more than likely old-timers, gay bar habituées or working-class women'. This statement posits a 'middle-class, upward mobility of the lesbian feminist identification and shifts the sense of community from that of working-class, often women of colour, lesbians in bar culture'.

This shift to the more correct point of identification of an androgynous, middle-class, white, homogenised lesbian identity in which the too visible eroticism of sexual lesbianism became the (homophobic) othering of lesbian-ism within feminism was also an othering of the stereotypical naturalness or unrepressed sexuality attributed to blacks and working-class people. The representation of black butch lesbians gets easily conflated with stereotypes of black male sexuality and 'contaminated' by the association. This symbolic exchange is especially set into circulation when black and white lesbians are represented together.

What pleasures can this scene in *Sweet Sweetback's Baadasssss Song* offer black lesbian spectators against the grain of racist and heterosexist ideology and myths? The distance opened up by the camp transvestite play with gender as self-parody, but also as critique of the stereotypes, can be filled with her fantasy and desire. Her engagement is clearly summoned because the repres-entation is of a black lesbian and a black butch-femme coupling in which the femme is visibly satisfied with the lovemaking and the butch's dildo.

In a reversal of the usual castration of the phallic woman, for a fleeting moment of the transsex transformation, she does have the penis. The shock of this sudden rupture of the gender/sex sign and the collapse of the boundary between polarised sex positions might also be a thrill for the black lesbian spectator. But on the screen the transformation happens quickly and in that same moment she ceases to be a lesbian and becomes a man, and the transgressive charge abates.

The heterosexual audience is probably relieved by the reattachment of the stolen penis back onto the male hero and is reassured by the audible pleasure it obviously gives the girl, who is saved from her lesbian wanderings. The lesbians have vanished from the screen but the shock waves linger.

For the black lesbian viewer these waves resonate with the internal oscillation of desire which, according to Mulvey, 'lies dormant waiting to be "pleasured" in stories of this kind'.[27] And there is a lesbian residue in *Sweetback's* hero after the transformation which seems to add to his mythical power.

In Van Peebles' script he is the 'man alias lesbian'. If lesbian is one of his aliases then stud, faggot and whore are others. All marginalised black people are invited to identify with this outlaw white-cop-killing black stud. The empowerment of black people is the other side of the coin to the stereotype into which white negrophobics read their annihilation.

Sweetback, made in 1971, anticipates Spike Lee's characterisation of Opal Gilstrap, the predatory lesbian in *She's Gotta Have It*, made fifteen years later. Although she is more contemporary and slightly developed as a character, Lee portrays desire between the two women as impossible, refused, blocked. The name Gilstrap free associates to strap-on. But the promise – or is it a threat? – of a lesbian dick being revealed in action is suppressed.

Opal is made impotent when questioned by Nola Darling, the 'she' of the title, about what lesbian sex is and Opal answers, 'I can tell you what it's not.' Lesbian sex becomes not-sex. And so Opal has nothing to offer Nola, for whom getting her fill of the sex of males is everything. Opal's function seems to be to appear in order to disappear – and this through erasure by another woman, mirroring a self-subtraction. It is interesting that this most deflated and desexed representation of a black lesbian should appear in a film by a black male film-maker when he feels he must respond to Alice Walker/ Spielberg's attack on black men and heterosexuality in *The Color Purple*.

There is no camp interchange between outlaw, queer and black positions here as in *Sweetback*, no transgressive meeting or articulations at the frontiers of race and gender and sexuality. The categories are kept well distinct and nothing strange can happen.

GHOST

What happens when a similar device of gender transformation is used in a mainstream Hollywood film and across race as well as gender? Is the potential for the transgressive charge as great as it was in Van Peebles' cult film, which addresses a specific subcultural audience?

Queer readings are as dependent on intertextual information that the spectator brings to bear on the film as on a queer subtext. A Hollywood text, therefore, should be ripe for queer readings. *Ghost* is a big budget romantic comedy thriller, directed by Jerry Zucker in 1990. In one particular scene from the film, issues about boundaries between black and white are played out beneath the love story between a young white couple, Sam (Patrick Swayze) and Molly (Demi Moore).

Early in the film, Sam is murdered but his ghost is trapped on earth, doomed to wander in limbo until his death is avenged. He tries to communicate with Molly but she cannot see him or hear him. The only person who can, he discovers by chance, is Oda Mae (Whoopi Goldberg), a black woman who makes a living by posing as a medium.

In the scene in question, Oda Mae, seeing the strength of the love between the couple, how powerful their yearning to physically touch each other again, offers her body for Sam to use. Sam's ghostly form superimposes itself over Oda Mae's body and is then absorbed by it. Sam and Oda Mae have merged. Oda Mae's body becomes the vehicle of Sam's desire for Molly. Oda Mae's consciousness seems to have been evacuated, but where does it go?

The erotic tension in the scene builds quickly by returning to the romantic music that had played over the couple's love scene earlier in the film. Heavy breathing is also audible on the sound track. Oda Mae's black hands, with their long red nails, clasp Molly's hands. The camera pans up to Molly's face, across her heaving breasts and up to her love-softened face as she closes her eyes.

In the next shot, when they stand up to dance, we expect to see Oda Mae but instead see that Sam's body is in her place. We see him in Molly's mind as she experiences his reappearance. Sam touches her face and kisses her hair. A long shot shows just the two of them in the room where there had been three. Oda Mae has completely disappeared – until a violent knock at the door disrupts the atmosphere of erotic tension and Molly and Oda Mae are thrown apart as Sam is expelled from Oda Mae's body.

Hollywood can only let us see what Molly imagines – Sam's face and body next to her own. But the disorienting shock of Oda Mae's hand on Molly's, along with the intense erotic charge between them, is not quickly forgotten by the spectator. This may be disturbing and unpleasant for white heterosexual viewers. It is interesting to speculate whether white women recoil with horror at this scene, unable to get the image out of their minds, remaining mingled with the erotic feelings that the music had brought on in the first instance.

But for the black lesbian spectator, certainly, there seems to be a frisson, a ghost of desire between the two women which does not require the suspension of disbelief. Add to this the intertextual reference of Whoopi Goldberg's lesbian exchange as Miss Celie in Steven Spielberg's film of Alice Walker's novel, *The Color Purple*, and the circulation of lesbian desire runs riot in the scene.

The gesture of self-effacement and self-sacrificing exploitation which could be read into a character giving up her body for a white man to inhabit and use is an ambivalent image for a black lesbian audience. But the transgressive result of not knowing whose point of view and whose desire is being expressed through Oda Mae's eyes opens the reading up to uncertainty for the white and heterosexual spectator as well. 'The psychic-social boundary ... is transgressed, crossed and disrupted precisely by the super-imposition of two ways of seeing, which thus throws the spectator into uncertainty and undecidability, precisely the experience of ambivalence as a structure of feeling in which one's subject-position is called into question.'[28]

The use of dissolves in the genderfuck sequence in *Sweetback* reinforces the transsexualness of the transition. In *Ghost*, the superimposition of Sam over Oda Mae and his disappearance as he slips under her skin, so to speak, gives the impression of a struggle to blend impossible and incompatible elements – male/female and black/white into a composite whole while retaining glimpses of each component part – she's there and not there, he's there and not there. But mostly the result is the 'noise' of uncertainty and denial – like static from two wavelengths interfering with each other on the same channel.

The effect is the 'splitting of the subject in the construction of white identity, entailed in the affirmation and denial of racial difference' for part of the audience.[29] For the black lesbian spectator, this simulates the struggle she usually has trying to get her desire to fit the shape of the white or male hero in mainstream cinema. The pleasure in this instance comes from the fact that, through the static, the struggle of presence and absence, she can make out her image and her desire from time to time in the weaving.

The superimposition challenges the fact of the body as the principal boundary site of both gender and race. In his article 'White'[30] Richard Dyer suggests that 'whites and men (especially) become characterised by "boundariness".' Although an effort is made to assimilate and define the threat of otherness in the colonial fantasy that a black person can become 'white', Dyer argues that 'this is in fact deeply disturbing, setting in motion the anxiety attendant in a loosening of the fixed visibility of the colonised other'. The problem of 'unfixed appearances' opens up the white person to the possibility of deception and takes away his power to name, define and keep categories separate and pure – deception leading to a possible pollution and feared annihilation. The black person passing as white hides the threat of mixing and miscegenation. They would wear whiteness as a mask, a masquerade which hides their difference.

It is interesting, then, that the most evil character in *Ghost*, the killer, is presented as not black but not white either, a more alien or other-raced person in his foreignness. Although he is identified as Puerto Rican, this seems to hold a stigma of foreignness which, when coupled with racial indeterminacy, a miscegenated blurring of boundaries, is evil incarnate. The other two races remain good because they keep their purity and distinctness. When Sam first speaks to Oda Mae she says: 'You're white, aren't you?' And when Oda Mae and her sisters watch the Arsenio Hall show on television, the presenter opens the programme by announcing: 'Don't adjust your TV; I'm black.'

When blacks accuse other blacks of racial inauthenticity, this introduces into the idea of a bounded dichotomy of race defined by body/skin/pigmentation the possibility that race or 'blackness' is a more complex and amorphous quality than can be strictly coded by colour or a single, simple social class condition. The innocent notion of the essential black subject has been brought to an end. The stereotypes and 'master codes' of the dominant culture, the assumption that 'all black people are the same' which reinforces the view of black communities as monolithic and homogenous, and that black subjectivity is defined exclusively by race and nothing but race, have been undermined. It is precisely the hybridity of Black British, African-American and other diaspora cultures which have encouraged cultural critics like Paul Gilroy and Stuart Hall to observe:

> Once we recognise blackness as a category of social, psychic, and political relations that have no fixed guarantees in nature but only the contingent forms in which they are constructed in culture, the questions of value cannot be decided by recourse to empirical common sense about 'colour' or melanin.[31]

This opens a space for the white negroes, alienated and renegade whites who want to be 'black'. Doesn't their very existence point to the complexity of what race is?

WITHOUT YOU I'M NOTHING

Intertextuality is a very important way for lesbian, black and working-class spectators to bring their cultural experiences and discourses into the textual and symbolic exchanges with the mass media. It is with two contrasting intertextual references to the circulation of Sandra Bernhard's 'blackness' that I'd like to begin the analysis of her film, *Without You I'm Nothing*, an independent US comedy/musical directed by John Boskovich in 1990. I think these examples together throw some light on the meaning of the enigmatic black women who haunts the extra-narrative edges of the film. Bernhard almost says with this motif, there's a story to be told, on the margins, while I'm taking up centre stage, claiming to be more black than the black woman, because white people find my blackness more palatable – or do they?

The first reference is in *VIBE*, a magazine dedicated to hip-hop music and culture, the second is in *Playboy*. In *VIBE* the issue is actually foregrounded and dealt with directly. It is with an accompanying article on the phenomenon of whites who 'wanna be black', an interview with Bernhard entitled: 'Sandra's Blackness'.

The article opens: 'In the beginning of the summer, an ad appeared in the LA Weekly for "Divas: Simply Singing! II" (a benefit concert for the Minority AIDS Project in Los Angeles), featuring photographs of various black women who were expected to perform: Patti LaBelle, Marilyn McCoo, Stephanie Mills, Martha Wash, Cherelle, Siedah Garrett, Lalah Hathaway, Marva Hicks, Mary Wilson, and so on. Nestled among all of these divas was a photograph of Sandra Bernhard. No explanation. No apparent sense of irony. Just a head shot of Miss Bernhard, her hair all pumped up, a sweater tied around her neck, her head resting in her hands, her lips as full as ever. One couldn't help but ask a few questions: How did this happen? Who decided to put her on the bill? Do they know she's white? Does she know she's white?

'Of course she does. But Sandra Bernhard is different from other white performers who admit to a black influence. She wears hers on her sleeve like a badge of honour – and then often uses it to make fun of white people.'[32]

The central feature is the visual description of Bernhard 'nestled among' the black divas and with 'her hair pumped up' and 'lips as full as ever'. The reference to her hair and lips immediately throw up the signs usually read as racial signifiers of blackness: woolly or frizzy hair and full lips. Is she or isn't she? The description points to the idea that she could be, almost, by the way she looks. But though she isn't black, the racial instability alarms don't go off just yet because of the stabilising effect of Bernhard's Jewishness – she's not a gentile, so she's not white either.

The confusion of the image stems more from her being 'nestled' among blacks. She is clearly not black in that context. Don't they know, doesn't she know? What is she then? The word 'nestled' has an association with nurturing or mothering. The answer to what she is, then, is perhaps infused by blackness – embodying the qualities that she's learned from the black divas, in their honour. And maybe the key to this intimacy is in the biographical information in the interview, about Bernhard growing up near Detroit in the 1960s with the thriving black music of Motown and with a black housekeeper named Marie. Bernhard: 'She was a really rich, warm, wonderful, emotionally available person that I feel affected my life. She was amazing. And she also played a mean jazz riff on the piano.'

In this way Bernhard is a daughter of blackness as personified by Marie and by the black divas like Diana Ross and Nina Simone. And this is a different register of identification than those white negro masquerades which owe more to Hollywood and the music hall blackface minstrels.

The 'White Negro' of Norman Mailer's famous essay, written in 1957, lived his ambivalent identification with blacks in the American context of the bohemian subcultures of the beatniks and jazz clubs. Mailer asserted that 'It is no accident that the source of Hip is the Negro for he has been living on the margin between totalitarianism and democracy for two centuries.'[33]

Kobena Mercer describes the white negro: 'Like a photographic negative, the white negro was an inverted image of otherness, in which attributes devalorised by the dominant culture were simply revalorised or hyper-valorised as emblems of alienation and outsiderness, a kind of strategic self-othering in relation to the dominant cultural norms.'[34]

Mailer's white negro takes the modernist position of 'racial romanticism' – existential white hipsters on the margins of society, the impulse for which can be seen in Western cultural history since the nineteenth century. Its expression reflects the negotiations of the social and political state of relations between the races at that time.

Lou Reed, in his song *I Wanna Be Black*, parodies youth culture's adoption of 'cultural signs of blackness in music, clothes and idioms of speech' as emblems of 'cool'. Although his intentions are an attempt to understand, or empathise, the resulting lyrics, in their uncritical reproduction of stereotypes, seem like just another version of racism: 'I wanna be black, Have natural rhythm, Shoot 20 feet of jism, too. I wanna be black, I wanna be a Panther, Have a girlfriend named Samantha, And have a stable of foxy whores, Oh, I wanna be black.'[35]

Putting on signs of race – masks of stereotypes – this blackface is a 'deeply ambivalent mixture of othering and identification'.[36] As in the iconic images of minstrels, when whites 'assimilate and introject the degraded and de-valorised signifiers of racial otherness into the cultural construction of their own identity' this imitation seems to have more to do with a 'masquerading of white ethnicity'.[37]

In the way that, as Laura Mulvey points out, the pervasive presence of fetishised images of women throughout the whole of the mass media – with which we are constantly bombarded – have nothing at all to do with woman and everything to do with man and his fears and desires, so the 'true exhibit is always the phallus'.[38]

And so this parade of stereotypes, imitations and fetishes also has little or nothing to do with blacks and everything to do with whites, which brings me to the second context circulating Bernhard's blackness.

Playboy magazine[39] had found another way to digest and neutralise the symbolic racial instability provoked by Sandra Bernhard's performances and black appearances (impersonations). *Playboy* is aimed at a male audience with the goal of providing objects for male fantasy, voyeurism and porno-graphic stimulation. Sandra Bernhard's lesbianism and her particular predi-lection for high fashion models is portrayed by *Playboy* with an image of her in bed, her naked body flanked, covered and entwined with the bodies of four nude female models.

The image is spread over nearly two pages, as if it is too packed with bodies to fit onto one. Bernhard's face is at the top of the page and her mouth is open. All the other models, on their backs, supine, their eyes closed as if sleeping, are fanned out along the bottom edge of the image at about the level of Bernhard's knees. Then all of a sudden one notices something strange and shocking. A dismembered black hand appears from the fold between the pages, not at first clearly attached to a black body, or *any*body. It does seem, however, to be emerging from between Bernhard's legs, but this usually privileged place in *Playboy* is hidden from view behind the draped body of one of the models.

In search of the body which belongs to the hand, the viewer's eye then happens upon the bald head of a black model. Her face is completely obscured and the rest of her body disappears into the fold between the pages or is submerged under the bodies of Bernhard and the other models. The other strange thing is that, unlike the other models, she is not passively on her back, but facing forward, as if ready for action.

It doesn't take much to decipher the fears and obsessions which abound for the creators of this image. The sleeping beauties languish in postcoital sensuality, all equally satisfied by Bernhard's prowess in the bed, the emblem of which is the phallic black hand. In case we should miss the reading of the hand it is reinforced by the baldness of the model which scrambles signals about whether or not this is a man or a woman, with no other signs like a face or breasts to corroborate. But more, it is reminiscent of one of Robert Mapplethorpe's photographs of a black male nude whose head, neck and torso are framed in such a way as to make the whole look like a penis. Further down Bernhard's leg another, smaller hand of one of the white models seems to echo this reading of active, phallic hand with its erect thumb and black leather fingerless gloves (in the black skin of an animal).

For *Playboy*, Sandra Bernhard's power and appeal is that of a top-femme, a masculine or phallic woman, and her lesbianism is one obvious outcome of this. Her identification with blackness complicates the picture. Doesn't that make her a black man masquerading as a Jewish dominatrix? And so the result for the white male reader of *Playboy* must be erotically fascinating but highly ambivalent.

The result for the black lesbian viewer is also ambivalence. And the question remains how much is this about white people using black signs to provoke white fears and fascinations in order to exert white mastery over them and reinforce white myths about white supremacy? In other words, how much of this is about the construction of white ethnicity and how much of this is about Bernhard – and other white people like her who resist the racist and heterosexist status quo – trying to set up political and ethical alliances with black people who are fighting racism in their everyday lives. I think that in the making of *Without You I'm Nothing*, Bernhard has tried to go some way toward clearly answering that question, though her race-bending provokes a great deal of ambivalence and anxiety for some.

Without You I'm Nothing is John Boskovich's 1990 screen adaptation of Sandra Bernhard's 1988 one-woman off-Broadway show of the same name. The title of the film itself is loaded with associations about the dialogues, relationships and negotiations between the 'you' and 'I' of the title, depending on whether a black or a white person is positioned in one or the other positions or in both. It brings into view the 'politics of enunciation'[40] where the contextual relations between author, text and reader effect different readings by different readers.

But it also provokes shifting and multiple points of identification for each spectator, problematising a fixed and simple race identity as if black, white, Jewish were pure and separate categories, sealed off from one another biologically, culturally and symbolically.

The title of the film ironically points to the fact that although there is, of course, still economic and social apartheid for blacks in America today, whites have always pillaged black culture and music and profited disproportionately from their imitations. Culturally, materially and symbolically, white America's dependence on black America for its continued existence and domination resonates in the title.

Richard Dyer describes how whiteness as an ethnic identity, because it is naturalised by ideology as the norm, becomes invisible, both everything and nothing.[41] He says further, 'Whites hold power in society, but are materially dependent upon black people. It is this actual dependency of white on black, in a context of continued white power and privilege, that throws the legitimacy of white domination into question. What is called for is a demonstration of the virtue of whiteness that would justify continued domination, but this is a problem if whiteness is invisible.'

Whiteness requires black subordination for its own domination, black poverty for its own riches; it claims virtue by defining itself as civilised and repressed to black's naturalness or savagery, technological to black's primitive, ordered to black's chaos and degeneration, cerebral to black's physicality.

Bernhard deconstructs whiteness, reveals 'the political unconscious of white ethnicity', laying bare 'the constitutive ambivalences that structure whiteness' by splitting the subject's identification. White ethnicity is based on a disavowal of difference, fixing the phobogenic black object by stereotypes which are endlessly repeated. And, ambivalently, white ethnicity is based on the assertion of blackness as difference in an expression of white dominance and mastery. What happens when they cross into the position of the other in a relationship of awe or equivalence instead of mastery? Doubts about the legitimacy of white domination are circulated by the statement, *Without You I'm Nothing*.

The other 'I' and 'you' of the title are embodied in the film by Sandra Bernhard as the performer and the bored black audience for whom she's performing, and especially the beautiful and dignified black figure played by model Cynthia Bailey, who enigmatically haunts the margins of the film until she enters the space of the performance as the last and only member of the audience at the end. It is she who answers the question and resolves what is undecidable in the ambivalence of the text.

There is a lot of pleasure in the recognition of the range of black personae that Bernhard brings to the screen in a series of sketches and in the celebration of blackness and the life and soul of black music as an unavoidable cultural force in American history. All the taboos and stereotypes and typical cross-race encounters are paraded out or parodied to the utter boredom of the black audience. White personae are also mocked, debased and deconstructed. In the process race categories reverse, collapse, merge and dissolve. In the final scene, Sandra Bernhard strips off her costume and personae and, wearing only an American flag, admits to being a fraud and a liar. She says to the audience: 'Without You I'm Nothing.'

Literally stripping to expose herself completely to the audience, she ends to find that everyone has left except for the Cynthia Bailey character who, at intervals throughout the film, we have seen going about her daily life. Bernhard waits at the end of her performance for the black woman's verdict. Bailey writes in red lipstick on her white tablecloth, 'Fuck Sandra Bernhard'. Then, as epic music wells up on the soundtrack, and wearing a white flowing dress that floats around her body, infused with light and billowing in the breeze as if full of emotion, she goes out through the door into a blinding white light. The screen dissolves to white, and African music plays on the soundtrack.

In this final scene, then, this beautiful black woman, who summons the identification of the black, lesbian spectator, does not reflect Sandra Bernhard back to herself as the alienated ideal, the whole raced existence to the white nothing, but displaces the debased white self-exhibition of the stereotypes and imitations with an heroic and mythical bitch. But this, at last, leaves us with an open book and a clean page for symbolic relations between the races. The infusing of the black woman with light refers to cinema's tradition of Hollywood lighting codes, developed in relation to white woman's representation 'to endow them with a glow and radiance'. When a black character is lit like this, it thus has the effect of a 'reversal of the good/bad, white/black, light/darkness antinomies of Western culture'.[42]

The continuation of the African music on the soundtrack, having displaced the Western classical music, seems to echo a statement made by Bernhard earlier in the film about rhythm, the beat, the funk as the libidinal and revolutionary life force common to all humanity. 'The funk fights fascism, racism, sexism, homophobia . . .' And then, challengingly, 'You are gonna funk, you ingrate motherfuckers, you must funk with me.'

This film speaks to black audiences about an ending of the fraud of white supremacist myths and degrading black stereotypes. It speaks to white audiences, the new generation of whom have grown up in a miscegenated and multicultural world, through the media if not in their own neighbourhoods, about a hope for resolving the 'racial gap which they don't feel responsible for'. And it does so by crossing over, by loving instead of fearing blackness, by having black heroes, by refusing racism, and ultimately by embracing African-American culture which is all Americans' culture. This has been called the Afro-Americanisation of American youth: 'A potent thought since [the] country is fast headed toward a non-white majority for the first time since its colonisation.'[43]

CONCLUSION

These four films potentially offer a new kind of pleasure for black lesbian spectators who can seize queer readings from them. It is the ambivalence which causes a queer feeling. Pleasure and threat co-exist in the shattering of fixed categories and stereotypes. Black lesbian spectators must renegotiate their own stereotypes.

Conscious of themselves individually and collectively as a critical and 'strategic audience', black lesbian spectators make impatient demands on current texts. They seek to open a space for the articulation of black lesbian desires and fantasies which operate, from subjective experiences, at the borderlines of race, class, gender and sexuality.

Queer readings differ from other forms of oppositional readings. Although the spectator's response indicates something is strange or disturbing about the text, it may be undecidable whether or not its representations are hostile or valuable. Undecidable signs in queer subtexts may at first appear hostile to pleasurable black lesbian identification. However, transgression and collapses of fixed categories which limit potential black lesbian representation can give pleasure and empowerment and allow as yet unimaged new images and narratives.

Indeterminacy opens signs up as a site for struggle and so to the appropriation by any political discourse, as in the appropriation of radical feminist anti-pornography arguments by the Moral Right. It also allows hybridity, ambivalence and the co-existence of multiple and shifting points of identification to open up the field of subjectivity and a space for play, self-invention, polymorphous perversity and jouissance.

NOTES

1 Jacqueline Bobo, 'The Color Purple: Black Women as Cultural Readers', in E. Deidre Pribram (ed.), *Female Spectators: Looking at Film and Television*, Verso, London, 1988, pp.95–6.
2 ibid., p.96.
3 Gina Marchetti, 'Subcultural Studies and the Film Audience: Rethinking the Film Viewing Context', in Bruce Austin (ed.), *Current Research in Film: Audiences, Economics, and Law*, vol.2, Abex Publishing Corp., Norwood, NJ, 1986, p.73.
4 ibid., p.73.
5 Laura Mulvey, 'Visual Pleasure and Narrative Cinema', *Screen*, vol.16, no.3, Autumn 1975, p.8.
6 Vern L. Bullough and Bonnie Bullough, *Cross-Dressing, Sex and Gender*, University of Pennsylvania Press, Philadelphia, 1993, p.325. They also refer to Marjorie Garber, *Vested Interests: Cross-Dressing and Cultural Anxiety*, Routledge, New York, 1992.
7 'Jouissance' is a French word rich in connotations. Its simplest translation in English is as 'pleasure'. The noun is derived from the verb *jouir*, which means to enjoy, to revel in without fear of cost, and also to have an orgasm.
8 J. P. Telotte, 'Beyond All Reason: The Nature of the Cult', in J. P. Telotte, (ed.), *The Cult Film Experience – Beyond All Reason*, University of Texas Press, Austin, 1991, p.16.
9 ibid., p.16.
10 Gayle Rubin, 'Of Catamites and Kings: Reflections on Butch, Gender, and Boundaries', in Joan Nestle (ed.), *The Persistent Desire – A Femme-Butch Reader*, Alyson Publications Inc., Boston, 1992, p.473.
11 Michel Foucault, *The Order of Things – An Archaeology of the Human Sciences*, Tavistock Publications, London, 1970, p.xv.

12 Jean Baudrillard, *The Transparency of Evil: Essays on Extreme Phenomena*, translated by James Benedict, Verso, London, 1993, p.21.
13 Oprah Winfrey's interview with Michael Jackson, 15 February 1993, BBC2.
14 Mulvey, op. cit., pp.6–7.
15 Chris Straayer, 'The She-man: Postmodern Bi-sexed Performance in Film and Video', *Screen*, vol.31, no.3, Summer 1990, p.280.
16 Foucault, op. cit., p.xviii.
17 Laura Mulvey, 'Afterthoughts on "Visual Pleasure and Narrative Cinema" inspired by *Duel in the Sun* (King Vidor, 1946)', *Framework*, vol.6, nos 15–17, Summer 1981, p.13.
18 ibid., p.15.
19 Mandy Merck, 'The Feminist Ethics of Lesbian s/m' in *Perversions: Deviant Readings*, Virago, London, 1993. She quotes Catherine Millot, 'The Feminine Superego', in Parveen Adams and Elizabeth Cowie (eds), *The Woman Question*, MIT Press, Cambridge, MA, 1990.
20 'Top femme' is a variation of the S/M classification 'dominant/submissive' or 'sadist/masochist' which indicates the initiator of a sexual scene. 'Top' is associated with the one who has power or controls the direction and goal of the encounter. The positions express the relationship 'doer/the done to'. 'Butch/femme' is the lesbian identity style in which 'butch' is traditionally detached, the sexual initiator, the one who chooses in relationship to the available, vulnerable, to-be-looked-at femme. 'Top-femme' highlights the self-confidence of the lesbian femme who actively invites the gaze by orchestrating desire through consciously sexual display. Uncompromising, she gets what she wants though she may remain untouchable. She knows just what buttons to push to stretch her bottoms to their limits.
21 Marusia Bociurkiw, FEMINALE 6, Internationales Frauen Film Festival (Catalogue), Köln, 27–31 May 1992, p.46. She quotes Judith Butler, 'The Force of Fantasy: Feminism, Mapplethorpe and Discursive Excess', *Differences: A Journal of Feminist Cultural Studies*, vol.2, no.2, 1990, pp. 105–25.
22 ibid., p.46.
23 Gilles Deleuze, *Masochism: An Interpretation of Coldness and Cruelty*, George Braziller, New York, 1971.
24 Parveen Adams, 'Of Female Bondage', in Teresa Brennan (ed.), *Between Feminism and Psychoanalysis*, Routledge, London and New York, 1989.
25 Melvin Van Peebles, *Sweet Sweetback's Baadasssss Song* (shooting script), Lancer Books Inc., New York, 1971, pp.23–4 and pp.113–15.
26 Sue-Ellen Case, 'Towards A Butch-Femme Aesthetic', *Discourse*, vol.11, no.1, Fall–Winter 1988–89, p.58. She quotes Del Martin and Phyllis Lyon, *Lesbian/Woman*, Bantam, New York, 1972.
27 Laura Mulvey, op. cit., 1981, p.15.
28 Kobena Mercer, 'Skin Head Sex Thing: Racial Difference and the Homoerotic Imaginary', in Bad Object-Choices (ed.), *How Do I Look? Queer Film and Video*, Bay Press, Seattle, 1991, p.187.
29 ibid., p.189.
30 Richard Dyer, 'White', *Screen*, vol.29, no.4, Autumn 1988.
31 Mercer, op. cit., p.204. He quotes Stuart Hall, 'New Ethnicities', in *Black Film/British Cinema*, ICA Document 7, ICA/BFI, London, 1988, p.28.
32 Jonathan Van Meter, 'Sandra's Blackness', *VIBE*, Preview Issue, Fall 1992.
33 Norman Mailer, 'The White Negro: Superficial Reflections on the Hipster', in *Advertisements for Myself*, Putnam, New York, 1959 (originally published in *Dissent*, Summer 1957).
34 Mercer, op. cit., pp.207–8.
35 Lou Reed, on the album *Street Hassle*, 1978.

36 Mercer, op. cit., p.207.
37 ibid., p.208.
38 Laura Mulvey, 'Fears, Fantasies and the Male Unconscious or "You don't know what is happening, do you, Mr Jones?"', in *Visual and Other Pleasures*, Macmillan, London, 1989, p.13.
39 'Not Just Another Pretty Face', *Playboy*, vol.39, no.9, September 1992. Photography by Michel Comte, text by Sandra Bernhard.
40 Mercer, op. cit., p.195.
41 Dyer, op. cit., p.48.
42 ibid., p.61.
43 James Ledbetter, 'Imitations of Life', *VIBE*, Preview Issue, September 1992, p.110. He quotes Cornel West.

3

THE GAY GAZE,
OR
WHY I WANT MY MTV

Steven Drukman

INTRODUCTION

Since the publication in 1975 of Laura Mulvey's ground-breaking essay, 'Visual Pleasure and Narrative Cinema', much debate has centred on the validity and usefulness of psychoanalytically based film theory, particularly within feminism. Most of the debate concerns itself with the concept of the spectator as historically constructed (rather than solely gender-specifically subject to a given text) and the idea that any theories posited about a universal 'male' or 'female' spectator are necessarily reductive. Moreover, feminists have pointed out that there is no 'female' spectator in Mulvey's essay, and have concentrated on 'phallocentrism' as a point of departure within feminist debate.

However, as Janet Bergstrom and Mary Ann Doane point out in a 1989 issue of *Camera Obscura*:

> It was Laura Mulvey's 1975 essay which acted as a catalyst for considerations of sexual difference and spectatorship *per se*. . . . For a while it seemed (and often still seems) that every feminist writing on film felt compelled to situate herself in relation to Mulvey's essay. The structure of psychoanalytic concepts – fetishism, voyeurism, castration – and their articulation within the aesthetic categories of narrative and spectacle generated a tremendous amount of rethinking and discourse. (7)

As of yet, there has been little or no writing that has undertaken the reformulation of the gaze (heterosexual and male, as theorised by Mulvey) into a formalised model of a 'gay gaze'. I aim to do just that: limiting an examination to psychoanalytic tenets – fetishism, scopophilia, ego-identification – I will reimagine Mulvey's gaze model in a gay male context.

In the issue of *Camera Obscura* excerpted above, Laura Mulvey offers an overview of feminist film theory dating from her 1975 essay to the present. In addition, many of the most notable theorists in the field offer their views on the state of psychoanalytic spectatorship. David Rodowick (1989: 269) writes:

> Despite the achievements of psychoanalytic film theory and textual analysis in the past twenty years, I would insist that all claims made about processes of identification in actual spectators, powerful and important as they may be, are speculative. . . . To assert that film theory describes positions of identification that are ultimately undecidable with respect to any given spectator is, for me, an indispensable political *a priori*. . . . It is incumbent upon feminist theory – and in fact all critiques of domination – to attempt to create new positions of interpretation, meaning, desire, and subjectivity even while acknowledging they sometimes stand on shaky philosophical legs.

My essay, then, will necessarily generalise a universal gay male spectator to create a new position of interpretation, desire, meaning and subjectivity. In an attempt to schematise from scratch a new taxonomy for gay male spectatorship I humbly concur with Rodowick's *a priori* of ultimate undecidability. It is my hope that, like post-Mulvey theorists have done, scholars will continue work in gay studies that will round out the psychoanalytic discussion offered here.

Furthermore, I believe that a psychoanalytic methodology is useful to a study of gay spectatorship in much the way feminism has made psychoanalytic theory useful in film *à la* Mulvey, Cook, Penley, Silverman and others. Mulvey's original intention was to 'challenge this cinema of the past. Psychoanalytic theory is thus appropriated as a political weapon, demonstrating the way the unconscious of patriarchal society has structured film norm' (1975: 16). My aim is far less tendentious, but at the same time I recognise the uneasy relationship between the burgeoning field of gay studies and much of the psychoanalytic literature.

This uneasiness is due mostly to psychoanalysts' views of homosexuality as a deviant psychopathology. Until 1973, the American Psychiatric Association listed homosexuality as a mental disorder in its *Diagnostic and Statistical Manual* (*DSM*–III). Even when the APA removed homosexuality from its nomenclature it was 'for scientific, not ideological, reasons. Psychoanalysts were held scientifically accountable for the claim made by many that homosexuality was pathological; the scientific database supporting their assertion was inadequate' (Friedman 1991: 270). However, despite cultural and socio-medical (post-Freudian, orthodox APA) conservatism, a psychoanalytic model that adheres to the actual Freudian model is more liberating for gay men. Michael Warner, in an essay attempting to separate homosexuality from a pathological narcissism, acknowledges that for gay men 'the first difficulty lies in appropriating psychoanalysis' (Warner 1990: 192). The sticking point is Freud's restrictive reliance on a heterosexual, teleological norm: an idea incompatible with many of Freud's own psychoanalytic premises. Among these premises are the separation of a normative genital/ object choice from instinct ('triebe', or 'drive'), the belief in an inherent bisexuality and, as Warner points out, the incongruence of psychoanalytic explanations linking homosexuality to narcissism (1990: 193).

These incongruities are taken up by Jeffrey Weeks in his *Sexuality and its Discontents: Meanings, Myths and Modern Sexualities*. Weeks points to the cultural conservatism of Freud and his followers whose

> attitudes towards homosexuality could, indeed would, change, but it would always have to be judged by the norm of heterosexuality. That was the organisation of sexuality that culture demanded and there seemed to be no alternative to that.
>
> (Weeks 1985: 156)

So although Freud recognised the seeds of homosexuality in all men and women, 'a heterosexual genital organisation of sexuality . . . demanded their subordination to the norm' (155). It is just this dichotomous clash, between its radicalism and conservatism, that leads Warner to remark:

> Although it is uniquely equipped to analyse the slippage in our culture between understandings of gender and understandings of self and other, traditionally psychoanalysis has been the principal site of that slippage.
>
> (1990: 192)

This is what prompts Mulvey's (and other feminists') appropriations of Freud toward 'a political use of psychoanalysis' and why I think a gay male appropriation of psychoanalysis *per se* is integral to the future of gay studies.

My work owes a great debt to Freud even as I grant that psychoanalysis and gay studies are uneasy, if not strange bedfellows. As I formulate a gay way of gazing, I am aware that a psychosexual essentialism is at cross-purposes with a constructivist agenda. However, as Wayne Koestenbaum explains in his essay on gay reading:

> My description of a limited point of view – mine – as if it were universal shares with the drag queen a taste for absolute gesture . . . the (male twentieth-century first world) gay reader, like the female spectator, knows the rewards of looking from the outside in. He reads resistantly for inscriptions of his condition, for texts that will confirm a social and private identity founded on a desire for other men.
>
> (1990: 176)

While Koestenbaum is far more brazen and unapologetic when 'submitting to a dangerously comfortable essentialism – as if gayness transcended gender, class, race, nationality or epoch', I feel compelled to be self-reflexive about the shaky philosophical legs on which this project (possibly) stands. Lacking the drag queen's bravado, and stating outright the *a priori* of ultimate undecidability, I offer one gay man's rendering of the gay gaze.

WHY I WANT MY MTV

E. Ann Kaplan, feminist cultural studies theorist and pre-eminent MTV analyst, speaks of MTV's 'varying types of gender address' and concludes that 'MTV does not speak anything like a monolithic sexual discourse (whatever one might think by turning the channel on for half an hour from time to time)' (1986: 9). These varying addresses are unique to the televisual construction of MTV, where a panoply of video clips reflect, in a visual performative medium, the richly (and sexually) varied world of popular music. This relatively new form is an open field for any and all spectatorial positioning, and its symbiotic intersections with the gay community (from the many gay/video bars to Madonna's *Vogue* video) are already apparent. Before I can apply the 'gay gaze' to this form, however, I will trace the trajectory of feminist theory on the subject, to lay the foundation for a gay way of looking.

Laura Mulvey's 'Visual Pleasure and Narrative Cinema' has been considered pioneering in its fusion of feminist and psychoanalytic theory with theories of film spectatorship. Although criticised for her liberal readings of Lacan and Freud and for conflating elements of both in forming one psychoanalytic paradigm,[1] the essay has had far-reaching effects in the field of film theory. In establishing a taxonomy of dual (and occasionally contestatory) drives for the male spectator, Mulvey set into motion new ways of thinking about ways of looking, especially for feminist film theory. The first drive, scopophilia, arises from 'pleasure in using another person as an object of sexual stimulation through sight. The second, developed through narcissism and the constitution of the ego, comes from identification with the image seen' (Mulvey 1975: 18).

While innovative in its virtual invention of the male heterosexual gaze, Mulvey's essay also generated some questions. How does one politicise this psychoanalytic model in order to subvert the spectator's usual modes of pleasure? How does one break from cinema's phallocentrism and still speak in a language that is understood? More to the point, if one is not a male heterosexual spectator, why pay the price for the ticket?

Teresa de Lauretis, more than a decade after Mulvey, and in an article of similar import, asked, 'What manner of seduction operates in cinema to procure the complicity of women in a desire whose terms are those of the Oedipus?' (1985: 14). Must not this question be asked of gay men, too, since their desires must inherently resist Mulvey's analysis? According to Mulvey, the object of scopophilic pleasure is the woman and the subject of ego-identification is the man. For the gay male spectator, the object of scopophilic pleasure is the man and the subject of ego-identification is, I propose, in constant flux between the woman and the man. This twist on the traditional reception of Oedipal diegesis is central to understanding what I will call the 'gay gaze'.

In her 1981 'Afterthoughts on "Visual Pleasure and Narrative Cinema"' Mulvey frees up possibilities for the gaze, formerly incongruent with her original restrictive analysis. Still content with an essentialist masculinisation of the gaze, Mulvey's revision now allowed for a resistance to traditional heterosexual diegesis. She says that the female spectator 'temporarily accepts "masculinisation" in memory of her active phase' (1981: 15). While this acknowledges the possibility of variable spectatorial positions, it still rests on a masculine propulsion of narrative, leading the man (for our purposes, even a gay man) to be the 'maker of meaning' while the woman remains 'bearer of the look'.

Recent feminist film theory has taken advantage of the 'gaze-shifting' space allowed by Mulvey's later essay, trying simultaneously to reformulate the passive positioning of the female. Mary Ann Doane, in a 1982 essay, wonders if the female gazes in the same way that a man gazes and concludes that 'sexual mobility would seem to be a distinguishing feature of femininity' (1982: 81). Leaving the scopophilic drive behind (which she equates with the male gaze), she posits two possibilities of ego-identification for the female spectator: narcissistic identification with the female or a transvestite identi-fication with the male. This oscillation allows for a different sort of pleasure – one that has 'potential to manufacture a distance from the image which is manipulable' (1982: 87) – allowing for a resistance to the dominant (hetero-sexual) male gaze.

Other feminist theorists have challenged Mulvey's male/female, active/passive model, some previous to Mulvey's 1981 essay, some after. In 1978, B. Ruby Rich, calling Mulvey 'pessimistic' (Rich 1990: 279), put forth the idea of a pleasurable and resistant female spectatorship. Janet Bergstrom's 'Enunciation and Sexual Difference' (1979) emphasised Freud's belief in an inherent bisexuality, allowing for 'trans-gendered' identification. Finally, E. Ann Kaplan, extending the hypotheses of Doane's essay asked, 'Is there the possibility of both sex genders occupying the positions we now know as masculine and feminine?' (1983: 28).

The essay that synthesised many of these disparate notions was Teresa de Lauretis' 'Oedipus Interruptus' (1985). In this essay, de Lauretis tries to deepen the analysis around male-propelled Oedipal narrative to pinpoint more concretely the moment(s) of feminine identification. While Mulvey's 1975 project was written to subvert the phallic gaze ('It is said that analysing pleasure, or beauty, destroys it'), de Lauretis' project is not out 'to destroy vision altogether, as it is to construct another vision and the conditions of visibility for a different social subject' (1985: 38). In stressing the social side of the gaze, de Lauretis foregrounds interpretation as existing in a moment of enunciation: an interaction between the actual text and the desires of the socially constructed spectator.

Much of feminist film theory is useful in pinning down the gay gaze. I would suggest that gay/male/gazing pleasure resides in the id's scopophilic faculty as well as the ego's mode of identification (Mulvey). I would argue that there is room for resistance within traditional. heterosexual diegesis, but that narrative is still propelled via the phallic gaze (Doane). Finally, I maintain that gay men are historical subjects and that 'film's images are not neutral objects of a pure perception' (de Lauretis 1985: 36) but that images have different valences as filtered through the sensibility of the gay male spectator. It is to this third aspect – actually an augmentation of the gay gaze – that I would now like to turn.

Various theorists have written about this ineffable gay sensibility[2] and some (most notably Richard Dyer and Vito Russo) have used the cinema as a logical site of application. Whereas Russo's analysis is concerned mostly with the shrouding of homoerotic content within filmic narrative, Dyer comes closer to formulating a hermeneutic philosophy informed by homosexual experience. A brief examination of these writers is useful to identify the components of a gay sensibility, and then to synthesise them into a more or less specific gay gaze.

In *The Celluloid Closet*, Vito Russo writes:

> People say that there can be no such thing as a 'gay sensibility' because the existence of one would mean that there is a straight sensibility, and clearly there is not. But a gay sensibility can be many things; it can be present even when there is no sign of homosexuality, open or covert, before or behind the camera. . . . It is a ghetto sensibility, born of the need to develop and use a second sight that will translate silently what the world sees and what the actuality may be.
>
> (Russo 1981: 92)

Although clearly less sophisticated than Mulvey's paradigm of the straight male gaze, Russo's is one of the earliest suggestions that there may be a gay way of looking (in Russo's words, a 'second sight'). This passage is anomalous to much of the book, however, which is less concerned with the gay decoding process than it is with the encoding of homosexuality, veiled or otherwise, by film directors, writers, etc. *The Celluloid Closet* is best read as 'an impressive act of gay archaeology' (Medhurst 1984: 59) that, despite an overtly essentialist analysis, is an invaluable resource for gay cultural studies. For my purposes here, it is useful in its claiming of a gay sensibility, one that has enabled 'lesbians and gay men to see . . . something on the screen that they knew related to their lives in some way. Often it was the simple recognition of difference, the sudden understanding that something was altered or not what it should be' (Russo 1981: 92).

A somewhat more scholarly project than Russo's book, Richard Dyer's recent *Now You See It*, is a compilation of films made by lesbians and gay men with lesbian and gay subject matter. Dyer's focus is the interaction of 'historically specific lesbian/gay subcultures and particular filmic traditions, as worked through in the texts of the films' (Dyer 1990: 2). Although not concerned with a gay gaze *per se*, he acknowledges a gay awareness of 'the construction of appearance – as a perception of the straight world, as an ironic distance from it, as a strategy of survival within it' (Dyer 1990: 284). Throughout his analysis he emphasises the enunciative cinematic process, concluding:

> [Gay films] are, like all ideology, necessary fictions . . . part of the ceaseless process of construction, reconstruction and deconstruction of identities and cultures. . . . Lesbian/gay culture is different only to the degree to which the erasure of the gap between construction and experience is less naturalised than with many other human categories (notably race, gender and, supremely, heterosexuality) and thus in its high degree of awareness of that gap.
>
> (Dyer 1990: 285–6)

This differs slightly from the Russo excerpt quoted above. Russo is speaking of a type of gay savvy: the notion that a gay spectator could detect 'reality' about sexual pleasures even when obfuscated by a smokescreen of 'appearance'. Dyer's gay sensibility is far less cloak-and-dagger (and far more postmodern) in recognising that constructions are 'necessary fictions' to which we all adhere and that gay women and men are simply part of (albeit more aware of) these fictive constructions. Where Russo sniffs out the sham of heterosexuality in certain texts, Dyer says that heterosexuality is a sham to begin with.

Both writers are cited here not to elevate one analysis over another but to isolate these modes of perception as aspects of gay reception. In other words, both of these awarenesses (of the duality of appearance/reality and of the duality of construction/experience) inform and deform the pleasure paradigm set up by Mulvey to create a singular gay gaze. This gay sensibility enables the twist of traditional Oedipal narrative that makes the gay male want to gaze at all, and may be why MTV is so appealing.

Discussions of a gay sensibility inevitably lead to discussions of camp; the subject seems, in fact, unavoidable given the tenets of contradiction, irony and subterfuge integral to the sensibility. Camp is a 'natural' response to the polarisation of appearance and reality, of social constructions and lived experience, and thereby derives its humour from these opposites. Camp is important to this discussion because, in the cinema, on television and in the theatre, camp is a primary hue through which the gay gaze is filtered.

This metaphor of mediation is used on purpose: Sontag writes (and I agree) that camp is 'a sensibility that, among other things, converts the serious into the frivolous' (1966: 276) and 'one that is alive to a double sense, in which things can be taken ... between the thing as meaning something, anything, and the thing as pure artifice' (281). Inextricably linked to a gay sensibility, it is only incidental to the gay gaze. Like a rose-tinted pair of glasses kept in the breast pocket of the gay male spectator, camp is ever handy, but used more for cosmetic reasons than for clarity of vision. In other words, camp allows for a more seamless shifting (between object of scopophilia and subject of ego-identification) for the gay gaze. Rose-tinted lenses blur the rigid constraints of 'straight' heterosexual narrative, making it easier on the eyes.

But even tinted lenses are capable of transformative vision. In his essay 'Camp and the Gay Sensibility', Jack Babuscio writes that camp reflects 'the strong strain of protest that resides in the gay sensibility' (1984: 43). Contrary to Sontag's emphasis on the frivolous nature of camp, Babuscio points to a more serious side. Camp is 'a means of defiance: a refusal to be overwhelmed by unfavourable odds. It is also a method whereby one can multiply personalities, play various parts, assume a variety of roles – both for fun as well as out of need' (43). Camp, then, can be a 'means' or a 'method' for the gay gaze: both a placating/passive 'solvent of morality' (Sontag 1966: 290) and an emancipating/active way to 'project one's need' (Babuscio 1984: 43).

Camp also exerts a unique appeal in popular music, and may help to explain the gay male fascination with music video. As Jon Savage points out, 'The tacky shimmer of lurex flouncing now looks primitive. Camp has become an all-pervasive ingredient in a pop culture [that] has become reified, ironicised, once-removed from the impulses that called it into being. . . . In America, this has been marked by the influence of MTV' (1989: 168). Music video, a performative form that, by its very nature, exposes identities as necessary fictions, is already imbued with camp. Because MTV began as promotional advertisements for pop stars, the artificial constructedness of persona is so obvious that it is rarely commented upon. This is a large part of MTV's gay draw – the chance to gaze at a 24-hour world where artifice is a way of life.

Furthermore, MTV is a logical site of application for any gaze, gay or otherwise, delineated by a psychoanalytic model. Marsha Kinder, writing in *Film Quarterly* suggests that the appeal of music videos is congruent with the act of dreaming. Here, psychoanalytic pleasure is doubly imbricated: in the video's dreamlike narrative structure and in the spectator's always deferred gratification – an aspect of most of television programming – for something better after the commercial break. Moreover, the very nature of the dream experience, where 'reality' and 'appearance' are thrown into question, echoes one aspect of the gay sensibility.

Turning now to this dreamlike world of MTV to illustrate the gay gaze in action, I will consciously mirror the form of Mulvey's 1975 essay. Whereas her subsections were headed 'Man as Maker of Meaning/Woman as Bearer of the Look' (followed by examples in Hitchcock and Sternberg), reimagined in a gay context my headings will read '[Gay] Man as Maker of Meaning/

Man as Bearer of the Look' (followed by examples in Madonna and George Michael).

[GAY] MAN AS MAKER OF MEANING . . .

The ever-shifting ego-identification (from gender to gender) is one part of what differentiates the gay gaze from Mulvey's postulation. Similarly, the world of MTV is a televisual enunciation of shifting gazes due to the varied addresses of different video clips as well as the diversity of contemporary popular music. Simon Frith has called the current state of popular music, with its excess of appropriation and fragmentation, a 'culture of margins around a collapsed centre' (1988: 5); For the gay spectator, already used to modifying his gaze to the codes of traditional filmic narrative, this ex-centric way of looking is nothing new. It is the opportunity to make his gaze centric that appeals to the gay male spectator when watching MTV.

This is not to suggest that MTV has flooded the airwaves with homoerotic imagery. It is merely to reiterate that the absence of a dominant sexual discourse in MTV 'make(s) it impossible to pin down any solid stance toward sexuality' (Kaplan 1983: 9).[3] MTV thus grants freedom to the gay (re)-visioning of Mulvey's gaze, a freedom unsanctioned in mainstream cinema.

Open Your Heart, a 1986 video by Madonna, explicitly addresses the various gaze/address enunciations allowed by MTV. Madonna, calling attention to her 'to-be-looked-at-ness' (Mulvey 1975: 19), enacts the role of a woman employed in a peep show. Immediately pointing up this illusory construction by removing a black wig (changing from the peep-show girl to Madonna), she ensures that our gaze is already decentred. This is followed by shots of the various spectators behind the plexiglass, presumably patrons who are gazing to satisfy their own scopophilic drives. The peep show, then, is an obvious metaphor for MTV, with the patron/spectators representing all of us who tune in and turn on.

Noticeable at once is the variety of gazes being addressed in this clip. Those addressed are, in order of each patron's appearance: two male sailors, hand in hand, identical in appearance (represented by twin mannequins), a leering man, a smiling, apparently aroused black woman, a young 'cowboy', a critic, complete with notepad, scribbling furiously, and an old man, somewhat shocked, gulping bromide tablets. Madonna, then, makes her performance available to many gazes, even as she acknowledges the different responses contingent upon the different spectators' desires.

The gay sailors (the only couple in the video) are brought closer together as the dance progresses, first shown hand in hand, then almost kissing. Despite their deadpan expressions (they are, after all, mannequins), their gazing on Madonna's release of sexual drives apparently enables their desires to be met. It is difficult to celebrate this as wholly liberating for the gay gaze: the gay male spectator is asked to ego-identify with a mannequin, a non-human representation. It may be granting Madonna too much credit to suggest that it was intended to be further commentary on the 'constructed-ness' of gender and sexual identity. More likely, it is a wink and nod to Madonna's gay male following while conceding to the more repressive aspects of MTV and popular culture. (To Madonna's credit, though, the black female spectator is shown at the end of the video smoking a cigarette, her lesbian gaze seemingly sated.)

But even more room is provided for the gay male spectator's shifting ego-identification in the larger narrative of *Open Your Heart*. Lisa Lewis, concerned with a feminist reading, breaks it down this way:

> A young, preadolescent boy dawdles outside the sex parlor, wanting to go inside, but unable to convince the ticket master. The boy's motiva-tions are not altogether clear, although his young age and inquisitive gestures suggest that his interest is pre-sexual. In his innocence, he is fascinated with the act of looking, and covers one of his eyes and then the other, exploring the bounds of vision. His gaze emanates more from an identification sensibility than a sexual voyeurism, and is therefore linked to female rather than male spectatorship. He strikes poses and dances erotically in front of a distortion mirror for his own pleasure . . . [Madonna] re-enters the frame, dressed not as the erotic dancer, but in the clothes and hat of a boy – of the young boy who identifies with her. As she leans over to kiss him, the similarities in their faces, in their facial type, are apparent. His naive, playful fascination with sexual performance is void of the maliciousness and perversity implied in the adult male consumer's pleasure and it is with this wonderment that Madonna chooses to align herself. She abandons the role of adult erotic dancer, retreating to a vision of life in which gender is undelineated, and representation and performance uninformed by hierarchical regimes of looking.
>
> (Lewis 1990: 142–3)

I quote Lewis at length not only for her insight and thoroughness but to show that the gay gaze experiences pleasure in ways similar to the female spectator's enunciation of oscillating identifications. The gay spectator first identifies with the young boy as in traditional phallic-driven diegesis. The boy's sexual otherness, what Lewis calls 'pre-sexual', is enunciated by the gay gaze as homosexual. Therefore, his 'innocence' is read as a lack of sexual engagement even as he is 'fascinated with the act of looking'. The gay gaze 'emanates more from an identification' with Madonna, but also with the gay sailors, who fade in instantly after the fade out on the boy. From our immediate entrance into the peep show, then, the gay spectator has the availability of shifting identifications between three parties: the boy, the sailors and Madonna.

Finally, I have chosen to analyse this video because of its satisfying narrative closure for the gay gaze. As our oscillating identifications are volleyed between the boy and Madonna, through cutaways from her erotic dance to the boy's in front of the mirror, we await the video's climax. Madonna, dressed like the boy, kisses him, in a close-up that shows the 'similarities in their faces'. Mirroring the twin sailors left inside, their kiss seals the MTV narrative for the gay spectator in the manner that the climactic kisses of mainstream cinema satisfy traditional Oedipal diegesis.

MAN AS BEARER OF THE LOOK

Like it or not, MTV has allowed us to get a really good look at our pop idols. As a consequence, more men are feeling the glare of what Mulvey called 'to-be-looked-at-ness'. Traditionally, men had to maintain a phallic hardness to combat the softness associated with being the gaze's object (read: 'woman'). Remarking on the imagery associated with this macho fear of passivity, Richard Dyer notices in the objectified male pin-up the 'clenched fists, the bulging muscles, the hardened jaws, the proliferation of phallic symbols' (1982: 71).

On MTV, these images find constant reinscription in the heavy metal, 'headbanger' video clips. E. Ann Kaplan labels this type of music video as 'nihilist' and its stylistic cachet as 'phallic and homoerotic'. Although the antics of the band members are often replete with stroking guitars and inventive uses for the microphone, these videos are not the ideal site of application for the gay gaze. The reason may lie in the bands' uses of their 'to-be-looked-at-ness'. More often than not, the performers work to subvert the spectator's pleasure, usually through methods of visual distraction. Often this involves constant cutaways to adoring (usually female) fans in the 'audience', allowing for a shift in gaze to diffuse the one-on-one relationship of MTV spectator and spectacle (e.g. Poison's *Ride the Wind*, videos by Ratt, Whitesnake and countless others). Occasionally, the objectification is justi-fied by random displays of athletics: Bon Jovi's gymnastics in *Living on a Prayer* or the high-wire antics of Van Halen's *Avalon*. These videos, therefore, are only somewhat satisfying to the gay gaze. As in much of televised sports, they offer up male spectacle for eroticisation but disavow the gaze entirely.

But this is not always the case on MTV. Aerosmith's *Dude Looks Like a Lady* actively stalks the gay gaze even as it thwarts it. Images of men enjoying Steve Tyler's androgynous form are interwoven with images of their being nonplussed at finding out that he is, indeed, a 'dude'. Motley Crue invites us in to share some phallic imagery by *Smoking in the Boys' Room*, only to be punished for it by the repressive figure of a school-teacher at the end of the video. Other examples abound of MTV artists who acknowledge but subvert the spectator's pleasures (e.g. David Lee Roth, Twisted Sister) proving that 'like so much else about masculinity, images of men . . . are such a strain.

Looked at but pretending not to be – there is seldom anything easy about such imagery' (Dyer 1982: 72).

No video artist has felt this strain more (or so he would have us believe) than George Michael. I would suggest that it is the gay gaze along with MTV that has given Michael's career its remarkable buoyancy. Michael is a performer who, from the very beginning, actively seduced the gaze while infusing his act with a gay sensibility. As a member of the duo Wham!, Michael was usually the object of the gaze in their videos. As Suzanne Moore and others have noted, Andrew Ridgley's role in Wham! was, in fact, never really determined. He didn't compose the music, nor did he sing or play any instruments. Casting loving glances from the sidelines, his presence allowed embodied ego-identification for the gay male spectator as he/we gazed at George Michael. (I am tempted here to note that Hall and Oates have a similar homoerotic appeal, but at least John Oates ostensibly performs a musical function – even if nobody can figure out precisely what it is.) Upon seeing Wham!, Simon Napier-Bell, popular music impresario, 'immediately picked up on the homoerotic tension between the boys and saw it as a marketable phenomenon' (Moore 1988: 55).

George Michael soon embarked on a career as an object of gay scopophilic pleasure. After imploring Ridgley, *Wake Me Up Before You Go-Go*, it was Michael who broke up the relationship to drift toward MTV superstardom. His 'look' was crystallised in the 1985 *Faith* video, where he was fetishised perhaps like no other male performer, before or since, on MTV. Indeed, in much the same way Madonna's *Open Your Heart* addresses shifting gaze identifications via both theme and style, *Faith* seems to be only about George Michael-as-object as the camera objectifies him.

Totally devoid of narrative, the video is a series of shots photographing Michael shaking his hips, holding a guitar. Dressed in faded blue jeans and a distressed leather jacket, he does not strain against male objectification through the 'phallic hardness' mentioned above. On the contrary, Michael softens his image just enough to actively invite the gaze, gay or otherwise. 'Just enough' – without tipping over into what Kaplan calls 'soft' androgyny or what Aufderheide calls the 'daring statement'(1986: 126) of MTV androgyny. The softness of the faded blue jeans, earrings and jacket are contraposed with the phallic imagery of a jukebox, cowboy boots and guitar. Michael appropriates the look of the gay denim/clone sensibility, making *Faith* a 'gay window' video.[4] But *Faith* actually invites the gay gaze as a 'gay mirror' as much as a 'gay window'. Wearing mirrored sunglasses, our gaze is reflected back at us, amplifying the autoeroticism of Michael's preening – therefore, when Michael sings, 'Before I touch your body/I know not everybody/ Has a body like you', the meaning is a pure expression of gay male enunciation. With Michael posed as scopophilic object par excellence, the only identification possible is with the gay gaze's own drives. The lyrics, then, are the gay male spectator's, fantasising through

MTV's 'solipsistic, dreamlike structure' (Kinder 1984: 5) about touching George Michael. As the lyrics plaintively suggest, the gay spectator 'needs someone to hold' but, by holding off for the next video, will 'wait for something more'.

With George Michael, gay men are still waiting. In his video *Freedom 90*, Michael works to divorce himself from the objectification he had eagerly solicited for so long. Unlike Madonna, who transforms her 'to-be-looked-at-ness' into a resistant mode of empowerment, Michael tries to clean the slate, deconstructing his pop persona so that fans can simply *listen* without prejudice.[5] To deflect the gaze from him, the lip-synching is performed by renowned fashion models, male and female. To erase his former identity, the leather jacket, guitar and jukebox (all from *Faith*) are set ablaze or exploded. The lyrics lament that when he 'got a brand new face for the boys on MTV' there's someone he 'forgot to be'. George Michael is asking for the freedom to not be looked at for a little while. (Curiously, this is a very popular video with gay men. This may be due in part to the scopophilic pleasure in watching the male models, as well as the song's theme of the construction/experience duality [Dyer], mentioned above.)

So what does this all mean for the gay spectator of MTV? Does he await the resurrection of George Michael and continue watching for more male spectacle? Does he seize glimmers of same-sex images occasionally thrown his way? (Sinead O'Connor and Sheila E. have both shown tender images of men dancing arm-in-arm in their videos.) Does he hope for more complete satisfaction of the gay gaze's dual drives by openly gay MTV artists? (The Communards and Dead Or Alive acknowledged male-to-male address in their songs' lyrics, but failed to in their videos.)

The gay male spectator, whether in his living room or at the new video bar, keeps watching. The absence of MTV's monolithic gender address still encourages, as does the lack of traditional/Oedipal narrative forms. The sheer abundance of floating signifiers allows for gay enunciation unavailable to the male gaze in mainstream film and television. The dreamlike structure of MTV, pitting 'appearance' against 'reality' excites the gay sensibility as it defers ultimate gratification to the next video.

MTV's beat keeps the gay gaze alert. P. F. Grubb has stated, in a 1982 Gay Studies Conference in Amsterdam, 'that if there is such a thing as a gay sensibility, it is to be found in a preparedness to find certain sign material relevant for perception-forming processes related to homosexuality'. The gay spectator must be vigilant, watching, questioning, reformulating . . . ever ready to claim and enunciate gay desire in music videos. As Madonna Ciccone warns: 'Poor is the man whose pleasures depend on the permission of another.'

NOTES

1 In particular see Marsha McCreadies's *Women on Film: The Critical Eye*, Praeger, Westwood, 1983, pp.61–2.
2 Michael Bronski's *Culture Clash: The Making of a Gay Sensibility* (1984) is perhaps the best known book-length text on the subject; however the 'gay sensibility' turns up even in journals more aligned with a psychoanalytic, gaze-oriented methodology than with an ethnographic one (e.g. Mark Finch's 'Sex and Address in *Dynasty*', *Screen* vol.23, nos 3–4, September–October 1982).
3 See also Kaplan 1987, Fiske 1989, and particularly Hsing Chen's article 'MTV: The Cultural Politics of Resistance' in *Journal of Communication Inquiry*, Fall 1986.
4 Michael Bronski writes in *Culture Clash* that 'mainstream ads which carry a gay subtext are called "gay window" ads' (1984: 187).
5 *Editor's note: Listen Without Prejudice, Volume 1* is the title of George Michael's second solo album, released in 1990. *Faith*, his first, was released in 1987. *Listen Without Prejudice, Volume 2* was supposed to have been released in 1991; instead, Michael has been engaged in a prolonged contractual dispute with his record company, Sony. In November 1993, the case came to court in Britain, with Michael making a series of well-publicised appearances in an attempt to gain release from his contract with Sony on the grounds that it constituted a 'restraint of trade'. In June 1994, Michael lost his case in the High Court – he promptly announced his decision to mount an appeal.

REFERENCES

Aufderheide, Pat (1986) 'The Look of the Sound', in Todd Gitlin (ed.) *Watching Television*, New York: Pantheon.
Babuscio, Jack (1984) 'Camp and the Gay Sensibility', in Richard Dyer (ed.) *Gays and Film* New York: Zoetrope.
Bergstrom, Janet and Doane, Mary Ann (1989) 'Enunciation and Sexual Difference', *Camera Obscura*, 3–4: 33–65.
Bronski, Michael (1984) *Culture Clash: The Making of Gay Sensibility*, Boston: South End Press.
de Lauretis, Teresa (1985) 'Oedipus Interruptus', *Wide Angle*, 7(1–2): 34–40.
Doane, Mary Ann (1982) 'Film and the Masquerade: Theorising the Female Spectator', *Screen*, 23, (3–4): 74–88.
Dyer, Richard (1982) 'Don't Look Now', *Screen*, 23(3–4).
—— (1990) *Now You See It: Studies on Lesbian and Gay Film*, London: Routledge.
Fiske, John (1986) 'MTV: Post-Structural Post-Modern', *Journal of Communication Inquiry*, 10, (1): 75–81.
Friedman, Richard (1991) *Male Homosexuality: A Contemporary Psychoanalytic Perspective*, New Haven: Yale University Press.
Frith, Simon (1988) *Music For Pleasure*, New York: Polity Press.
Kaplan, E. Ann (1983) *Women and Film: Both Sides of the Camera*, New York: Methuen.
—— (1987) *Rocking Around the Clock: Music Television, Postmodernism and Consumer Culture*, London: Methuen.
Kinder, Marsha (1984) 'Music Video and the Spectator: Television, Ideology and the Dream', *Film Quarterly*: 2–15.
Koestenbaum, Wayne (1990) 'Wilde's Hard Labor and the Birth of Gay Reading',

in Joseph Boone and Michael Cadden (eds) *Engendering Men: The Question of Male Feminist Criticism*, New York: Routledge: 176–89.

Lewis, Lisa (1990) *Gender Politics and MTV*, Philadelphia: Temple University Press.

Medhurst, Andy (1984) 'Notes on Recent Gay Film Criticism', in Richard Dyer (ed.) *Gays and Film*, New York: Zoetrope.

Moore, Suzanne (1988) 'Here's Looking at You, Kid!', in Lorraine Gamman and Margaret Marshment (eds) *The Female Gaze*, London: Women's Press.

Mulvey, Laura (1975) 'Visual Pleasure and Narrative Cinema', *Screen*, 16: 6–18.

—— (1981) 'Afterthoughts on "Visual Pleasure and Narrative Cinema" inspired by *Duel in the Sun* (1946)', *Framework*, 6, (15–17), Summer.

Rich, B. Ruby (1990) 'In the Name of Feminist Film Criticism', in Patricia Erens (ed.) *Issues in Feminist Film Criticism*, Bloomington: Indiana University Press.

Rodowick, David (1989) *Camera Obscura*, 20–1: 268–73.

Russo, Vito (1981) *The Celluloid Closet*, New York: Harper & Row.

Savage, Jon (1989) 'Sex, Rock and Identity', in Simon Frith (ed.) *Facing the Music*, New York: Pantheon.

Sontag, Susan (1966) 'Notes on Camp', *Against Interpretation*, New York: Delta.

Warner, Michael (1990) 'Homo-Narcissism, or, Heterosexuality', in Joseph Boone and Michael Cadden (eds) *Engendering Men: The Question of Male Feminist Criticism*, New York: Routledge.

Weeks, Jeffrey (1985) *Sexuality and its Discontents: Meanings, Myths and Modern Sexualities*, London: Routledge.

Part II

QUEER
GENRES?

4

LA BELLE DAME
SANS MERCI?

Tanya Krzywinska

We traverse the length of the galleries the underground tunnels the
crypts the caves the catacombs you singing with victorious voice the
joy of m/y recovery.[1]

(Monique Wittig, *The Lesbian Body*, 1973)

Early in my teens, along with my best friend, I was seduced by a beautiful
vampire who went by the name of Carmilla (Ingrid Pitt in *The Vampire
Lovers*, Ward Baker, 1970). This vampire fed our growing curiosity about
our bodies and presented us with the beginnings of a shared fantasy in whose
arms we could begin to explore our sexualities. The vampire offered an
articulation for our fantasies, and as a result my fantasy life has been imbued
by the icon of the 'Hammer Horror' female vampire of the 1960s and early
1970s. This essay is an exploration of the dynamics of desire which
construct this holiest of unholy icons. The female vampire has never yet
been properly buried, her shifting, intangible form fits any scene at any time;
the mirror cannot reflect her, and she needs my fantasy to keep her from the
patriarchal stake.

The female vampire, like her sister icon the Virgin Mary, mediates between
the world of the living and the otherworld of the dead. The key to the
seductive and fascinating powers of the female vampire, from Coleridge's
Christabel (first published in 1816) to Catherine Deneuve in *The Hunger*
(Tony Scott, 1983), is their overt queer sexuality which is constructed as a
metaphysical, and supernatural, phenomenon. Rather than see the female
vampire within the feminist tradition as the reproduction of patriarchal fear
of women as 'other', I want to expand the theorisation to take into account
the seductive power of the vampire and show how it is that she still seems to
maintain a place, at some level, within the fantasies of many women with
diverse sexual identities. This fascination is borne out by contemporary
reworkings of the vampire genre in the short stories of Pat Califia (*The
Vampire*), Angela Carter (*The Lady of the House of Love*), Anne Rice
(*Interview with a Vampire* trilogy), the presence of vampire imagery in
Monique Wittig's *The Lesbian Body* and in the film *Mark of Lilith* (Fionda,

Gladwin and Nataf 1986). I will argue that the queer female vampire presents us with a duplicitous message – she is both the production of patriarchal and heterosexist fear and, at the same time as she foregrounds the fears and terrors of the dominant ideology, she is also a popular articulation which breaks the silence about same sex desire. Later in this essay I will look at two vampire films in detail. These are *Crypt of Horror* (Camillo Mastrocinque, 1965 and rated 15 in the UK) and *Vampyres* (Joseph Larraz, 1976 and rated 18 in the UK) which I believe best exemplify queer desire at work in mainstream vampire films, and which are absent from Andrea Weiss's chapter on the Vampire genre in *Vampires and Violets*.

Many feminist and structuralist critical responses to the vampire genre have been governed by the need to deconstruct the political agendas that construct women characters and women viewers as victims of a text. The legacy of this form of criticism is a disavowal of the possibility of any female desire or sexual response to the texts, and also the disavowal of the idea that texts can, as Jacqueline Rose says, be 'transgressive as well as the site (*the* site) for production of the norm'.[2] It is possible to see the queer female vampire as a cipher for the abject and 'abnormal' but at the same time, by sleight of hand, the same cipher can become a powerful and empowering emblem of same sex desire. The critical approaches that deal with the vampire as merely a construction that re-establishes patriarchy and heterosexuality can be interpreted in the same way that Luce Irigaray and Jane Gallop see Freud's theory of sexuality: 'it is a theory of sexual function (ultimately the reproductive function) and questions of pleasure are excluded, because they have no place in the economy of production.'[3]

The 'production' of the vampire is only half the story. Another version which undermines this reading of the vampire is as an explosion of the subversive that, once articulated, cannot again be buried without trace by a neat 'happy ever after' ending. If a spectator, such as I am myself, cannot resist the pleasure of the vampire's brief freedom then the patriarchal resolution has not been achieved. Is our fascination with the vampire based purely upon her ability briefly to evade compulsory heterosexuality and patriarchy, especially when we know that it was these institutions that breathed life into her form, or is it built upon a precarious tension between the two?

Critical responses that precede Andrea Weiss's *Vampires and Violets* and Sue-Ellen Case's 'Tracking the Vampire' dealt with the vampire film within the terms of the horror genre. Andrew Tudor, in his book *Monsters and Mad Scientists*,[4] acknowledges the presence of a 'lesbian subtext' within these films and argues that the presence of 'lesbian sex' is used negatively to establish a positive state of 'normative' heterosexuality; but Tudor does not allow for the possibility of a queer pleasure dynamic in the 'Hammer Horror' vampire film. The problem of this reading of the female vampire in the romantic tradition of 'la belle dame sans merci', which Mario Praz identifies in *The Romantic Agony*, is that she is only seen as a narrative device by which the vampire hunter and the prospective husband can overcome the 'excesses' of an 'unnatural' sexuality that threaten the stability of the patriarchal system. This construction proposes a simplistic polarity which disallows other readings of the text, and neglects the possibility that the spectator can celebrate the brief freedom of the vampire which, I would argue, ironises the use of female same sex desire as a signifier of 'unnaturalness'.

It would seem that Tudor's view is based on a narrow reading of feminist critical theory. In forgetting that spectators are not merely recipients of the text, but bring to bear different fantasies (not only a heterosexual male purient and interventionist interest in a 'lesbian scene') to the site of reception, Tudor dangerously underestimates the diversity of spectators and appropriates feminist theory to uphold a monolithic reading of the text. It would seem that in his view the pleasure gained from these texts can only be through simple identification with those agents in the text that re-establish the patriarchal order. It is too easy to see the pleasure of these films as merely an explication and reinforcement of male, heterosexual fantasies. This kind of criticism gives no space for, specifically, the female spectator and for the 'interchange of female fascinations'[5] and allows no gap for alternative forms of desire and fantasy.

What seems to be required is a notion of pleasure that is robust enough to deal with the possibility of complex and, perhaps, recalcitrant desires and pleasures. Within both feminist and lesbian theoretical writing there has been a tendency to dismiss the presence of some forms of fantasy and desire. At best this can be seen as deferral; censoring difficult fantasies and physical responses until we have the theoretical apparatus to deal with them. Teresa de Lauretis argues that 'Queer Theory' expands the discussion of sexuality and same sex desire by counteracting increasingly rigid definitions of lesbian and gay sexualities; she aims to maintain a radical agenda through the acknowledgement of different erotic 'mappings'. She says:

> In a sense, 'Queer Theory' was arrived at in the effort to avoid all of those fine distinctions in our discursive protocols, not to adhere to any one of the given terms, not to assume their ideological liabilities, but instead to both transgress and transcend them – or at very least problematise them.[6]

Queer Theory offers a means through which it is possible to begin to talk about the complexity of sexualities and desires. It also seeks to make conscious the contradictions and proscriptions that have emerged within lesbian, gay and feminist discourses. Queer Theory counteracts what has seemed, at times, as the closing down of certain areas of our experience and desire, through different forms of censorship, and helps instead to confront the dissonances engendered by desire. My queer fascination with the vampire is predicated precisely upon the dissonance and tension between patriarchal 'feminine' signifiers – cleavages, red lips, velvety skin, etc., and the subversion of patriarchal and heterosexist norms. A similar tension presents itself in the 1992 film *Basic Instinct* (Paul Verhoeven) in which an apparently 'femme' woman is not represented as the nurturer of the male, but instead, as his nemesis. Although my queer desire may temporarily spring the vampire out of the function of representing male constructions of 'otherness' it is also apparent that the vampire is the product of a patriarchal signifying system that sees women as both alien and 'other'.

An interesting and productive problem that Queer Theory presents to a radical feminist agenda lies in the argument that mainstream films coerce women spectators into a male system of desire. Many theorists have sought out strategies for identifying and overthrowing the asymmetry of the patri-archal controlling gaze. Christine Gledhill's notion of 'negotiation' helps to open up a space which allows for differently desiring positions:

> As a model of meaning production, negotiation conceives cultural exchange as the intersection of processes of production and reception, in which overlapping but non-matching determinations operate. Mean-ing is neither imposed, nor passively imbibed, but arises out of a struggle or negotiation between competing frames of reference, motiva-tion and experience.[7]

The spectator is not always the passive victim of the text, but may, with a polymorphously perverse pleasure, seek out contradictions and hiatus. It would seem a braver expedient to fantasise a critical position that allows for the possibility of variable and shifting textual readings and accounts for the possibilities of recalcitrant, in feminist terms, fantasmatic relations to the text.

The complexities of both desire and pleasure in relation to fantasy have been the subject of recent psychoanalytic theory. This work broadens the psychoanalytic conception of the 'male gaze' originally proposed by Laura Mulvey. Laplanche and Pontalis suggest that we do not read a 'scene' in a specific and stable way, but in a shifting manner. The implication of this is that the spectator's unstable reading often works to defy the 'classical narrative' attempt to structure the spectator's response in a particular way. Laplanche and Pontalis argue that in scenes of primal fantasy there is an 'absence of subjectivisation'. Taking Freud's essay, 'A Child is Beaten',[8] they suggest that in a child's fantasy of being beaten by the father, the child may fantasize herself into any aspect of the fantasy: 'nothing shows whether the subject will be immediately located as daughter; it can as well be fixed as father or even in the term seduces.'[9] I would argue that this model of multiple and shifting identification is at work within the process of textual spectatorship. Identification not only with the textual characters is located during the moments of reception but also retrospectively; a subject can be then inculcated into a scene or narrative in a multiplicity of ways which can also shift in time.

The implication of Laplanche and Pontalis's work is that labyrinthine network of conscious and unconscious desiring processes that are present at the different moments of reception, are simplified at the expense of the different desiring positions of the spectator. It is only by writing this into spectatorship theory that racial, cultural and sexual specifics and difference can be taken into account. The theoretical positions that argue that mainstream films are closed books that are not open to fantasy and different mappings of desire are, I would argue, monolithic and, in originating from the institutions of patriarchy and compulsory heterosexuality, undermine sexual plurality and difference. While the unconscious effect of these two institutions is invasive at the level of language, resistance remains crucial. The presence of the closed monolithic theory within academic theory in its solemnity of purpose culminates in texts that lack acknowledgement of the writer's desire. Playfulness is perhaps the crucial tool of queer theoretical practice which allows barriers and thresholds to crossed, sexual and gendered roles to be explored, and, importantly, the acknowledgement of the role of fantasy within different discourses: 'the theoretical text could become a moving simulacrum of desire in movement – a carnival, a masked ball.'[10]

Engagement with any text is a dance with desire – the desire to appropriate, ironise, or equally, to reject meaning. Our desire and fantasy is, undeniably, always cast through the ideological meanings that are inherent in the systems of signification that are available to us at any given time. Laplanche and Pontalis point out that fantasy is always 'reworked through the material of the everyday'.[11] The implication of this statement is that our continuous reworkings of fantasies and desire are hooked onto the images or icons that in some way are related to early questions about our own identity, particularly our sexual identity. The vampire's power to haunt is as an image of the wound of femininity that is inflicted by patriarchal structures and the intrusion of 'compulsory heterosexuality'.[12] The image is a place onto which experiences and meanings cluster, which then inevitably, feed back into our rendering of the real.

This leads into the question of how it is that the vampire has attained the status of icon. Anyone who is even very slightly familiar with vampire-lore will know that the vampire cannot be seen in the mirror. In *The Lost Boys* (Joel Schumacher, 1987), a 'rite of passage into masculinity' vampire picture, the dissolving image of the boy-hero in the mirror becomes the visual sign of his transformation into a vampire. The mirror's role in both masking and unmasking 'otherness' is a key concept in Lacanian psychoanalytic theory. In the essay 'The Mirror Stage as Formative of the Function of the I as Revealed in Psychoanalytic Experience',[13] Lacan uses the mirror as a metaphor to expose the fictional sovereignty of the ego. The recognition or misrecognition of the image in the mirror acts as a promise of a future stable totality. Lacan writes:

> The mirror stage is a drama whose internal thrust is precipitated from insufficiency to anticipation – and which manufactures for the subject, caught up in the lure of spatial identification, the succession of phantasies that extends from a fragmented body-image to a form of its totality that I shall call orthopaedic.[14] [15]

The image in the mirror offers an illusion of completeness but its nether face is the fragmented, dissembled body. The fragmented body is repressed but emerges in fantasy and engenders the staple fare of horror movies including the revenant, death-defying vampire. Malcolm Bowie says of the Lacanian child, 'The child itself so recently born, gives birth to a monster: a statue, an automaton, a fabricated thing.'[16] The sexual power of the vampire leans on the notion that sexual ecstacy dissembles our 'normal' mappings of a unified and stable body and so the body becomes monstrous and unfamiliar.

The desire for unity is crucial to our sense of self as an active agent in the world, but ironically, also gives birth to unconscious fantasies of disunity. The return of the repressed, in the form of a fear of bodily disunity, is a common theme of such uncanny tales as Poe's 'The Sandman' and in the dismembered and re-assembled body of Frankenstein's monster. The language of Lacan's text has, as Bowie points out, the excessive, elaborate patina of the Gothic novel. The use of this excess as the *mise-en-scène* of Lacan's conception betrays the investment of desire in that which exceeds containment. The vampire's polymorphous sexuality belongs to the fragmented body of the 'other' which lies outside the gendered heterosexual identity of the fictive complete ego. The vampire may be the 'nightside' of the ego but its seductive manifestation is a representational means of making a link with the 'other', the monstrous, fragmented and uncontrollable body, and, with this articulation, is offered a fictive possibility of its control. Control is carried out through representation – projection on to that which is believed to be 'other' to the self.

In order to link the monstrous being in Lacan's mirror and the use of the female body as a signifier of disunity and, therefore, death, I turn to Freud's conception of the death instinct. The death instinct begins to take speculative shape in *Beyond the Pleasure Principle* and recounts Freud's observation of his young grandson playing with a cotton reel. The boy's solitary game consisted of throwing the cotton reel out of sight and then pulling it back into view once more. Freud used this game of 'Fort/da' to show how the boy used the cotton reel to represent his mother and her absences. Freud argues that the game was a means by which the boy could control and master the absences of his mother and thus gain control over the mother's body. The repetition of the unpleasurable experience allows the boy in some way to reduce the tension produced by the mother's absence, but in so doing further opens up the gap between the maternal body and himself which confirms his autonomous state. Freud says:

At the outset he was in a *passive* situation – he was overpowered by the experience, but, by repeating it, unpleasurable though it was, as a game, he took on an *active* part. . . . Throwing away the object so that it was 'gone' might satisfy an impulse of the child's, which was suppressed in his actual life, to revenge himself on his mother's going away from him.[17]

The achievement of obtaining 'active' status, which must be related to the acquisition of gender identity, is predicated upon the fear generated by the absence of the mother. As it is the unpleasurable absence of the mother that is the event that propels the infant into the act of mastery, the construction of the unified subject always implies its other face – the dissembled body and the death of the subject. The coalescence of the figure of the vampire acts as a safety valve – projecting the monstrous outside of the body and using the notion of 'fiction' to support the projection.

Jacqueline Rose uses Kristeva's notion of 'abjection' to expand upon the Freudian and Lacanian model to show how the fear of fragmentation and the disunity that threatens to overwhelm the conscious self is unconsciously always mapped directly onto the female body.

Abjection is a primordial fear situated at the point where the subject first splits from the body of the mother, finding at once in that body and in the terrifying gap that opens up between them the only space for the construction of its own identity, the only space for the constitution of its own identity, the only distance which will allow it to become a user of words.[18]

To become a 'user of words', through which the subject consolidates an experience, albeit fictive, of a complete and unified self, Julia Kristeva argues that it is necessary to banish that which is considered unacceptable and unclean. The vampire film offers a non-disruptive means by which to assimilate and control the threat to the unified self. The death of the vampire stands in for a supposed victory of the threatening force but nevertheless is resurrected in fantasy or in later movies. Grosz writes:

what has been expelled from the subject's corporeal functioning can never be fully obliterated but hovers at the border of the subject's identity, threatening apparent unities and stabilities with disruption and possible dissolution.[19]

The vampire's undead body defiantly resists the boundaries of 'good taste' including the rules that govern the threshold between life and death. Vampirism becomes a disease (dis-ease) which must be held at bay by the rigid containment of sexuality within heterosexual and patriarchal institutions. As a signifier of abjection the vampire confirms that these parameters are really social constructions and are the effects of 'desire and not nature'.[20]

Through a queer theoretical position, the transgression of the patriarchal and concomitant heterosexuality, becomes liberating – but at the same time is allied to death. Sexual identity is heterogeneous and is gleaned from many cultural sites, including bad, old movies. The representation of abjection through the vampire and specifically the queer female vampire betrays the social projections that determine the inscription of boundaries and thresholds. Hand in hand with the representation of the sexual transgression of these boundaries is the threshold of subject and object that is presented by bodily waste and fluid. The fear of bodily fluids, in particular the blood of menstruation, takes on a renewed force with the fear generated by HIV and AIDS. The vampire takes on yet another ideological encoding of the fear of the 'other' (a new threat to the sovereignty that assumes it is immortal) demonstrating that the vampire's 'power' as an icon lies in her ability to 'stand in' for a multiplicity of meanings.

The queer female vampire of 1960s movies (a reworking of the figures in Gothic poems and novels of the early nineteenth century) is a male construction designed to master, duplicitously, the fear and pleasure represented by women as 'other' within patriarchal and heterosexual structures. A love affair with the vampire can be seen as a desire to make whole and complete a sexuality that is constructed as a signifier for fragmentation and which is disavowed by patriarchal and heterosexual discourses.

The Spanish film *Crypt of Horror* is a reworking of J. Sheridan Le Fanu's 'Carmilla'; the plot hinges on the figure of the witch who will not stay in her grave until revenge has been levelled against her persecutors. A sense of melancholic Gothicism is maintained through the use of shadowy black and white filmstock, which evokes a sense of the 'other' place of fantasy that is not represented in the same way in the colour Hammer films. The invocation of the heroine's melancholia through the *mise-en-scène* illustrates Linda Bayer-Berenbaum's notion that 'Gothicism includes all that is generally excluded; it reveals the shadow and the stranger, exploring their immanence within this life and within the self.[21]

Our heroine is plagued by bad dreams; her secret history, locked into her unconscious, leaks out while she sleeps. These bad dreams mark her off as 'different from the other girls'. The isolation that arises from what she is told is her special 'gift' (the sight/the *site*) is broken by the arrival of a mysterious woman to whom she is deeply attracted. At the same time a man also comes to the castle and falls in love with our heroine. In the most memorable scene of the film, the male suitor begins to propose to her, but during the course of his pretty speech, the desired woman appears in the frame over his shoulder; spectator and heroine can see her but the male suitor cannot. All our attention is on the other woman. Our heroine no longer hears his words and he walks away, leaving the two women gazing longingly at one another. A question that is often asked in recent feminist film criticism is what happens when two women look at one another within the cinematic frame. In *Crypt of Horror* the spectator is offered this look which seems to occupy and signify a space not shared by any other of the film's protagonists and it is this space that is the space of my fantasy and my pleasure. The 'look' between the two women recurs frequently, including a scene in which our heroine gazes at the other woman while she sleeps. When she wakes she asks, 'Why do you look at me so?' The reply is: 'How beautiful you are.' The women forget what is happening around them and are totally absorbed in a fascination with one another. I, like the protagonists, forget the plot, the ostensible reason for the film. I watch them as they watch each other and forget the narrative's need to destroy their relationship to restore the Karnstein family to 'health and heredity'.

A similar look of fascination is also present in *The Vampire Lovers* but here the transfixed look of the innocent victim directed at the vampire is the result of hypnotism and not desire – her gaping mouth and wide eyes look plain silly. The look in *Crypt of Horror* offers me a possibility – the possibility of a different story, whatever the intention of the film-makers and the unsatisfactory, conventional ending to the tale. The narrative is predicated on the secret history of a family which is made manifest in the heroine's dreams; the heroine has a complex internal life which revolves around her quest for her own history. I would argue that the subtext of the film acts as a safety valve for the secret history that lies beneath the family romance. The whole Karnstein family are implicated in the crucifixion of the transgressive witch (her crime is 'killing' young girls, a crime of which she professes innocence) and they attempt to wipe her image out of the family archives. The heroine's fantasy life implicates her in the scenes of seduction so that it is always unclear whether she is the seduced or the seducer.

The way in which *Crypt of Horror* constructs its sexual signifying space differs a great deal from *Vampyres*. The latter film uses very little of the vampire lore employed by the vampire hunter in earlier Hammer films. *Vampyres* has no van Helsing figure; instead it seems to take up the scene in Stoker's *Dracula* (1897) where Jonathan Harker almost succumbs – only the count's arrival saves the day – to the charms of three very beautiful but halitotic female vampires in Dracula's library:

> Lower and lower went her head as the lips went below the range of my mouth and chin and seemed to fasten to my throat. Then she paused, and I could hear the churning sound of her tongue as it licked her teeth and lips, and I could feel the hot breath on my neck. Then the skin of my throat began to tingle as one's flesh does when the hand that is to tickle it approaches nearer – nearer. I could feel the soft, shivering touch of the lips on the super-sensitive skin of my throat, and the hard dents of two sharp teeth, just touching and pausing there. I closed my eyes in a languorous ecstasy and waited – waited with beating heart.[22]

In quoting this passage out of context it becomes clear that the language has shifted into the register of pornography. This passage is a seductive tease which teeters on the delicious edge of expectation that is the genre of the pornographic writing. *Vampyres*, moves from an appropriation of the written pornographic text to the appropriation of the cinematic pornographic text. *Vampyres*, in parallel to the erotic seduction of Jonathan, is a soft-core meditation on the life of two queer female vampires. There is a great deal of nudity, including pubic hair. The whole movie is structured around quite graphic sexual episodes, or as Linda William's puts it, sexual 'numbers' (as in a musical).[23]

It is suprising, given the constraints of the soft-core pornography genre, that the sex scenes between the two women are shown with no 'model' male voyeur present. This differs from most 'heterosexual' hard-core pornography, in which a man will generally watch, then intervene, participate and conclude, through his orgasm, the 'action'. Other vampire movies that hinge upon a supposedly palatable heterosexual 'love story' are in a sense a displaced pornography, relocating the genitals in the 'super-sensitive' neck. The blood that spurts out of the neck to be drunk by the vampire invariably ends up by dribbling down the chin, in the same way that the conclusion of a 'blow job' in hard-core porn movies ends up with the 'proof' of the orgasm running out of someone's mouth and down the chin. The effect of this is that one bodily fluid stands in for another – the blood belonging to the horror genre is more acceptable than the visual representation of real semen of the hard-core porn genre. Both are hinged on a dichotomous fear and desire for the body's monstrous 'otherness' which cannot be contained by the fictive unified self. The representation of this 'otherness' by the queer vampire; who signifies death to the established order is, of course, located within the terms of patriarchal and heterosexual discourses.

Vampyres does not, however, portray the two female vampires as simply 'monsters', in the way that the female vampires in Dracula's library are merely voracious, sexualised extensions of the head male vampire. These vampires are not only blood-crazed, but retain the passions of mortal women, and as such they can, on their own terms, take sexual pleasure from their prospective victims. They do not use their bodies merely to lure their lunch, but also to satisfy their own sexual hunger. The displacement of genitality onto the neck or breast that occurs in many other vampires films does not occur here. The feeding scenes, instead of being a seductive glide into the waters of oblivion, are, instead, a vicious and gory feeding frenzy that is only eroticised by being placed next to the sexual 'numbers'.

Although the film is, in some ways, partially constructed like a porn film, the heterosexual sex within the film would seem to offer a palliative for the heterosexual, probably male, spectator. By virtue of this palliative it is possible to represent the private queer lives of the vampire in which they have a commonality of experience; a shared life governed by the rhythms of night and for the quest for blood. The sex between the two women differs from other vampire films of this time, in that they both desire one another. It is by virtue of this sisterhood that the relationship between the two women can be appropriated by a queer reading of the text.

The vampire, throughout its history, functions as a means of articulating what is epistemologically constructed as both 'unnatural' and unspeakable. This construction can only be achieved through the use of mythological creatures and scenarios. Myths, in the form of stories about the individual or in a wider societal context, often seem to provide illusory answers to questions about who we are. They do not, however, exist outside a social praxis. Such mythic models often claim to be archaic, outside history and beyond ideology. The paradox of representing the 'unnatural' in the form of the queer vampire is that of fascinating, rather than repelling, a female spectator. When I watch the two vampires in *Vampyres* gliding hand in hand through the dawn mist to their daily resting place I am transported out of my own mortality and consumed by the play of death defying erotic signifiers.

The gap created through a queer reading of the female vampire is duplicitously predicated upon a patriarchal and heterosexual articulation of 'otherness'. What creates the difference is in extracting the vampire from inhabiting a monolithic, patriarchal discourse and placing her within the context of a gloriously transgressive, but fleeting, celebration of 'otherness'. 'You have only to look at the Medusa straight on to see her. And she's beautiful and she's laughing.'[24]

NOTES

1 Monique Wittig, *The Lesbian Body*, Beacon Press, Boston, 1973, pp.20–1.
2 Jacqueline Rose, *The Haunting of Sylvia Plath*, Virago, London, 1991, p.163.
3 Jane Gallop, *Feminism and Psychoanalysis: The Daughter's Seduction*, Macmillan, London, 1981, p.67.
4 Andrea Weiss, *Vampires and Violets: Lesbians in the Cinema*, Jonathan Cape, London, 1992; Sue-Ellen Case, 'Tracking the Vampire', in Naomi Schor and Elizabeth Weed (eds), *Differences*, vol. 3, no. 2, Summer 1991, pp.1–20; Andrew Tudor, *Monsters and Mad Scientists*, Blackwell, London, 1989; Mario Praz, *The Romantic Agony*, Oxford University Press, Oxford, 1970.
5 Jackie Stacey, 'Desperately Seeking Difference' in Lorraine Gamman and Margaret Marshment (eds), *The Female Gaze*, The Women's Press, London, 1988, p.114.
6 Teresa de Lauretis (ed.), *Differences – Queer Theory: Lesbian and Gay Sexualities*, vol. 3, no. 2, 1992, p.v.
7 Christine Gledhill, 'Pleasurable Negotiations', in E. Deidre Pribham (ed.), *Female Spectators*, Verso, London, 1988, p.68.
8 Sigmund Freud, 'A Child is Being Beaten: A Contribution to the Study of the Origin of Sexual Perversions', in *The Standard Edition of the Complete Psychological Works of Sigmund Freud*, vol.XVII, pp.175–204.
9 Jean Laplanche and Jean-Bertrand Pontalis, 'Fantasy and the Origins of Sexuality', in Victor Burgin, James Donald and Cora Kaplan, *Formations of Fantasy*, Routledge, London, 1986, p.22.

10 Malcolm Bowie, *Lacan*, Fontana Press, London, 1991, p.200.
11 Elizabeth Cowie 'Fantasia', in Burgin, Donald and Kaplan, op. cit., p.22.
12 Adrienne Rich, 'Compulsory Heterosexuality and Lesbian Existence', in Elizabeth Abel and Emily Abel, *The Signs Reader*, University of Chicago Press, Chicago, 1983.
13 Jacques Lacan, *Ecrits: A Selection*, Routledge, London, 1966.
14 Catherine Clement notes that Lacan uses orthopaedic to mean that 'which helps the child stand': Catherine Clement, *The Lives and Legends of Jacques Lacan*, Columbia University Press, New York, 1983, p.90.
15 Jacques Lacan, *Ecrits: A Selection*, Tavistock/Routledge, London, 1977, p.4.
16 Malcolm Bowie, *Lacan*, Fontana Press, London, 1991, p.26.
17 Sigmund Freud, *On Metapsychology – Beyond the Pleasure Principle*, Penguin, Harmondsworth, 1984, p.86.
18 Jacqueline Rose, *The Haunting of Sylvia Plath*, Virago, London, 1991, p.33.
19 Elizabeth Grosz, 'The Body of Signification', in John Fletcher and Andrew Benjamin (eds), *Abjection, Melancholia and Love*, Routledge, London, 1990, p.87.
20 ibid., p.90.
21 Linda Bayer-Berenbaum, *The Gothic Imagination*, Fairleigh Dickinsen University Press, 1982, p.146.
22 Bram Stoker, *Dracula*, Bantam Books, London, 1981, p.39 (first published 1897).
23 Linda Williams, *Hardcore*, Pandora Press, London, 1991.
24 Hélène Cixous, 'The Laugh of the Medusa', in Elizabeth Abel & Emily Abel (eds), *The Signs Reader*, University of Chicago Press, Chicago, 1983, p.289.

5

JUST A GIGOLO?

Narcissism, Nellyism and the 'New Man' Theme

Paul Burston

> Oh he wears such a thin disguise
> Look a little closer and unmask his eyes
> See right through him, see him oozing with lies . . .
> (Hazel O'Connor, *Gigolo*
> Albion Music, 1980)

There is nothing about gay people's physiognomy that declares them gay, no equivalents to the biological markers of sex and race. There are signs of gayness, a repertoire of gestures, expressions, stances, *clothing* and *even environments*.[1]

(Richard Dyer [my italics])

This essay is the story of a gay man's obsession with gigolos, in particular with those men Hollywood paid to drop their pants during the 1980s. The *Collins English Dictionary* defines 'gigolo' as 'a man who is kept by a woman, especially an older woman; a man who is paid to dance with or escort women'. I take it for granted that the men who signed the cheques for Richard Gere's exhibitionism in *American Gigolo* (1980) and Tom Cruise's posturing in *Top Gun* (1986) would insist that the stars' bodies were put on display for the sole purpose of pleasuring women. But as Yvonne Tasker recently pointed out, 'the meaning of the body on the screen is not secure. but shifting, inscribed with meaning in different ways at different points.'[2] And as I intend to show, both films relied heavily on a tradition of homoerotic textual codes which, though hardly securing the male body as the exclusive object of homosexual desire, certainly invited gay men as well as heterosexual women to grab their share of visual pleasure.

Historically, popular cinema has shied away from presenting sexually explicit images of its male stars. Of course this is no accident. Socially and cinematically, male authority is bound up with the act of looking. Any representation of masculinity denoting 'to-be-looked-at-ness' is therefore perceived as a threat to dominant notions of what it means to be a 'real' (i.e. rigidly heterosexual) man. Still Hollywood has always had its share of male

111

narcissists, from Valentino to Schwarzenegger, actors whose bankability was (and is) dependent precisely on an audience's desire to look at them. And cinema audiences, as we all know, are not composed entirely of swooning heterosexual women. The knowledge that male viewers might enjoy the spectacle of the male body is a constant source of anxiety; men are not supposed to function as objects for one another's erotic gaze. Which is why displays of male flesh are usually given an alibi (e.g. 'this man isn't posing for our pleasure, he's demonstrating his brute strength'), and accompanied by acts of sadism and/or punishment. As Steve Neale observes, 'Were this not the case, mainstream cinema would have openly to come to terms with the male homosexuality it so assiduously seeks to denigrate or deny.'[3]

If the look of the male viewer is cause for concern, the look between men on the screen can provoke all kinds of hysterical reactions. Yet many of the film genres targeted specifically at male audiences, from the traditional Western to the modern buddy cop movie, invite us to inhabit a man's world where the 'innocent' pleasures of the homosocial are constantly under threat from the homosexual. Discussing the buddy movies of the late 1960s and early 1970s, Cynthia J. Fuchs describes how 'the exclusion of women compelled overt condemnation of implicit and even explicit homoeroticism, as the texts worked precisely to keep such frightening feelings "below the surface."'[4]

Fast forward to 1980. Westerns are out, wardrobes are in. Richard Gere's well-dressed portrayal of a male narcissist in *American Gigolo* signalled the dawn of a decade in which pleasures previously branded taboo or feminine would be sold to men on a grand scale. A full five years before Nick Kamen dropped his Levi's in that launderette, Richard Gere offered us a tantalising peek at what the so-called 'New Man' might look like under his designer clothes. A marketing phenomenon analysed by media commentators and advertising executives, the New Man has, for the most part, been spared the scrutiny of film theorists.[5] Newspapers and women's magazines may have devoted considerable copy-space to discussions of where the New Man's priorities lay (in the bed or in the bathroom?); surprisingly little has been written about how the images of 'New' masculinity presented to us at the cinema might relate to questions of homosexuality.

Yet on the face of it, the rise of Richard Gere, Tom Cruise, and all the brazen young dudes who followed in their footsteps appeared to signal a measure of acceptance of the male body as an object of desire, a challenge to tradition through a redefining of masculinity which created space for homoerotic desire. Suzanne Moore, writing about the New Man advertising phenomenon in 1988, observed that many of the images used to denote the New Man were 'culled in both form and technique from a long tradition of soft-core homoerotica'.[6] This is hardly a surprise. Historically-speaking, women have been denied the social power to examine, let alone market erotic images of masculinity. Gay men, on the other hand, have enjoyed the economic strength necessary to articulate their erotic pleasures through the celebration and marketing of the male physique, from the coy *Athletic Models' Guild* studio shots of the 1950s to the booming gay porn industry we see in the present day. Rowena Chapman, in a stimulating discussion of 'Variations on the New Man Theme', agrees that the increased availability and acceptability of nude male images in advertising during the 1980s was due largely to a thriving gay economy which 'had an influence on hetero- sexual men, enabling them to treat other men as objects of desire and to give vent to suppressed homoeroticism'.[7]

But as she also takes care to point out, the manipulation of recognisably homoerotic imagery was usually accompanied by 'moves to ensure that male models [are] presented as images of desire for women alone'.[8] This comment not only serves as a timely reminder of the obvious (but often neglected) fact that gay men do not automatically respond to the same erotic stimuli as heterosexual women; it also challenges us to expose the 'moves' applied to protect the boundaries of heterosexual viewing, and to examine the film industry's attempts to incorporate the forms and techniques of gay erotica into the presentation of its male stars and still deny, if not a homoerotic, then certainly a queer reading of the film text.

AMERICAN GIGOLOS DON'T DO FAGS

Nowhere is this tension between the employment of homoeroticism and the denial of homosexuality more clearly illustrated than in *American Gigolo*. Paul Schrader's visually stylish, emotionally sterile thriller ushered in the new decade with a false promise of available male sexuality – pampered, preened, and (herein lies the crux) on offer exclusively to those who can afford it.

Richard Gere plays a high-class male prostitute, Julian Kay, who is framed for the murder of a client. The detective assigned to the case, while displaying an over-active interest in the nature of Julian's employment, decides that he is 'guilty as sin' (of murder?). Our poor hero finds himself in the unfortunate position of being unable to come up with an alibi, since the woman he was with at the time of the murder refuses to put her marriage on the line. On the level of narrative alone Schrader's film functions as a warning of the dangers inherent in the male body being eroticised. Julian is taught the error of his ways, and undergoes a remarkable conversion just in time for the closing titles. In the film's final scene, Michelle (Lauren Hutton) visits him in prison. The wife of a senator, she has been in love with our hero since their first encounter, following him around by day and turning up at his apartment in the middle of the night. Throwing caution and reputation to the wind, she announces that she is willing to provide Julian with an alibi. She places her hand against the glass that separates them. He leans his head against it, whimpering poignantly 'My God, Michelle! It's taken me so long to come to you.'

Within this cautionary narrative, a paranoid fear of homosexuality is expressed in a variety of ways, most overtly in Julian's repeated assertion that 'I don't do fags'. The first disclaimer is issued within the first few minutes of the film – indicative, surely, of the depth of anxiety provoked by the subject. From here on in, the denials fly thick and fast. Not wishing to be sidetracked into a debate on 'positive' and 'negative images', it is still worth pointing out, as Vito Russo does, that the only gay characters to appear in the film are 'a lesbian pimp, a black pimp, and a closet case who hates women and has his wife beaten while he watches'.[9]

Russo neglects to mention also the blond boy who appears towards the end of the film, and is supposedly guilty of the murder for which Julian stands accused. Moreover, Russo contents himself with the suggestion that the deployment of such stereotypes is simply another example of the sort of Hollywood homophobia he is committed to cataloguing. Not wanting to defend *American Gigolo* against such charges, it none the less seems to me that, within the scheme of the film as a whole, the presentation of a series of stereotyped images of gay men serves as more than simply an excuse to vent a prejudice.

This should become clearer if we consider for a moment the scene where Julian escorts one of his regular clients to an auction. Catching sight of another, older woman, who has a reputation for being something of a gossip, his client warns Julian that he is about to become subject to unsolicited advances. Our hero's immediate response to the problem is to adopt an exaggerated German accent and camp manner, complete with limp wrist and mincing gait, and to rush up to the woman, kissing her ostentatiously on both cheeks and remarking on her 'beautiful dress'.

The comic appeal of Richard Gere 'acting the fag' is, to say the least, limited, and the scene serves little other purpose. Certainly, it has no part to play in the forwarding of the narrative. What it does provide, however, is an alibi, an opportunity to remind the audience of what a 'real fag' is. In a film, which ostensibly sets out to challenge familiar models of masculinity, it should hardly come as a surprise to discover such comforting clichés strategically positioned along the way. 'Don't worry,' the film is saying, 'this is what fags are like. Our gigolo is nothing like this.' Within the precarious framework of gender relations (which the eroticised male threatens to disturb), stereotyped images of gay men serve to reassure the audience of what Gere's character is *not*. The film's construction of overt, exaggerated homosexuality acts as a decoy, directing us away from the conclusion that this gentleman protesteth too much, and towards the preferred (i.e., hetero-sexual) reading of the text.

Of course Richard Gere wasn't the first or last screen idol to 'act the fag' in order to maintain a straight face.[10] Still *American Gigolo* is noteworthy (if not exactly unique) for the extent to which it actively courts that which it also seeks to deny. For as I have already suggested, the film's reconstruction of a purportedly heterosexual man as a source of erotic spectacle borrows extensively from a catalogue of textual codes which have their roots in gay male culture. Inevitably this presents a problem: how to transpose the technique and form of homoerotica into a convincingly heterosexual context? I would argue that Schrader employs two main tactics: tacit denial and autoeroticism.

Before discussing these, it would be useful to establish the fact that Schrader's protagonist exists in what was in 1980 an identifiably gay world. It is a world of sun-kissed bodies and swimming pools, of pastel interiors and micro-blinds. It is the world revealed in the paintings of gay artist David Hockney. Of course Hollywood has always exploited the attraction of exotic, unfamiliar locations. Still there is something very specific riding on Schrader's choice of settings. The deployment of late 1970s gay iconography is part of a wider strategy to establish a context which makes it possible, if not imperative, to view the male as erotic spectacle. Framed within this world, Julian is coded as an object-to-be-looked-at.

As if to underline the fact of his object-ivity, the first glimpse of his naked torso is directly preceded by a series of establishing shots which do more than simply alert us to the particulars of time and place. The camera focuses on a pile of paintings, then a collection of vases, a sofa, a pair of dumb-bells, a pair of feet, hands gripping a bar, feet locking on the bar and finally the torso extended downward. The fetishisation of Gere's body – the way in which he is set up as a commodity, the fragmentary quality of the camerawork – suggests a reworking of traditional film strategies for viewing women. At the same time, the precise way in which he is coded for visual pleasure borrows heavily from a long tradition of homoerotica. The shot of his fully extended naked torso is a classic example of gay soft-porn posturing. Artfully lit, with a glistening coat of sweat highlighting his straining pectorals, he hangs upside down, arms outstretched, a dumb-bell clutched in either hand.[11]

Having established a scene charged with ambiguous eroticism, Schrader then has the object of desire issue a statement of intent, designed to remove any sexual ambiguity. 'I am not interested in that,' Gere says, ostensibly as part of his Teach Yourself Swedish home-cassette course. Issued at the time it is, preceded by a titillating survey of his musculature (complete with standard gay iconography), and immediately followed by a phone call from Leon (the black pimp who is constantly pressurising Julian to do 'fag tricks'), such a declaration functions as a tacit denial of homosexuality and an attempt to reaffirm the frontiers of heterosexual viewing.

And yet to what extent is Gere's sexuality really on offer to anyone? He may be stripped and fetishised, but would it be true to say that he was disempowered? An invitation to feast our eyes upon his well-oiled torso hardly constitutes a surrender of all will and autonomy. It is clear from the way in which the scene is framed that the pleasure is not exclusively, or even predominantly, ours. As Rowena Chapman comments, when discussing the erotification of the male form in calendar-shots, 'The images presented are peopled by paragons of male aesthetics . . . expressive of action, power and control. Everyone knows you don't get a body like that just by whistling, it requires effort, patience and commitment. Even in passivity it articulates action and potential, identifying the participants as active subjects.'[12] In Gere's case, the overall impression is of some kind of superman, capable of stretching both his physical and mental limits simultaneously.

Evidently, the erotic potential of the scene is conditioned as much by Gere's character as by our voyeuristic position to him. He is clearly depicted as deriving autoerotic pleasure from his activity, and certainly not as relinquishing all power to the spectator. Faced with the 'threat' of homo-eroticism, Schrader struggles to deliver Gere from the hungry eyes of the proverbial predatory gay male viewer by overstating the narcissistic side to Julian's nature. Since there is no female character present in the scene to provide the much-coveted proof of heterosexuality, the male subject himself takes control of the gaze, pre-empting our erotic interest and claiming the pleasure as his own. In a peculiar sense, the gaze becomes self-centred. Autoeroticism is offered as the last safeguard against homoerotica.

Throughout *Gigolo*, Schrader takes pains to regulate the male spectator's reading of the film-text. Attention is repeatedly drawn to the distinction between Gere as the male viewer's ego-ideal and the female viewer's source of erotic visual pleasure, most explicitly in the scene at the Ryman's house. When Julian arrives he is greeted by Mr Ryman, to whom he trots off the by-now-familiar line, 'I don't do fags'. Ryman, whom we are led to believe is a repressed homosexual, responds by insisting that he watch while Julian has intercourse with his wife. It is hardly surprising that Ryman (who in some sense embodies the active, gay male gaze within the subsequent scene) is portrayed as a nasty piece of work. Why would any self-respecting gay male viewer want to identify with him?

Still Ryman's plaintive 'I can still look' serves as a reminder that neither the queer gaze nor the processes of queer identification are fixed. As Kobena Mercer points out, 'The gendered hierarchy of seeing/being seen is not so rigidly coded in homoerotic representations, since sexual sameness liquidates the associative opposition between active subject and passive object'.[13] It may be possible, in fact, for the gay male viewer to identify with the gigolo while at the same time adopting the spectator position represented by Ryman, or else to oscillate between the two positions, enjoying the various pleasures offered by each.

A simple extension of the denial strategies outlined above explains why mirrors figure so consistently throughout *American Gigolo*, and brings us to a consideration of one of the film's most self-conscious (and, I believe, revealing) scenes. Suspecting Julian of the Ryman murder, Detective Sunday turns up at a hotel lobby where Julian is discovered having his shoes shined in preparation for meeting a 'special' client. They settle into a conversation,

Julian offering the detective 'a few pointers to picking up women', Sunday responding by questioning the ethics of Julian's occupation. Their relative social, sexual and legal positions are made abundantly clear. 'Doesn't it bother you, Julian, what you do?' asks Sunday. 'Giving pleasure to women?' retorts Julian. 'I'm supposed to feel guilty about that?'

Throughout the exchange, the camera is centred on Julian's face, with the detective's face reflected in the mirror behind him. Sunday is clearly intended to represent what we would have to call the 'Old Man'. Uncultured and unkempt, he lacks dress-sense and pays little attention to the finer details of his appearance, as Julian is quick to point out. The composition of the scene – Julian in the foreground, the detective reflected behind him – invites us to compare the two, the Old with the New Man. We are also clearly asked to identify with Julian, since it is he who expresses the views with which the 'modern', 'liberal' male spectator would surely align himself. 'Legal is not always right,' Julian says. 'Men make laws. Sometimes they're wrong. Stupid. Or jealous.'

Stupid? Perhaps. Jealous? Possibly. One thing we are left in no doubt about is the threat Julian's lifestyle poses to patriarchal norms. Condemned by the senator as 'a whore', he represents the antithesis to the whole concept of family, the promotion of which has provided the basis of the politician's election campaign. Such is the threat embodied by the male sex-object that no man will come near him (with the notable exception of a criminally motivated black gay pimp). Julian's only real friends in the film are women, and these relationships are, to say the least, fraught. His salvation lies in the fact that he recognises the error of his ways and forges a commitment to a woman we know to be 'good wife material', a woman who is prepared to forsake her reputation for her man, a woman who fulfills her role as one half of the traditional gender equation. Any pretence at exploring a new, liberated version of masculinity is dropped. Male-bonding – the stock theme of 1980s Hollywood – could find no place in the turn-of-the-decade, autonomous, autoerotic world of the all-American gigolo.

THE ICEMAN COMETH?

Top Gun, Tony Scott's 1986 *Boy's Own* story, was memorable on two accounts. It established Tom Cruise (an aspiring brat-packer whose previous experience included dropping his trousers at regular intervals throughout 1983's *Risky Business*) as a major box office attraction, effectively eclipsing the more mature Gere in the heart-throb stakes. And it brought the fetishisation of flying jackets out of the gay clubs and onto the high street.

Cruise plays Maverick, a new recruit at Fighter Weapons school (referred to by the recruits as 'Top Gun'), whose tempestuous temperament makes him a hazard to all around him. 'I'm dangerous,' he boasts to rival recruit Iceman (Val Kilmer), whose frigid demeanour and blond-boy good looks confirm him as Maverick's polar opposite. If the Iceman is impressed, he doesn't let it show, but an intense and intimate rivalry between the two is established from the point at which they look each other in the eye and issue challenges across a crowded room.

Like every good *Boy's Own* story, *Top Gun* has its share of heterosexual love interest, provided here in the shape of Charlotte (Kelly McGillis), who goes by the name of 'Charlie' and gradually falls for Maverick's cheeky-boy charms after overcoming her reservations at being his instructor. True to her name, Charlie spends half the film dressed in unisex naval uniform, complete with peaked cap, though she does have the courtesy to let her hair down and put on a frock for her big love scenes. Her first conversation with Maverick, which starts in the bar and ends in the ladies' room, serves to underline the fact that flying fighter planes isn't all that different from having a good fuck. 'So, are you a good pilot?' asks Charlie. 'I can hold my own,' replies Maverick with a lecherous grin. On this occasion, Charlie holds her own. She would have been well advised to do so on each subsequent occasion, too, though this would have made things a bit difficult for poor Tony Scott, whose valiant attempts to defend the frontiers of heterosexual viewing against the onslaught of homoerotica are already failing hopelessly. The romance may be firmly on the ground, but the passion is anchored in the cockpit.

The coding of the young fighter pilots as erotic spectacle relies heavily on cockpit to locker room editing techniques and the camera's lingering looks over torsos and precariously held towels. In the first locker-room scene, one man is laid out on a bench next to Iceman, who appears to be contending with an erection through his towel. As the scene changes, a senior officer's voice is heard shouting 'I want somebody's butt and I want it now!' Mere coincidence? A later scene, in which Maverick and Iceman compete in a game of volleyball, is lifted straight out of the homoerotic portfolio of Herb Ritts. Stripped to the waist, the men jump in the sunlight, their torsos glistening under the customary coat of sweat, their pleasures heightened by a rock rendition of *Playing with the Boys*. The homoerotic charge between the pilots is exemplified by the language used whenever they are together, whether it be in the air, the locker room or the instruction room. Iceman's first words in the film, offered as an aside to his buddy Slider during an instruction on flying technique, are, 'This gives me a hard-on' – to which Slider replies: 'Don't tease me.' Once we're up in the air, the *double entendres* fly thick and fast, borne by phrases like 'this guy's hot on my tail', 'this boy's all over me', 'I've given him the finger' and 'my dick, my ass'. (With all this testosterone flying about, Charlie's sexually coded advice to Maverick – 'it takes a lot more than just fancy flying' – seems oddly out of place in a heterosexual context.)

Generically, *Top Gun* has all the trimmings of the male action movie, including the traditional buddy scenario, though here the homoeroticism is more pronounced. Maverick's buddy throughout the film is Goose, who is prepared to be Maverick's wing-man in spite of his hot-head reputation. 'You're the only family I've got and I'm not going to let you down,' promises Maverick. Ten minutes later he's apologising to Goose for losing his cool and coming within an inch of securing their joint dismissal. 'It'll never happen again', says Maverick solemnly in the locker room. 'I know,' says Goose, barely audible over a swell of harp strings.

But it does happen again, and Goose is killed, leaving poor old Maverick to stand around in his jockey-shorts, look deep into his troubled soul and wonder about his dear old pop (whose death in action is surrounded by rumours of misconduct and whose memory prompts his son to behave as though 'he's up there flying against a ghost'). Charlie's efforts to talk him out of quitting the force are unsuccessful. After dismissing her, Maverick rides off into the night, finally showing up at Commander Metcalfe's house on Sunday morning, where it is revealed that Maverick's daddy was Metcalfe's sidekick and 'a fine pilot'. One ghost thus laid to rest, Maverick returns to the locker room, where Iceman extends the hand of friendship. Following a half-hearted return handshake at the graduation ceremony, where Iceman is honoured as 'the best of the best', fire and ice are finally joined in symbolic union during a real life battle situation, during which Maverick rescues Iceman from possible death. The two land side by side, are met by a crowd of emotionally charged men, and indulge in the kind of physical male-bonding normally reserved for the football pitch. 'You can be my wingman anytime,' offers Iceman. 'Bullshit! You can be mine,' replies Maverick, before wandering off and throwing his last token reminder of Goose into the ocean.

As Cynthia J. Fuchs has observed, the paradox of homosexual attraction between men claiming to be heterosexual is 'rehearsed in the buddy film's movement from conflict to resolution (between the two men or between them and a hostile environment)'.[14] In *Top Gun*, the sexual tensions already implicit in the male-to-male bond are further exacerbated by the order of the narrative, which implies that emotional ties between men are both (a) exclusive and (b) reproductive. Just as Commander Metcalfe becomes, in a sense, Maverick's father figure, so Ice replaces Goose in the young pilot's affections. This transference of intimacy between men is so powerfully inscribed that any relationship not subject to its thematic conditions lacks credibility.

In the film's penultimate scene, Maverick heads off for a romantic reunion with Charlie. Determined to reaffirm his hero's heterosexuality, the director throws in every known romantic cliché. Framed against a blood-red sky, the couple repeat their first-ever conversation, only this time with the roles reversed – the suggestion being, presumably, that any tension between them has now been successfully negotiated. But even as the scene fades (to the strains of *You've Lost That Loving Feeling*), there is no indication of the kind of emotional physicality we witnessed when Maverick and Ice 'made up'.

The final shot is of two fighter planes soaring together into the sky. Love is very clearly in the air. But where on earth is Charlie?[15]

CONCLUSION: 'ALL IN THIS TOGETHER'?

Jane Fonda apologised, but not Barbarella.
(Sandra Bernhard)

Queer readings of popular culture can take many shapes, drawing as they do from a wide range of disciplines (psychoanalysis, constructionism, reception theory, considerations of authorship, stars, etc.). What they all share is the understanding that cultural texts do not have single meanings, that what is denied at the level of narrative (i.e., queerness) can often be deciphered through closer inspection of the textual codes.

A critic who adopts this kind of approach is often accused of 'reading against the text', of taking an 'oppositional' or (better yet) an 'alternative' view. Such allegations are founded on the assumption that all cultural production is, by its very nature, straight, unless it proclaims itself otherwise (and sometimes even then its queerness is passed over, played down, or called into question – a heterosexist response Eve Kosofsky Sedgewick character-ises as 'Don't ask; You shouldn't know. It didn't happen; it doesn't make any difference; it didn't mean anything; it doesn't have interpretative consequences.'[16]) A similar thing happens whenever a lesbian or gay man dares to suggest that another (closeted) person might be lesbian or gay. 'How could you possibly know that?' the heterosexual interrogator demands. The answer, more often than not, is desperately (and unhelpfully) simple: some things you just know.

Another way to argue this would be to point out that queerness (precisely because of its 'invisibility') has managed to pervade popular culture to such a degree that it hardly makes sense to draw distinctions between what is 'mass culture' and what is 'queer subculture'. Or as the British playwright and author Neil Bartlett recently put it: 'The history of mainstream entertainment is the history of gay culture.'[17] Considered in this light, queer readings are hardly 'oppositional'. Rather, they represent an attempt to point out what really ought to have been clear to everybody from the start.

The pleasures of such readings are simple: what better revenge on a culture which seeks to exclude you than to demonstrate how you were there all along? The problems – by which I really mean the politics – are rather more complex: if queers devote their time and energies to the interpretation of popular texts (texts which, however queer they may be, still represent the interests and ideologies of a heterosexist society), where will the support come from for openly queer cultural production by and about queers? Isn't all this 'textual fetishism' simply an excuse to shrug the responsibilities of *Realpolitik*?

The answer depends on whether or not you regard pleasure and politics as mutually exclusive – depends, in fact, on whether you accept that criticism is itself a form of activism, with its own activist strategies and political goals. My readings of *American Gigolo* and *Top Gun* concentrate far more on the potentially queer pleasures of the texts than on the politics of their production. Still this isn't to say that such readings aren't political.

In *The Celluloid Closet*, Vito Russo expressed his fears that 'reality will never be profitable until our society overcomes its fear and hatred of difference and begins to see that we're all in this together'.[18] It seems to me that queer readings are part of a wider project to prove that we are 'all in this together' precisely by demonstrating the presence of that 'difference'. It is only by declaring our position in relation to popular cultural texts that we can ever hope to expose the myth that the only profitable forms of cultural production are those which express a uniform straightness. Then, perhaps, we can hope for a bit of 'reality'.

NOTES

1 Richard Dyer, *The Matter of Images*, Routledge, London, 1993, p.19.
2 Yvonne Tasker, *Spectacular Bodies: Gender, Genre and the Action Cinema*, Routledge, London, 1993, p.165.
3 Steve Neale, 'Masculinity as Spectacle: Reflections on Men and Mainstream Cinema', *Screen* vol.24, no.6, November–December 1983, p.15.
4 Cynthia J. Fuchs, 'The Buddy Politic', in *Screening the Male*, Routledge, London, 1993, p.196.
5 Steve Neale's ground-breaking essay concentrates on images of masculinity prior to the period under discussion.
6 Suzanne Moore, 'Here's Looking at You, Kid!', in Lorraine Gamman and Margaret Marshment (eds), *The Female Gaze*, The Women's Press, London, 1988, p.51.
7 Rowena Chapman, 'Variations on the New Man Theme', in *Male Order: Unwrapping Masculinity*, Lawrence & Wishart, London, 1988, p.236.
8 Ibid.
9 Vito Russo, *The Celluloid Closet*, Harper & Row, New York, 1987, p.238.
10 Rumours surrounding Gere's own sexual orientation were rife as early as 1979, when he played one of the two homosexual prisoners in the Broadway production of Martin Sherman's *Bent*. Given the potentially catastrophic effect of such speculation on a young actor's career in Hollywood, we oughtn't to underestimate the degree to which *Gigolo* might have served as a cinematic 'right to reply', providing Gere with the perfect opportunity to set the record 'straight'.
    In an interview in *Vanity Fair* (January 1994), Gere refused to confirm or deny rumours that he is gay. 'The accusation is meaningless', he was quoted as saying, 'and whether it's true or false is nobody's business. I know who I am; what difference does it make what anyone thinks, if I live truthfully and honestly and with as open a heart as I can?' Shortly afterwards, he and his wife, Cindy Crawford, took out a full page advertisement in *The Times* newspaper, reassuring the world of their heterosexuality.
11 Interviewed in the US lesbian and gay magazine *The Advocate* (issue 609, 13 August 1992), Schrader confirmed that the employment of homoerotic images had been 'a kind of current in my life'.

12 Chapman, op. cit., p.237.
13 Kobena Mercer, 'Skin Head Sex Thing: Racial Difference and the Homoerotic Imaginary', in Bad Object-Choices (ed.), *How Do I Look? Queer Film and Video*, Bay Press, Seattle, 1991, p.182.
14 Fuchs, op. cit., p.195.
15 For further discussion of homoeroticism in *Top Gun*, see Mark Simpson, *Male Impersonators*, Cassell, London and New York, 1994. For an example of how openly queer cultures appropriate the effects of mass culture, it's worth noting how *Top Gun* provided the scenario for a gay porn flick released within a year of the film's release. Matt Sterling's 1987 best-seller *Big Guns* picks up on Maverick's first meeting with Iceman in the bar. Rejected by 'Charlie', Maverick follows Iceman outside for some serious horseplay.
16 Eve Kosofsky Sedgwick, *Epistemology of the Closet*, University of California Press, California, 1990, p.53.
17 Neil Bartlett, interview with the author, published in *Time Out*, 24 November 1993.
18 Russo, op. cit., p.323.

6

THE TRANSGRESSIVE
SEXUAL SUBJECT

Cherry Smyth

It's time to seize the power of dyke love, dyke vision, dyke anger, dyke intelligence, dyke strategy. It's time to organise and incite. It's time to get together and fight. We're invisible sisters and it's not safe . . . it's time for a fierce lesbian movement and that's *you*: the role model, the vision, the desire.[1]

As an act of vengeance, I want to take what could be mine from Hollywood, put myself in the picture as it were, reinvent the story of the gaze. Wish-fulfilment, you may say, as I wrest the homo-subtext from its cosy hetero-complacent form and make it the major discourse. Maybe so, but then reading against the grain began as a wish for inclusion by marginalised, under-represented people and ended up as a strategy essential for our survival. The exercise of harnessing the text for purposes for which it was not intended also involves a level of whimsy, of ironic layering and deconstructing, that builds on a developing tradition of new dyke camp.

At no point do I wish to suggest that we can or ought to replace an essentialist hetero-reading with an equally essentialist dyke reading, for as Marusia Bociurkiw outlines: 'Absence is both a plausible and a dangerous starting-point for representation, for it can lead to false universals, to an essentialism that predicates a homogenous, undifferentiated "we".'[2] My reading is informed by my whiteness and also shaped by a socio-historical specificity which determines my relation to popular culture, film theory, feminism and queer politics – a dynamic that has shifted significantly in this decade and reshapes how contemporary and past filmic texts, once readily dismissed, are reinterpreted.

INTERROGATING THE POPULAR

I realised I'm not a lesbian anymore. I realised that women don't have fun together . . . I realised that men are heroes after all.[3]

Reading mainstream films subversively, lesbians have constructed heroines who do not officially belong to them, not only by disrupting the authority of the heterosexual male gaze, but also by appropriating the heterosexual woman as a homosexual object. From Marlene Dietrich, Greta Garbo and Bette Davis, to Catherine Deneuve, Jamie Lee Curtis, Jodie Foster and Whoopi Goldberg, there has been long tradition of lesbian appropriation of actors who've played strong, autonomous women. In a 1989 Channel Four *Out* television series' survey of lesbian spectators, the favourite 'lesbian' movie cited was *Alien* (Ridley Scott, 1979) with Sigourney Weaver, which never explicitly acknowledges the existence of lesbianism. As Chris Straayer points out:

> within the construction of narrative film sexuality, the phrase 'lesbian heroine' is a contradiction in terms. . . . The lesbian heroine in film must be conceived of as a viewer construction, short-circuiting the very networks that attempt to forbid her energy. She is constructed from contradictions within the text and between the text and the viewer, who insists on assertive, even transgressive, identifications and seeing.[4]

The persistence of the dyke invention of lesbian heroines urged me to reconstruct a mainstream Hollywood movie, a psychological thriller, in which the best thrills happen only if you impose a lesbian reading. At the time of its release, *Black Widow*, (Bob Rafelson, 1987) met with mixed (let's say heterosexual) press reviews, keen dyke response privately and severe dismissal from some dykes in public. For several reasons, I believe that *Black Widow* is ripe for another spin:

- Since there is a continued absence of recognisable lesbian heroines in Hollywood, it is important to continue archival revisionism to spot how and when we came close to a lesbian shero and why the narrative/s finally chickened out.
- The 1990s have brought much less suspicion of the popular. As B. Ruby Rich outlined at a queer cinema conference in London in 1992, lesbian and gay culture was once afraid of the contamination of the popular, a situation that was most visibly challenged and offset not only by the *Out* television series in Britain, but by the theatrical, commercial release of Derek Jarman's 1991 film *Edward II* in the US and the mainstream success of other queer boys' films, *Poison* (Todd Haynes, 1991) and *Swoon* (Tom Kalin, 1992). When Sandra Bernhard's character Nancy came out in *Roseanne* in 1993, the British gay press heralded this as a momentous victory for lesbian visibility – and it was. Could Bernhard take the heat, however? Think again.
- It continues to be necessary not only to challenge the heterosexist dogma of some feminist film theory and the intransigence of psychoanalytic theory, but also to confound lesbian orthodoxies. For example, the tyranny of positive images has shifted so much that lesbians who wield ice-picks, drive sports cars, and become senators and designer dykes can be embraced without the 'movement' collapsing under the burden of their irresponsibility.

A lesbian heroine who kills, such as Catherine in *Black Widow*, is not immediately dissed as an inappropriate role model. We are now more irreverent and robust and can use the term 'lesbian community' with irony, mocking its false homogeneity. Moreover, the reductive, infantilising grip of an anti-sex morality and notions of what a lesbian should look like are loosening.

• The advent of a queer movement which acknowledges the fracturing boundaries of sexual identification enables a narrative like *Black Widow* to be readdressed more easily. We no longer demand exclusive lesbianism of our heroines and a woman who fucks a man in a film's narrative can also be read as a dyke. As Alisa Solomon asserts, as we become more secure in our identities as queers, the need for a rigorous binary homo–hetero divide lessens.

As we feel freer to be ourselves, the useful organising fiction of the past – that a person's politics could be determined by his or her sexual orientation (or some other salient feature of identity) – no longer serves. We need a new way of thinking about identity, or at least a new appellation, one that preserves the promise of sexual liberation. It isn't enough to become parallel to straights – we want to obliterate such dichotomies altogether.[5]

KICKING THE THEORY

Many feminist rereadings of film have constructed arguments around male/female, masculine/feminine, active/passive, largely ignoring the potential intervention of a lesbian spectator, which may inject a text with a particular, subversive subtext, often unacknowledged by the film-maker and the heterosexual, feminist critic alike.

Traditional psychoanalytic approaches are far from adequate for discussions of female sexuality, not to mention lesbian desire. According to Lacan, both the masquerade of femininity and the penis signify the phallus, or male desire.

In her frequently quoted and highly influential essay, 'Visual Pleasure and Narrative Cinema', Laura Mulvey described how dominant cinema codes have been constructed by a patriarchal system of looking and the desire to obtain and consume. The gaze championed by Mulvey is assumed to be male (white and heterosexual) and therefore endowed with the power and privilege enjoyed by (white and heterosexual) men in a patriarchal society. Mulvey's account of the sexual hierarchy of narrative cinema has been challenged by many critics who have insisted that identification can also occur across gender and sexual demarcations. Mulvey herself readdressed the issue in a later article, in which she argued that when the central protagonist is female, the female spectator can enjoy 'the freedom of action and control over the diegetic world that identification with the hero provides' but that this identification is unsatisfactory since 'the woman central protagonist is shown to be unable to achieve a stable sexual identity, torn between the deep blue sea of passive femininity and the devil of regressive masculinity.'[6]

This analysis robs the unfeminine, female, active lesbian spectator of a point of entry into the text that operates as desire for, not identification with the female hero. For Mulvey, even if the woman identifies with the invulnerability of the male hero, this 'transsex identification is a *habit* that very easily becomes *second Nature*. However, this Nature does not sit easily and shifts restlessly in its borrowed transvestite clothes' (emphases in original).[7]

The use of the word 'transvestite' suggests that the female spectator feels more 'natural' in stereotypically feminine dress, and that clothes and gender can be conflated. It forecloses the options for the butch dyke spectator whose 'masculine' dress is her 'first Nature' and whose masculinity in the world is not a 'regressive' fantasy, but a constantly subversive reality. Any woman who steps out of her socio-cultural gender role by dressing as a man is not merely 'borrowing' these clothes, but disrupting the categories of male and female, as well as unhinging the function of category itself.

Although many lesbians find the psychoanalytic model redundant, it is beginning to be reinterpreted and subverted for lesbian purposes by theorists like Sue-Ellen Case and Elizabeth Grosz, in ways that neither pathologise nor invalidate our desire. For example, Case points out subtextual homophobia, castigating

> heterosexual feminist critics who metaphorise butch/femme roles, transvestites, and campy dressers into 'subject who masquerades', as they put it, or is 'carnivalesque' (note the fancy French endings) or even, as some are so bold to say, who 'cross-dresses'.[8]

Masculine women, and for my purposes, butch lesbians, have been seen as having failed in the masquerade of femininity. Masculinity is seen as 'stolen' and must be hidden for women to function unpunished in society in traditionally male roles. Womanliness and the masquerade are seen as the same thing, with masculinity as the norm and femininity its dissimulation.

However, the powerful and complex tightrope of masquerade is learnt by any woman the moment she realises that she does not reciprocate male desire. She must reconstruct an identity from a sexual space in between, fused by shame, secrecy and pleasure. We are constantly aware of our potential to destabilise the image of the woman, to explode or parody the confines of femininity, by parodic artifice – the high-femme, or disavowal – the lesbian boy. These skills inform our reading of any cinematic exchange between women.

In Straayer's words:

> Women's desire for women deconstructs male/female sexual dichotomies, sex/gender conflation, and the universality of the Oedipal narrative. Acknowledgement of the female-initiated active sexuality

and sexualised activity of lesbians has the potential to reopen a space in which straight women as well as lesbians can exercise self-determined pleasure.[9]

TRANSGRESSING THE SEXUAL SUBJECT

Elizabeth Cowie has written at length about the dangers of pilfering images and sequences from a filmic text and twisting them to our own discourse, for example, invoking feminist heroines in a film where the heroine capitulates to sexist stereotypes and never sees herself as feminist, 'For the film cannot be read as progressive in relation to definitions constituted outside the film, either alternative or dominant, which exist as contents given form, a representation, within the film.'[10] While I do not wish to argue that *Black Widow* is ultimately a progressive text, it does reveal ambivalences in the patriarchal order and in the heterosexist gaze and opens spaces for a transgressive lesbian sexual subject.

Lesbian theorists too have warned against the reclamation of heterosexual heroines as 'lesbian'. The fear of reclaiming an inscribed anti-feminist as a lesbian heroine has thwarted the development of a counter cultural wry wit, specific to dykes and analogous to the gay male camp tradition developed in between the spaces, the absences, of any reference to gay men and in the presence of homophobia.

> The survival tactic of hiding and lying had produced a camp discourse . . . (in which) gender referents are suppressed, or slip into one another, fictional lovers are constructed, metaphors substitute for literal descriptions, and the characters and narratives of pop culture replace personal ones.[11]

Sharon Stone's character in *Basic Instinct* (Paul Verhoeven, 1992) may be distinctly anti-feminist, but was cited popularly as a lesbian heroine. 'For me, a cute dyke with two Ferraris who kills men is a *positive* image,' claimed Clare Beavan, producer of the *Out* series, quoted in the *The New Statesman and Society*, 1 May 1992.

Black Widow lends itself to a similar kind of ironic reinvention. Here we have a rich, young beautiful woman, the eponymous Catherine (Teresa Russell), who picks up and poisons her husbands with the skill of a brain surgeon. She is discovered and sought after by a rather dowdy workaholic federal agent, Alex (Debra Winger) who needs a bit of hands-on excitement. It's a classic chase movie, with the familiar, and so compelling, ugly duckling motif thrown in. What's less familiar is that not only are there two female protagonists, but that Alex develops an obsession with Catherine, far beyond the call of duty.

The psychological motivation is thin. When Alex tells her boss that 'no one knows why anybody does anything', the gate opens and the psychiatrist has bolted, leaving the field of supposition totally accessible for a dyke interpretation of motivation. Alex's reply, which deflects her boss's concern that she is obsessed with Catherine, acts as a comic cypher for all the times dykes have no answers for the 'why'. 'Why do you always have your hair so short? Why don't you ever wear a dress? Why do you have to be so public about it? Why do you enjoy licking pussy?' Alex may be obsessed, but she's not going to see a doctor. She becomes a hunter.

As soon as a female character initiates and leads the action, whether it's Jodie Foster in *Silence of the Lambs* (Jonathan Demme, 1991) or Sigourney Weaver in the *Alien* trilogy (*Alien*, Ridley Scott, 1979; *Aliens*, James Cameron, 1986 and *Alien* [3], David Fincher, 1992), there is an immediate assumption of immunity for the protagonist which is immensely reassuring for the female spectator. As in *Question of Silence* (Marleen Gorris, 1982) and *The Awakening of Christa Klages* (Margarethe Von Trotta, 1978), the quest in *Black Widow* is initiated and structured through the female point of view, and the prize is another woman, or another woman's 'truth'.

In the pre-credit sequence, *Black Widow* constructs the act of looking as central to the narrative. The close-up of Teresa Russell's eyes as she applies eye-liner using a hand mirror has the effect of a split screen, in which both sections appear to be lit slightly differently (Figure 10). This suggests the duality of her nature, evoking bisexuality and the theme of merging with another woman, which recur in the narrative. It echoes Bergman's *Persona* (1966) in which two women battle for emotional and intellectual dominance. It also emphasises the potent role of masquerade, of making-up, of putting on a disguise.

As far back as 1929, in 'Womanliness as Masquerade', Joan Riviere comments: 'Women who wish for masculinity may put on a mask of womanliness to avert anxiety and the retribution feared from men.' In other words, if the woman operates as if she has a penis, she must disguise this by being ultra-feminine to avoid castration.

> Womanliness therefore could be assumed and worn as a mask, both to hide the possession of masculinity and to avert the reprisals expected if she was found to possess it – much as a thief will turn out his pockets and ask to be searched to prove that he has not the stolen goods.[12]

When Catherine then puts on sunglasses, thus making the make-up redundant, private, it establishes the bizarre anti-logic of a character who is clearly in the business of deceit. Teresa Russell as Catherine is young, stiff, bereaved and stylish, conjuring up the image of Catherine Deneuve, not only in *Belle de Jour* (Luis Bunuel, 1967) but also in the later and much more dyke-embedded *The Hunger* (Tony Scott, 1983).

As a widow, however, Catherine is not upset enough, which the spectator may read as betrayal or as an opening for a story of female revenge, of a husband killed because he deserved it, murdered because he tried to thwart

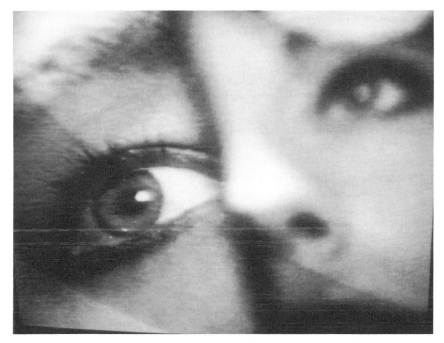

10 Eyeliner blues: Catherine, framed in split frame, applies redundant make-up
(*Black Widow*, Bob Rafelson, 1987)

his much younger wife. Catherine is already constituted as a 'bad girl', therefore, ripe for transgressive lesbian identification.

When the film cuts at once to Alex, the parallel positioning of the two protagonist's lives establishes the certainty that the narrative will propel them together. Anticipation kicks in. The suspense of the thriller, which relies on delay of knowledge, takes on a more acutely sexualised dimension for the dyke spectator.

Both women are constructed as single and available; in addition the thrill of 'opposites attract' works to heighten lesbian possibilities. Catherine is blonde, contained and sophisticated; Alex is dark, dressed in post-hippy casuals and with no knowledge of hair gel. The dichotomy of suave versus messy is well known to any romance spectator. Here it acts as a signal for a butch/femme, experienced/novice encounter which we've seen in *Personal Best* (Robert Towne, 1982), *Lianna* (John Sayles, 1982), *Another Way* (Karoly Makk, 1982) and *Desert Hearts* (Donna Deitch, 1984) to name but a few. This pattern intensifies the pleasure of the pre-meeting sequences.

To Catherine men are disposable. She swots up enough specialised knowledge to catch her professional mate, exposing hetero-desire as being as superficial and simple to mimic as a game show. Alex, by contrast, is constructed as operating in an adolescent, pre-sexual state of distraction. Her reluctance to socialise with her male colleagues (except when playing cards) reinforces the trope of Alex as a lesbian who doesn't know it. Yet.

It's a slow time-bomb of a movie whose formula is charmingly predictable and whose lesbian subtext is so unimaginable to itself that its frissons have endless repercussions. As soon as lesbianism is suggested it is quickly denied. For example, the moment Alex recognises photos of Catherine in her various disguises and decides to chase her, her male colleagues become more persistent in their wooing, as though to refute the idea that Alex might be a dyke. The slide projector scene is a gaze gem. Alex assembles slides of Catherine and smuggles them away to her home, where she blows them up and studies them in private. Her domestic environment is bare and functional, in need of 'a woman's touch'. She doesn't cook, eats boil-in-the-bag food and begins more and more to resemble a pre-hatched butch. The narrative's attempt to impose difference between the two women unwittingly suggests a butch-femme dynamic. As Alex superimposes different images of Catherine on the wall, she approaches them and touches them with her forefinger (Figure 11). Overplayed and extremely seductive, here we have a butch controlling the image of the femme in all her different masquerades.

Lesbian desire is always read as women wanting to be 'masculine', *to be men*, ignoring the dynamic of the femme dyke, whose conscious use of role/

11 Alex fingers the slide show (*Black Widow*, Bob Rafelson, 1987)

masquerade is directed at the butch. Catherine is acting out her desirability for Alex. In the case of Alex and Catherine, we have the masculine woman desiring the phallicised body of another woman.

> The femme foregrounds her masquerade by playing to the butch, another woman in a role; likewise the butch exhibits her penis to a woman who is playing the role of compensatory castration. This raises the question of 'penis, penis, who's got the penis', because there is no referent in sight; rather the fiction of the penis and castration become ironised and 'camped up'.[13]

For the lesbian spectator, it is a near-ideal opportunity to create her own transgressive sexual subject or hypothetical lesbian heroine, hampered only by the visual fact that both women appear as feminine/femmes. But if we are prepared to construct Alex as the pre-hatched butch, then Case's argument for a dynamic duo, offering strong subject positions, applies.

> They are the coupled ones who do not impale themselves on the poles of sexual difference or metaphysical values, but constantly seduce the sign system through flirtation and inconstancy into the light fondle of artifice, replacing the Lacanian slash with a lesbian bar.[14]

Elizabeth Grosz's essay on 'Lesbian Fetishism' wrestles with the notion of phallic desire in a butch–femme context which may illuminate how we read lesbian texts, or texts-lesbian. In her account she suggests that the femme phallicises or fetishises her own body, accepting her castration and seeking out a 'phallic'/masculine woman as a father-substitute.

The butch/masculine woman however, denies her castration and takes on a substitute for the phallus, an object outside her own body:

> the masculine woman takes an external love-object – another woman – and through this love-object is able to function as if she *has*, rather than *is*, the phallus . . . her 'fetish' is not the result of a fear of femininity but a love of it; it does not protect her from potential danger, for it introduces her to the effects of widespread social homophobia.[15]

The problem with both these approaches is that they presuppose an erotic attraction between women that is dependent on a butch–femme dynamic. Desire between two women who do not reinvent these roles is more difficult to read under the psychoanalytic model. They also presuppose that butch–femme identifications are as fixed as heterosexual roles, while in reality, lesbians often change their sexual role when they change their partners or their underwear.

To return to *Black Widow* where Alex is backlit by the projector beam which emphasises the construction of the gaze, magnifying it as on a cinema screen – eroticism bristling around the shadows on the wall. She moves to position herself in front of the two-shot of Catherine and her husband and stands opposite the image of Catherine, blocking the image of the male in the frame. Then, facing Catherine, she stands in for the male to 'look' at Catherine, who appears to 'look' at her. As she touches Catherine's image, it foreshadows the moment when she will touch the 'real' Catherine and reinforces the idea that Catherine is not real, but only Alex's illusion. Later this sense of Catherine as imaginary is echoed by Alex's boss, who says, 'You don't quit your job after six years to go chasing after some phantom.' 'She's not a phantom,' cries Alex, who goes on, 'You want to catch her you have to think like she thinks.' As she is still unable to articulate how much she wants to catch Catherine for herself, she does not use the first person pronoun, cannot quite give herself permission to claim the chase as her own.

The imminent merging of Catherine and Alex's personalities is evoked in this scene where the image of Alex merges with the projected image of Catherine which plays over her back. Alex then lays her hand gracefully on top of Catherine's, as if to see if it fits. The importance of hands as lesbian erotic signifiers is obvious to anyone who reads lesbian erotica/porn: hands that caress, excite, stimulate, penetrate, throb, fist, slap, finger, are lesbian sexual organs.

> I take your hand in my hand, take my courage in both hands and gently pull – not too much to my surprise you follow your hand and come . . . those delicate fingers holding my face to pull me to you . . . your fingers are in my hair . . . your nails scratch my back . . . fingers stroking downwards . . . my whole body moves around your fingers . . . you kiss me all over, lingering on my mouth, feeling the same sensation with your tongue as with your fingers. As your fingers explore me they find . . .[16]

Then Alex stands in front of the mirror, where we see her remove her shirt to reveal a man's grey vest and caress her own face as she has just touched Catherine's. She then pulls back her hair, as if to guess how she might transform herself as another, *as a butch*, signalling that she is willing to enter Catherine's game of masquerade on her own terms. The slides continue to flicker on and off in the darkened room, enveloping Alex in the private fantasy of the transformative agency of desire.

Teresa de Lauretis would undoubtedly disagree with this celebratory reading of the scene, as she dismissed *Black Widow* as an 'outright obnoxious commercial product . . . which unabashedly exploited the currently fashionable discourse on lesbianism to the end of an effective delegitimation of the lesbian – and perhaps even the feminist – politics of sexual difference.'[17] Because of the ubiquitous nature of lesbian scenes in heterosexual porn as preludes to the hetero-fuck, lesbian sexual images in the mainstream have often been constructed as pandering to some prurient need in the masses to disavow lesbians. I question the notion that lesbianism has ever been so fashionable and think the accusation of exploitation is too often used as an excuse not to explore/foreground explicit lesbian sexual subject matter. For

132

example, in a recent interview, lesbian heroine kd lang defended director Percy Adlon's choice not to make the lesbian content in *Salmonberries* (1991) more prominent.

> It would have been very different for him to have the two women make love, 'cause where does the story go from there? In some ways I wanted it to go that way, but in other ways I didn't, 'cause then it would have become a lesbian film. And what good is that? Then people just think you're being trendy or trying to sell the film through controversy.[18]

Contemporary reviewers of *Black Widow* were divided on the film's use of lesbianism. While Philip Bergson in *What's On* agreed with de Lauretis, that 'the film flirts coyly with lesbianism for the mass market' (30 July 1987), Nigel Andrews could not read the codes at all: 'no one seems able to nail Miss Russell, not even Debra Winger who hoofs after her and becomes involved in some weird relationship with her which I could not work out. Not lesbianism, something more kinky' (*Financial Times*, 24 July 1987).

Queer perhaps, as we might now read it. Pauline Kael was equally frustrated: 'You expect the women to share identities, or the picture to go lesbian, or *something*. But you're wrong. This is post-modernist *film noir* . . . you hope for something more pornographic in Russell's personality than you get.' Kael's conflation of lesbianism and porn is troublingly predictable (*New Yorker*, 23 February 1987). 'What is this delicate musk that Catherine radiates?' asks Richard Corliss in *Time*, 16 February 1987. 'Perhaps the scent of fulfilment through risk. And why does it attract Alex Barnes, a deskbound fed who determines to track Catherine down?'

The misogyny and homophobia of these readings are transparent. Most male bonding films have less motivational structure and as much homo-eroticism and yet the expression of 'kinkiness' and the bewilderment of the critics are rarely as apparent. Only one reviewer spied the butch potential in Alex: 'Catherine is beautiful, stealthy and detached, while Alex is *masculine* (my italics), loud and emotional . . . a curious relationship develops . . . a dangerous game, tinged by a strange mutual attraction beyond friendship, ensues as the two jostle for control' (*Films and Filming*, July 1987).

I believe that precisely because *Black Widow* does not know how to exploit lesbianism, it creates a space for a wild reading against the grain. Its construction of heterosexuality also works to delegitimate the great, white male as object of desire in that most of the men are greedy, gullible, naive and ultimately duped. Even Paul (Sami Frey), whom both women fuck, is used and disposed of.

In the aforementioned essay, de Lauretis also writes about the common confusion of desire with identification when female friendship films are discussed. In response to Jackie Stacey's article 'Desperately Seeking Difference' (*Screen*, vol.28, no.1, Winter 1987) she argues that both *Desperately Seeking Susan* (Susan Seidelman, 1985) and *All About Eve*

(Joseph Mankiewicz, 1950) are about identification, the first with a feminine
ego ideal, the second with an Oedipal mother/rival image. 'In psychoanalytic
terms, this "childlike" wish is a kind of identification that is at once ego-
directed, narcissistic and *desexualised*, devoid of sexual aim.'[19]

She goes on to assert that wanting to be like the object or seeing oneself
as the object (ego–libido) is very different from wanting to sexually have the
object (object–libido). While Alex does want to be like Catherine in order to
understand and therefore annihilate her, which fits the ego–libido model, the
slide show scene provides the characteristics of the object–libido model
which, although not fulfilled, provides an erotic context for the lesbian gaze.

In a later scene Alex's desire for Catherine is paralleled when Catherine
searches Alex's room for clues to her 'real' identity. She finds her initialed
handkerchief which she treats as an erotic object rather than a piece of
evidence, smelling it and rubbing it tenderly against her cheek (Figure 12).
Here again the question of identification versus desire is ambiguous: perhaps
she does want to be like Alex, a good girl federal agent, but it seems possible
to read the gesture as an attempt to articulate a desire for more intimacy, to
know and understand the 'real' Alex better. The fetishisation of Alex's
belongings in private echoes the fascination displayed by Alex in the slide
show scene.

12 Catherine fondles the handkerchief (*Black Widow*, Bob Rafelson, 1987)

The cross-cutting between the two women's lives continues, building up our expectation of their eventual meeting. Both are intellectually engaged in traditionally male roles, Catherine as an outlaw, a criminal, Alex as a government agent, a detective. Both are dedicated to their careers and constructed as worthy opponents. When Alex pleads with her boss to be allowed to investigate the case, she reveals how Catherine has disguised herself as different women using 'make-up, hair, attitude'. While men are completely fooled by Catherine's masquerade, it is obvious to another woman. Alex's awareness of the roles Catherine adopts proves that she too can use artifice and by implication is becoming more ready to become like Catherine by learning to seduce.

The moment the two women finally meet is redolent with the hetero-signifiers of lesbianism in that it is set in a swimming pool – all wet and no thrusting, in an archetypally feminine body of water. We enter the scene with Alex's knowledge of Catherine's presence, while Catherine still believes she is unseen. It is now Alex who is 'disguised' and the implicit references to 'passing' provide another lesbian entry point. Alex's passing as a tourist, as an 'innocent', evokes the thrill and anxiety of passing as straight. We are on familiar ground as we place ourselves in Alex's position, like the lesbian teenager in the all girl class who knows none of the other girls would play ball with her, *if they knew*.

The camera tracks slowly over pairs of women practising mouth-to-mouth resuscitation, coming to pause on a two-shot of Alex leaning over Catherine. 'You're not taking this personally, are you?' Alex asks. 'Don't worry,' Catherine laughs. Although this scene evokes the unspoken lesbian subtext, then disavows it by treating lesbian desire as a joke, it also operates at the level of a flirtation. In addition, the possibility of their desire is suggested more strongly by close framing and lip-to-lip contact, which encourages us to read them as 'a couple'.

The buddy movie narrative now asserts itself, though here the characters are not on the run, escaping bad men or chasing new dreams: rather the film is held in stasis, chasing its own tail. Neither woman can move until one of them lets slip her 'real' identity. Either Catherine is revealed as the killer, or Alex exposed as a fed. This layering of suspense and delay adds to the erotic tension as the women 'go on holiday' from their careers and male-defined roles – picnics, scuba diving, parties – which creates a sequence of erotic look exchanges that frames them as lovers.

> Conceptually, female bonding is a precondition for lesbianism. . . . So often female bonding has stood in for lesbian content, that lesbian audiences seem to find it an acceptable displacement at the conclusions of such 'lesbian romances' as *Personal Best* (Robert Towne, 1982) and *Lianna* (John Sayles, 1982).[20]

In one scene, both women, tousled after swimming and lying on sunbeds,

13 Girls by the pool: Alex framed by Catherine's leg (*Black Widow*, Bob Rafelson, 1987)

watch each other in the classic close-up shot/reverse shot. The shot of Alex is framed by the outline of Catherine's raised thigh and arm (Figure 13). Catherine is positioned as more physically relaxed and open, while Alex remains seated with her legs together. Alex trails her eyes down over Catherine's body in a gaze that is too overt to be 'polite'. Again the visual erotic tension is heightened by the dialogue as Catherine asks, 'What are you looking at?'

Alex is clearly embarrassed, hesitant, as if she has been caught looking in a way she shouldn't, i.e. 'as a fed', but we can read it 'as a lessie'. 'I'm sorry,' she blurts. 'I . . . no, it's just that we spent most of the day in the pool and you come out looking like that and I look like this.' Alex displays obvious flattery and makes a plea for guidance on her appearance. She acknowledges that she wants to be more like Catherine (ego–libido) but also wants to be more attractive to her (object–libido).

The narrative balances their power as active initiators as Catherine invites Alex up to her room 'for a couple of decent drinks'. By offering her a 'proper', i.e. 'strong', 'masculine' drink, we can construct Catherine as a 'top-femme', a sexually experienced woman offering to teach the novice. It works as a comic echo of Mae West, of countless *femme fatales* whose prey are men.

Hence Alex is reinforced as the baby-butch, the girl who needs help with her appearance and by extension with her sexual role. As Catherine lends Alex her clothes, the suggestion is that Catherine is as fascinated by Alex's lack of feminine artifice as Alex is seduced by Catherine's excess.

The intimacy of the bedroom scene, where both women are seen laughing (not giggling like pre-pubescent schoolgirls), with mutual respect for each other, is offset by their discussion of Catherine's boyfriend Paul, which works to re-establish the hetero structure. However, when Alex asks campily, 'Can I borrow your hair?' as she half-lies on the bed watching Catherine move around the room, she resembles a drag queen begging advice on a crumpled wig. This is Alex trying to bond in the only way she knows how, learning the 'make-up, hair and attitude' tricks of Catherine's trade and thus trying to disguise her masculinity.

According to Mulvey, the image of the woman in film is made glamorous, sexy and isolated until she becomes an erotic object for the male star, and by extension, for the omnipotent male spectator. However, as Mulvey states, the woman as icon connotes anxiety for the male due to her 'otherness' or 'lack of a penis'.

In order to avoid castration anxiety, the male chooses either sadism, by punishing and forgiving the woman or by demystifying her allure, or fetishism, by endowing her with a substitute penis such as breasts or high heels, or by phallicising her whole body into something reassuring.

Like a masculine hero, Alex seems to oscillate between wishing to fetishise Catherine as phallus and demystify her as icon. The formula usually ends in seduction – i.e. control or punishment and forgiveness – but here the erotic tension is sustained more than in most female bonding movies because the threat of mutual destruction injects a sharp edge of sadism into the dynamic, culminating in Catherine's kiss and Alex's eventual humiliation and entrapment of Catherine.

When Alex and Catherine make their entrance in the party scene, they are again coded as a couple. Alex, in Catherine's tight black dress and uncomfortably high heels, is unable to adapt to having a phallicised body. Stage one of the masquerade leaves her awkward, reinforcing the element of drag. Here the lesbian gaze can revel in the visual joke the narrative presents. Often in this kind of transformation, the novice embraces her role with immense satisfaction and can outdo her tutor, thus achieving her ego-libido identification to rival and win over the other woman. Alex's discomfort with this role reasserts the narrative drive that she wants Catherine, but since Catherine kills the thing she loves, i.e. men, Alex must entrap her using 'feminine' not masculine means. There is an increasing sense that Catherine will love Alex differently, in a way that will not lead to Alex's death. This sense of the omnipotence and 'difference' of lesbian desire also lends pleasure to the lesbian spectator.

Since both filmic and narrative desires are fuelled by sexual desire, films often introduce sexual signals to eroticise such framing which contains two women. Once eroticised, however, female bonding threatens to subvert or, worse, circumvent that heterosexual scheme entirely.[21]

In the scene in which Alex watches Catherine kiss Paul, she is presented ambiguously, as if she is jealous of both of them. Since we know that Catherine and Paul have not yet fucked, the erotic choices are still open: Catherine may choose to fuck Alex instead. While Catherine and Paul are safe, domesticated and sanctioned in the house, Alex is framed in the dark, outside in the lush tropical garden, which represents her otherness, her wildness. She is framed alone, singly, voyeuristic and excluded.

This scene recalls the scene with the slide show in which Alex also watched Catherine coupled with men, but was able to touch her and substitute herself for the male in the frame. On a psychoanalytic level, this encounter can be read as the one in which the infant Alex decides whether to continue to identify with the phallic mother and retain the masculinity of the pre-Oedipal position, or accept her castrated status and take the male as her love-object, as in 'normal' femininity.

Not only does the female bonding subvert the heterosexual scheme, it threatens Catherine's livelihood and freedom to seduce and kill. Will Catherine seduce Alex in order to destroy her, or discover in the seduction that she cannot kill a female lover?

In the notorious scuba diving scene, the male rival is eliminated from the action, which once again reverts to the well-worn metaphor of water as a signal of lesbian desire. Catherine rigs Alex's oxygen tank so that she almost drowns. However Catherine is unable to murder Alex and finally shares her own oxygen tank with her, giving her her life back, affirming that Alex has achieved Catherine's awe, if not her affection.

Hauled up breathless on the beach, Alex rebukes Catherine as if she's been accidentally betrayed by a lover or close friend, rather than having been the victim of attempted murder. Instead of leaving at once as any woman in her right mind would have done, Alex remains by the sea with Catherine until sunset, the two women watching the waves in a two-shot that replicates a thousand heterosexual love scenes. The tension between a structure motivated by the conventions of heterosexual desire and the non-heterosexual action is acute and the suspense of the thriller element becomes transferred to the delayed seduction between the two women. If Catherine has failed to kill Alex, the path of seduction is still an option.

In the next scene the two women are happily picnicking and sunbathing together, framed, as if in bed, lying on their bellies. Intimacy is built once more up by reverse close-up shots. Then Catherine rolls on to her back as she admits, 'I used to think of it as my job, making myself appealing. I was professional.'

The use of past tense intrigues the spectator, opening up the possibility of a different choice in the present. Then, as if to deflect these possibilities, Catherine offers Paul to Alex to fuck.

Cue the seduction scene between Alex and Paul which is wide open to a queer reading. Alex is wearing jeans with a red bandanna tucked in the back pocket. Paul mentions that he's surprised 'this attractive, intelligent, very, very strong' woman isn't married. Alex assumes he means Catherine, so absorbed is she in her identification/desire for her. When Paul embraces her from behind, Alex almost pulls away, then leans back into his body like a young gay man having anal sex for the first time (Figure 14). As the scene is located outside in a wild, overgrown location, it also evokes public gay male sex for the envious dyke whose cruising must usually take place indoors. Heterosexual intercourse is never shown and the *Village Voice* (17 February 1987) provides some extra-diegetic gossip, which again suggests that another film may have been trying to escape the rigid confines of the dominant narrative. This is an account of why Alex is not seen having sex with Paul:

> In *Vanity Fair*, Arthur Lubow reports that Winger ate a pizza with garlic before their (discarded) love scene; she unconsciously sabotaged it, the writer implies, because she knew the film should be Alex and Catherine, not Alex and her frog prince.

The Paul–Alex seduction scene is intercut with the scene where Catherine discovers Alex's handkerchief and 'real' identity, suggesting the erotic pull

14 Alex gives Paul the pre-fuck cold shoulder (*Black Widow*, Bob Rafelson, 1987)

between them and reinforcing the lesbian spectator's reading that they should be together.

When Catherine fucks Paul for the first time, inviting him into the swimming pool, we find the image of water so overdetermined diegetically by the 'lesbian' scenes that its powerful connotations overwhelm the hetero-narrative. In addition, that Alex has already had sex with Paul somehow serves to reinforce the bond between the two women. Catherine is fucking Paul to fuck Alex. Since Paul is constructed as other through his Frenchness and gentleness, the heterosexual love scenes are rendered less dominant in the overall structure.

Although Catherine later marries Paul, we see nothing of the ceremony or consummation; instead the passion is reserved for the 'goodbye' kiss between Catherine and Alex. The two women are situated apart from the rest of the wedding guests. Alex presents Catherine with a black widow brooch and Catherine suggests, 'She mates and she kills.' The camera cuts to Alex as Catherine goes on. 'Your question is, does she love? It's impossible to answer that unless you live in her world.' That Catherine puts the words in Alex's mouth by saying, 'your question is . . .' evokes their continued intimacy.

Catherine cannot expose herself to Alex to be understood, as it would mean removing her mask of femininity. 'It's not over yet,' asserts Alex. 'Till then,' promises Catherine. Again a male intermediary intervenes to separate the two women, asking for a kiss from the bride. Their kiss is cold, perfunctory, polite and again Alex is framed watching the heterosexual couple. The coyness of this kiss merely works to reinforce the passion with which Catherine then turns round and grabs Alex to kiss her abruptly and powerfully on the lips. The kiss works as an assault, a challenge and an invitation. Like the flick of a glove to signal a duel, it marks the countdown to victory. The force with which she grabs Alex by the back of the neck and pulls her to her unequivocally asserts her bisexuality and confirms their bond as sexual rather than simply a matter of identification (Figure 15). Catherine's masquerade of femininity is parodied deliciously as she kisses Alex, while wearing her bridal dress! 'Beauty is the desired one and the one who aims her desirability at the butch.'[22] At this point the conventional narrative structure explodes with the lesbian gaze.

Later, when Catherine believes she has conquered Alex and escaped discovery, she reveals that 'of all the relationships I'll look back on in fifty years' time, I'll always remember this one.' The suggestion is that they should/could have been lovers, their behaviour that of a couple splitting up. Finally, Alex outwits Catherine and as Catherine is led away, Catherine's final look bypasses Paul and focuses on Alex. Catherine has been topped for the first time – and by a woman to boot!

The last shot in the film fails to resolve the unstable heterosexual plot since Alex does not take Paul into her arms, but leaves the police building alone. She may retain her image as a phallicised woman-for-man, but has secured

15 The kiss like a knife (*Black Widow*, Bob Rafelson, 1987)

independence and shuns the approval of the press and colleagues. She may have upheld the patriarchal law, but has done so on her own terms.

While the male hero usually chases his prize and wins the female love-object at the end of his quest, thereby reinforcing heterosexual closure, in *Black Widow*, the 'happy ending' resolution of the dominant discourse in Hollywood film is refuted. *Black Widow* therefore avoids reinstating the unification of male and female, of the completion of the woman by the man (or vice versa). Instead Alex is framed in the hallway of the police buildings, walking outside, initiated, once-bitten, single and ready for more. Her assumption of the 'active' male role is neither punished nor rescinded. She achieves an integrity that is not dependent on male sexual approval and her singleness in the final image leaves her sexual choices open as protagonist and the ending open to a lesbian reading.

The heterosexual narrative is therefore problematised by the erotic exchange of looks between the two female characters, by the potent and irreducible use of erotic signifiers and the final failure of the dominant structure to reassert itself. Although *Black Widow* displaces rather than totally disrupts the heterosexist gaze, it foregrounds female bonding in a way that the text cannot ignore and has trouble subordinating.

When *Black Widow* was first shown in 1987 it was beset by the ideology of positive images (a man-killer is not the kind of lesbian we want to embrace), the rigid boundaries of sexual identity (Alex can't be a lesbian because she fucked Paul) and the feminist resistance to dealing with images of women grappling for power and control. As Marusia Bociurkiw asserts, 'The time for talking about our fear of representations of lesbian sexuality, or the damage done to lesbians because of them, has passed.'[23] Queer attitude has signalled that change, encouraging irony to bloom and marking the development of a multiplicity of readings of mainstream culture once unimaginable and fast being harnessed into a legitimised Queer Theory.

In the struggle to reclaim a popular narrative that we know is constrained by sexist and homophobic structures, we must use a reverse discourse that discharges both by identification against the grain, and sly humour that operates in much the same way as gay male camp has done. Precisely because the narrative of *Black Widow* is raw with contradictions and improbable as a political discourse, there is an interestingly queer friction set up when we examine how the lesbian gaze can make the desire between the women 'normal' and 'inevitable'. The heterosexual structure does not erase the alternative readings of the text, but allows room for the transgressive subjectivity of the lesbian spectator – the queer dyke who can laugh at herself in all her dis/guises.

NOTES

1 The Lesbian Avengers (eds), *Dyke Manifesto*, Lesbian Avengers, New York, 1993.
2 M. Bociurkiw, *Third Gender, Third Eye*, Internationales Frauen Film Festival, Köln, 1992.
3 S. Schulman, *Empathy*, Dutton, New York, 1993, p.6.
4 C. Straayer, 'The Hypothetical Lesbian Heroine', *Jumpcut* 35, April 1990, pp.50–7.
5 A. Solomon, *The Village Voice*, 30 June 1992.
6 L. Mulvey, 'Afterthoughts on "Visual Pleasure and Narrative Cinema", inspired by *Duel in the Sun*', *Framework*, vol.6, nos 15–17, Summer, 1981.
7 ibid.
8 S.-E. Case, 'Towards a Butch-Femme Aesthetic', *Discourse*, vol.11, no.1, Fall–Winter 1988–9, Indiana University Press, Bloomington.
9 Straayer, op. cit.
10 E. Cowie, 'Film as Progressive Text – A Discussion of *Coma*' in Constance Penley (ed.), *Feminism and Film Theory*, Routledge/BFI Publishing, London, 1988.
11 Case, op. cit.
12 J. Riviere, 'Womanliness as Masquerade', republished in Victor Burgin, James Donald and Cora Kaplan (eds), *Formations of Fantasy*, Methuen, London, 1986, p.38.
13 Case, op. cit.
14 ibid.
15 E. Grosz, 'Lesbian Fetishism', *Differences*, vol. 3, no. 2, 1991, Brown University, Providence.
16 C. Trusty, 'If It Doesn't Happen Soon', *Serious Pleasure*, Sheba, London, 1989.
17 T. de Lauretis, 'Film and the Visible', in Bad Object-Choices (ed.), *How Do I Look?*, Bay Press, Seattle, 1991.

18 kd lang, quoted in *Capital Gay*, London, 15 November 1991.
19 de Lauretis, op. cit.
20 Straayer, op. cit.
21 ibid.
22 Case, op. cit.
23 M. Bociurkiw, quoted in *How Do I Look?*, op. cit., p.278.

Part III

MASQUERADE

7

WE'RE HERE, WE'RE QUEER AND WE'RE NOT GOING CATALOGUE SHOPPING

Gregory Woods

Anyone who has been on a Gay Pride march in London will have heard the chant: 'We're here, we're queer and we're not going shopping!' Of these three assertions, everything one sees on the march will confirm the first two; but the third is likely to be open to doubt. Many of the women and men chanting, particularly those who have travelled to the city for the day, tend to be carrying shopping bags. The march does not start until the early afternoon – which leaves all morning for visiting shops.

Writing in *Marxism Today* in 1988, Frank Mort and Nicholas Green remarked that, 'Marketers and advertisers have always had designs on our images as much as our pockets.' After all, any company which can influence how we perceive ourselves, and how we want ourselves to be perceived, is guaranteed influence on how we spend our money. Mort and Green continued: 'The buzz word is *lifestyles* – a concept which goes hand-in-hand with the retail revolution. Lifestyle advertising is all about designer-led retailing which reflects changing consumer demand. In essence it is marketing's bid to get to grips with today's social agenda' (Mort and Green 1988: 32). Among the items on that agenda, of course, are the needs and demands of lesbians and gay men.

Since the late 1980s it has become increasingly commonplace to speak, not only of the purchasing power of the so-called 'pink economy', but also of the pink pound's extraordinary resilience during the recession of the early 1990s. A 1992 article in the London *Times* spoke rather enviously of 'a thriving subculture in which pink pounds are spent on pink services in a private micro-economy where spend, spend, spend! is still the watchword'. Intimidated by the homophobic Section 28 of the Thatcher government's Local Government Act (banning the 'promotion of homosexuality' with public funds) and by initial media responses to the AIDS epidemic – the argument goes – the gay community turned in on itself and unwittingly discovered economic virtue in old-fashioned solidarity (David 1992: 10).

The gay media are currently burgeoning, not only with advertisements for gay goods and services, but also with articles on the phenomenon of conspicuous gay consumption; and not all such articles are entirely taken in by the impression of general affluence. Bill Short, for instance, has questioned a number of rather slapdash assumptions shared by both straight and gay commentators, among them the myth that gay men necessarily have more spending power than their straight counterparts. He makes a point which is also evident in the fiction of contemporary writers like Neil Bartlett, that 'many gay men appear to be living the high life when in fact they have no disposable income at all'. However, Short agrees that, to a large extent, lifestyle is determined by economic considerations: 'Many of us who wish to maintain a gay identity, actually *buy* that identity.' The reason for this is fundamental, relating to how we meet each other and how we appear to the rest of society: 'We are forced to prove we exist by projecting a gay image or lifestyle' (Short 1992: 20). Thus, it is in quite a literal sense that one can say: I shop, therefore I am.

Speaking of the demise of the golden age of department stores, Harvie Ferguson has outlined a crucial shift in ways of showing off commodities: 'The larger propaganda aspect of display has been usurped by the more powerful, private and intimate form of television advertising. The shop window now opens directly into the home; the *flâneur* has become the somnambulist' (Ferguson 1992: 32). Indeed so. But the trouble with television advertising is that it tends to offer a limited range of goods, and it displays them for only a limited length of time between distractingly irrelevant programmes. To browse at one's leisure, one needs a catalogue; better still, a whole collection of competing catalogues.

With reference to sexuality, the cultural values and assumptions of mail order catalogues from Britain and the United States are not difficult to read. The consumer goods they advertise are arranged around implied narratives of heterosexual courtship and home-building. While it is clear that such catalogues as *Argos*, *Burlington*, *Index* and *Littlewoods* now make some slight genuflection in the direction of anti-sexism and multiculturalism, they exhibit no acceptance of any world order other than the strictly heterosexual. For a start, the nuclear family (father, mother, son, daughter) is always presented as being the ideal living arrangement. Whole catalogues are predicated on the assumption that no greater happiness can be found than in the combination of such a family and well-chosen consumer goods.

Many catalogues are friendly only to the family. Take the example of the *Avon* collection (Campaign 9), the front cover of which shows a father (dark) and mother (blonde) running in a shallow sea with their son and daughter. The catalogue opens with three double-page spreads of sun tan lotions, each illustrated with a photograph of a nuclear family. Cosmetics follow, all clearly aimed at women; there is even a page of 'Little Blossom' make-up for 'young ladies aged 5 to 8' – but none for boys or men. There are, eventually, four double-page spreads of toiletries for men; but each of these is conspicuously headed 'Father's Day Sunday June 21st'. There are no gifts here for the family's favourite bachelor uncle.

The *Ace* Christmas catalogue (1992) is aimed principally at the family, even if the written copy does not overtly push this fact. The cutesy cover photograph is of a boy and girl, cheek to cheek, evidently preparing for the kind of material future the catalogue then maps out. Roles are conventionally divided; for instance, there are only girl models playing with the advertised dolls. Sexuality is acknowledged – sex sells, after all, and in any case the company needs its buyers to produce new generations of buyers – but the nature of sexual pleasure is closely policed. On the bathroom page, opposite a family in co-ordinatred bathrobes (tall, dark father in royal blue; shorter, blonde mother in white; daughter in pink; son in pale blue), a teenage couple, he with his arm around her, are wearing personalised sarongs (Mike in 19 inches of royal blue, Susan in 29 inches of pink). Thus, exoticism and eroticism are reassuringly anglicised and tamed; even the lovers' towelling dictates their sexual roles.

A later page advertises musical boxer shorts for men: when you press the picture on the shorts (Santa Claus, a pink pig or a woman's lips) they play a tune. Three pairs are shown, but not on a model. Each is being pressed – by a woman's finger. God forbid that any man should press his own, or even get a male friend to press it for him. When a potentially disruptive item appears in the middle of this system of unquestioned heterosexualism, its use has to be firmly signalled and limited in the descriptive copy. So a Chippendales mug is captioned 'Ladies this is for you!' lest any of the gents should start buying them for each other.

This Christmas catalogue, finally, asserts its values in a double-page display of wedding stationery. What is being purveyed in these pages is a fresh-faced, jolly conventionality. Love is signalled here in a number of ways, since one is, after all, meant to be browsing for presents for one's 'loved ones'; but the company seems to have an oddly commodified idea of what love means. The material accompanying the catalogue is headed by the disturbing promise: 'You'll fall in love with your new *Ace* Christmas catalogue.' It is clear that we must add a new concept to our psychoanalytic lexicon: the phenomenon of catalogophilia.

The typical structure of a mainstream British catalogue (*Littlewoods, Janet Frazer, Burlington*, etc.) is as follows: women's clothes, children's clothes, men's clothes, sports clothes, soft furnishings, hard furnishings and leisure goods (an odd combination of jewellery, toys and bicycles). Because they segregate women and men for the sake of this schematic order, these catalogues end up subjecting themselves to a kind of semiotic panic about homosexuality. It must not appear that the lives the models in the photos are enjoying with such ostentatious pleasure are in any way abnormal. All items have to appeal to the average, even if when purchased they will be used as the currency for (un)neighbourly one-upmanship. You do not keep up with, still less outdo, the Joneses by adopting what are perceived to be eccentric or abnormal styles; you have to buy things that they will recognise and envy you for. You must not look lonely, of course. The best way of avoiding that is to create an impression either of sexual good fortune – in the case of single people – or of complete marital harmony. The one thing you must avoid is the slightest whiff of deviancy.

These worries manifest themselves in all kinds of ways: sometimes in the structure of the catalogue, sometimes in its written copy, most often in its illustrations. Many details, barely perceptible to the casual browser, become crystal clear when subjected to a moment's thought. For instance, the *L. L. Bean* catalogue genuflects to the anti-sexist tenor of our times by offering the 'River Driver's Shirt' – which is described as being 'Named for the rugged men who once worked the spring log drive on Maine's rivers' – to purchasers of both sexes. But although a wide range of colours is available to both women and men, women are offered one extra colour, 'Rose' – that is to say, pink. It is hard to imagine the kind of meeting at which such decisions are made; but even if the significance of the ban on pink shirts for men was not made explicit then, it cannot be attributed to anything but homophobia. Whether we attribute this fault to the L. L. Bean company itself or, more plausibly, to the prejudices they perceive in their customers, its name is homophobia none the less. Later in the same catalogue, silk underwear is offered to men in navy blue and 'natural' (the undyed fabric) but to women in 'natural' and pink.

The poses adopted by models seem to be under close scrutiny, particularly on the relatively uncommon occasions when two or more men appear together in the same photograph. Physical contact between them is clearly discouraged. They do, however, have to seem to be enjoying themselves, and it follows that they ought to look as though they enjoy each other's company. They should look like friends, even very good friends – but never lovers. Elaborate conventions, therefore, surround male bodily contact. Manly sporting activities are acceptable, of course. One man may place his fist, or less often his open palm, on the nearside shoulder, or less often the far shoulder of his friend. Ideally, they should look into the distance rather than at each other. Only very rarely do you see them looking into each other's eyes.

Given the difficulties raised by the juxtaposition of male bodies, many catalogues simply ration the number of times the difficulties arise. Take the example of two recent *Racing Green* catalogues. In the Autumn 1992 edition, as well as many photos containing single female or male models, there are seven photos of a male and a female; one of two males and two females, but arranged in the sequence male–female–male–female, so as not to suggest two queer couples; two of two women and a man, with the man in the middle, keeping the women apart; and just one of two women. In the whole catalogue there is no photograph of two men. Likewise, the Christmas 1992 edition contains many photos of single models, plus five of a man and a woman, just one of two women and, again, none of two men. Interestingly, *Racing Green*'s edition of Summer 1992 contains several pleasantly affectionate images of two women – perhaps because the models look sufficiently alike to be twin sisters.

While it is true that most kinds of commercial promotion are at pains to preserve conventions and not to violate the status quo, they must also create at least an impression of moving smartly with the times. After all, we buy new things because they are new. There is evidence, therefore, of the urge to change in most catalogues, particularly those aimed at young people. But such signs of change have a limited scope.

Despite a general tendency to subscribe to the values of its Littlewoods Group stable-mates, including the usual rigorous segregations and heavy semiotic hints (yet another bride who has donned her head-dress and picked up her bouquet while still only dressed in her underwear), the *Janet Frazer* catalogue shows unusual signs of relaxation on some of its informal mens wear pages. While there are still plenty of fist-on-shoulder shots of macho camaraderie, several poses allow an arm around the shoulder, once even around the neck instead. The context is of healthy beach sports, of course, but the general atmosphere is emotionally warmer than most catalogues seem to allow. There is even one shot in which a man appears to be affectionately patting his chum on the backside. The swimwear photos, although truncated in the usual fashion so that one cannot see nearly enough of the models' bodies, are group shots posed in what must have been very close groups, pelvis to pelvis, of up to five men; these contribute to the mood of unself-conscious friendliness which makes this section of the catalogue worth both looking at and commenting on. However, *Janet Frazer* soon reverts to type. We find that neither men's dressing gowns nor their underwear can be promoted without the admiring and endorsing gaze of an otherwise super-numerary female model.

Superficially modern and young in its values, the hardback *Next Directory*, for which one has to pay, turns out to be only a slight advance on its more dowdy competitors. The structure is conventional (women, men, children, household) and as you leaf through the pages you see that the compilers are suffering from familiar anxieties. Most models are pictured singly, lest they compromise each other by look or gesture. (In the women's section there is, however, one peculiar exception: two women appear together in bathing costumes, both evidently delighted that one has pressed her knee between the other's legs.) It is the male models, as usual, whose hetero credentials are considered more in need of endorsement. So several shirts and sweaters are shown to be huggable by women; as is the male body itself, on the swimwear pages and, later, the underwear pages. Although Next has gone to some trouble to present good-looking men in a relatively sexy range of shorts and briefs, the message is clear: these bodies are available to the female customer only. As if to prove that these signals are not merely fortuitous, the children's clothing section, which follows, shows a broad range of child models, both white and black, both female and male, in a wide variety of poses and degrees of affectionate physical contact, evidently unpoliced.

Even *International Male*, a catalogue plainly dedicated to the proposition that men can be mouth-wateringly sexy, only has a handful of photos of two men together, and in each of these cases the models are fully clad. In all photos of shorts, underwear and swimming trunks, each model is on his own. Although this catalogue does include instances of heterosexualisation by the otherwise superfluous presence of a woman, this occurs in only two out of several hundred images.

The problem, therefore, is not that such catalogues do not recognise the existence of non-heterosexual buyers. The signs are that, on the contrary, they do. Lesbians and gay men represent a significant absence from their pages, an absence which is enforced with evident nervousness. There is, for instance, a kind of desperation in the way photographic displays of goods for sale make claims on the heterosexuality of the models being photographed. Women modelling lingerie are shown wearing bridal veils. Single sex pairs of models are posed with detailed and obvious care so that the women are seen to be available only to browsing men, and the men do not conform to the myth that all male models are queer. Attractive individuals are often shown with a person of the opposite sex, in soft focus, in the background. One of the worst examples of this tendency occurs in the 1992–3 edition of the *Ciro Citterio* menswear catalogue. To start with, the written copy appropriates that most ungendered item of clothing, the pair of denim jeans, for exclusively male use: 'JEANS masculine, hard, brash, sexy, comfortable, cool, utilitarian.' This is accompanied by a photograph of a white and a black man, both shirtless, in jeans. Behind these two figures, a naked woman is lying face-down on a wall. In a subsequent photo, the men have more clothes on but the woman does not.

Given that lesbians and gay men are imagined as a small minority of the credit card-carrying population, no major company seems yet to have recognised a source of profit in representing any of its models – and, therefore, any of its customers – as likely to live in a single sex household. For obvious economic reasons, each catalogue is addressing a notional 'majority', and protecting that audience from any influence which might lead them to question their established values.

The closer a catalogue's implied narratives come to moments in which sexual events might take place, the more nervous their imagery seems to become. In a situation where sex has to be evoked, since everyone knows it helps sell consumer goods – it seduces customers into handing over money to buy the props for their fantasies – sex must also be kept under control. The wrong kind of imagery would evoke the wrong kind of sex, which would then taint the goods in question; and goods which seem queer will not be bought by people who do not want to seem queer themselves. So, if one imagines a typical narrative of seduction as proceeding logically through the various subdivisions of the domestic space – let us say from dining room to living room, then from bathroom to bedroom – each of these rooms will, in turn, cause the advertiser a bigger headache.

As far as one can tell, there is not a lot of difference between a man's and a woman's bathrobe; it would not seem to matter which gender modelled one. However, shoppers' insecurities are generally calmed with a photo of robes being worn by a woman and a man together (*Choice, Family Album, Kays*). To underline the point, such images may be accompanied by explanatory copy – 'Although made for men they are equally suitable for women' (*Sander & Kay's Mail Mart*) or, more pithily, 'Luxurious Unisex Towelling Bath Robe' (*Green Shield*). Adjacent to the latter is a display of His and Hers towels. The overall impression these pages leave is of bathtime as a shared experience, but shared only by opposite sex couples.

That there are sexual concerns behind these various idiosyncracies is further proved when one turns to pages concerning the bedroom. Anxieties surround what the consumer is expect to see there, to wear (and take off) there and, by implication, to do there. Again, these anxieties seem to be focused on unmarried men. Among their many pages displaying bed linen, most catalogues include one double-page spread intended to appeal to the single man – the so-called bachelor. Here, suddenly, instead of pastel colours, floral patterns, flounces and frills, the browsing eye encounters bold stripes, scarlet, a lot of black, and the trademark of the Playboy bunny. Three designs are offered: 'Bucks Fizz', an image of cascading champagne and bunny heads; 'Raffles', one large, black bunny head against a dark background; and 'Cabaret', a duvet-sized image of a woman's hat, face and gloved hand above the key word 'Playboy'. All this bedding can be matched with Playboy wallpaper and friezes, thereby making of the bachelor bedroom a perfect den for heterosexual seduction – or, perhaps more plausibly, a space in which to masturbate while fantasising such narratives.

An interesting accompaniment to this display is a bedding design called 'Censored'. This consists of a duvet cover in bold black and white stripes, with bright red highlights, down the full length of which is unambiguously printed, in black, the word 'PRIVATE'. On its other side, the reversible cover bears a large 'No Entry' sign. The complementary pillow case, mainly black, is liberally scattered with the legends 'Private', 'No Entry' and 'Keep Out'. Not surprisingly, this design is available only for a three-foot bed. It seems to be aimed at curiously demonstrative celibates.

Bedtime itself is, of course, the key moment for ideological and semiotic policing. Even more than the bathroom, the bedroom is desired and feared as the prime locus for the definition of sexualities. It is here that, perhaps under 'Frilled bedding with a floral stripe design and a contrast frill and trim', a groom might slip out of his 'PRINTED COTTON JERSEY PYJAMAS with fashionable classic motif', negotiate his way into his bride's 'WARM-HANDLE NIGHTDRESS with lace and ribbon trim' and ensure the survival of the species. (Thoughtlessly, however, most catalogues do not advertise maternity clothes.) But it is here, too, that the wrong combinations of bodies may occur: uncomplementary pairs – which is to say, of course, pairs which match. Queers.

In a display of bedtime wear for men which appears in several catalogues (*Burlington, John Moores*), on two double-page spreads, nine pictures of individual men in pyjamas or dressing gowns are accompanied by two in which a woman is kneeling or sitting on the bed behind the man, and two more in which the man is accompanied by a woman in a smaller version of the same dressing gown ('Judo-style robes IN SIZES TO SUIT BOTH OF YOU'). Yet the women's pages in the same catalogues are often significantly different. In the *Burlington* and *John Moores* catalogues, for instance, of thirty-five photos of women in nightdresses, pyjamas or dressing gowns, seven show two women together; and of these, two have them posing demurely together at the foot of their bed. Several catalogues promote garments which they describe as Samurai Yukatas, intended for use as dressing gowns, with an image of a man with his arm around a woman (*Home Free, Reader Offers from the Observer, Self Care*), ignoring or ignorant of the proudly homoerotic history of the Samurai themselves.

Only rarely do two men ever appear together in their dressing gowns or pyjamas. In the *J. D. Williams* collection, a catalogue aimed mainly at middle aged and old customers, two male models pose unproblematically, once with one in conventional pyjamas and the other in a bathrobe, then with both in pyjamas. Several facors seem to make these two images acceptable: because of its target age group, the catalogue does not seem much concerned to evoke sexual allure; the models, their clothing and their poses somehow look too conventional to be queer; photographed against a blank studio background, the models *look like* models, rather than the occupants of a real bedroom and bed.

A more daring image which appears in several catalogues (*Choice, Family Album, Kays*) shows two much younger models – both of whom also appear in a sexy display of underwear on an earlier double-page spread – dressed in Fido Dido and Spiderman 'short pyjama sets' (these being a combination which looks like tee-shirt and boxer shorts). One sits at a table, the other on it, with a portable backgammon board between them; behind them is a nondescript room with bare floorboards and a framed picture on the wall. Although ready for bed, these boys are not yet ready for each other: they are still concentrating on the game. But before long they will have to move: the one on the table has obviously not settled down for a protracted game. Although the marketers presumably do not intend this, the gay browser is prompted to ask one crucial question. In the unseen portion of the room, are the sleeping arrangements single or double?

It should be added that consumers are clearly expected to conform to company guidelines on sleeping arrangements even when on holiday. In the

L. L. Bean catalogue, sleeping bags are advertised with an image of a nuclear family, the four of them lying in a row, each in a single bag. Even here, members of the same sex are kept apart: the family has organised itself into a strict male–female–male–female sequence. A double sleeping bag is shown with a heterosexual couple in it. In the *Index* catalogue, even what is promisingly called a '2-man' tent is pictured being used by a straight couple. Needless to say, holiday brochures – apart from those few specifically aimed at gay tourists – indulge in the same appropriations of all spaces for the enjoyment of heterosexual couples and nuclear families.

Writing on the topic of recent advertising, Frank Mort has spoken of how 'male sexuality is conjured up *through the commodity*, whether jeans, hair-gel, aftershave or whatever' (Mort 1988: 201). It is worth taking into account, also, that 'through the commodity' is one of relatively few ways in which male bodies are acceptably conjured up in Western societies. Consequently one often hears of gay men whose first images of sexy men – their earliest masturbatory icons – were the men and boys in the underwear and swimwear sections of mail order catalogues. This use of catalogues as pornography seems to be tacitly accepted and, indeed, encouraged by companies selling 'exotic' underwear for men.

If one thing is clear about the promotion of men's underwear, it is that heterosexual men, although they constitute the major part of the market, are not the principal focus of the marketing. Because straight men apparently do not buy their own underwear – we are told that the majority of pants, pouches and shorts are bought by women for men (Blanchard 1992) – one even finds, on occasions, men's underwear in the middle of the women's sections of the catalogues. For example, on a page of women's knickers by Sloggi, a large photo shows a man and a woman with their arms around each other, his face laughingly pressed to her cheek, both clad in Sloggi underwear. The copy across the top of the picture says, 'Women know why MEN should wear Sloggi for Men' (*Choice, Family Album*). The unstated reason is, of course, that the gym-toned model looks delicious in his little white briefs.

It is difficult not to deduce from what we are told of straight men's indifference to their own underwear that the most appreciative browsers of the men's underwear pages of general catalogues, and of men's underwear catalogues, are straight women and gay men. Some companies – Body Aware and Shamian being two recent examples – may go so far as to acknowledge gay interest by advertising in the gay press; but their catalogues are still at pains to suppress all imagery of male interest in men.

The aim of such catalogues is, of course, mainly to sell knickers (or, at the very least, the next edition of the catalogue), but they need to do so by effecting or reinforcing a change in attitudes. Richard Dyer has spoken of how, in Britain, there used to be only two main ways of perceiving the very topic of male underwear, 'medical' and 'giggling' – the latter point emphasised by a proliferation of 'novelty' underwear emblazoned with jokey illustrations or slogans (Dyer 1989: 43). In common with 'high' fashion companies such as Calvin Klein and Nikos, the underwear catalogues are obviously trying to replace the therapeutic and comic images with the erotic. The more seriously sexy an item looks on the page, the sexier it promises to become when one puts it on or prepares to take it off. The seriousness of the focused eroticism is a major selling point. (I should add, however, that even in an intensely eroticised display of items for women and men, the *Bronson Collection* still includes such novelty items for men as the 'Chef's Special Pouch', the 'Old Man Pouch', the 'Indian Pouch', the 'Coco Pouch' and the 'Long John Plonker Pirate Pouch'. One item, an elephant's-head pouch called 'Williphants', is pictured being fed a cupcake by a semi-naked woman.)

The *Shamian* catalogue is relaxed enough to show two men in one photo – but only once, and both are wearing both vest and shorts. Only when on their own or with a woman do they wear any less. Similarly, *Body Aware* publish a catalogue of men's underwear with eighteen photos of male models on their own, and two of male models accompanied by a female. Since the women's clothes are not on sale, the women are clearly included only for what their presence implies about the men. The *Designs in Leather* catalogue of erotic underwear never has more than one man in any photo, though its rear cover does show that pet fantasy of straight males, two women together on a bed. Inside the catalogue, no man appears without one (seven times), two (five times) or three women (once) to endorse his heterosexual credentials. The catalogue thus promotes its wares within the narrow swingers' fantasy world whose unwaveringly straight men make it with eagerly convertible lesbians. In the *Kiniki* Catalogue, the majority of photographs are of single male models, but thirteen heterosexualise the display by including women in various stages of undress.

It is worth lingering on the *Kiniki* collection, to attend to the names with which all these briefs and pouches for straight men have been characterised. Some names are pithily descriptive of structure (Boxer, Ultrabox, Super-G, Contour, Zipper, Wispy); others bear the names of the men who might wear them, whether classy anglo (Marcus, Adam, Max, Barclay, James, Monty, Jasper), routinely suggestive (Roddy, Randy), continental or Latin (Pierre, Rico, Diego, Dino). The upper class theme is continued with underwear suggesting well-heeled leisure (Cabaret, Party, Stringfellow, Raffles, Ritzy), high status (Squire, Sloane, Top Notch, Elite) and dubious moral fibre (Charmer, Swinger, Dandy, Cad). Some briefs are named after the exotic locations they are intended to conjure up (Riviera, San Tropez, Brazil, Havana, Amazon, Hawaii, Mexico), others after the leisure activities one might enjoy in them (Sandtrecker, Windsurf, Beach Boy, Cruiser). Some are routinely macho (Beefcake, Tiger, Magnum) or evocative of macho narratives (Commander, Hero, High Flyer). Of these latter, the Hero briefs are shown in the silliest of photographs: he looks valiant in flying jacket, briefs, sun glasses and white silk scarf; she – the endorser of his sexuality – gazes into the sky beside him, dressed in nothing but the end of his scarf. One pair of padded briefs for men who do not measure up to requirements – 'Boost your credentials when you're eager to make an impression in this spectacular bulging brief' – is called Bandingo, presumably an intentional echo of the name of the West African tribe the Mandingo (Malinka), popularised in the developed world by the novels of Kyle Onstott. The racist message may be subliminal, but is perfectly clear: wear these pants and you will look as well hung as if you were black.

Eventually, anyone who browses the catalogues from a gay point of view must consider the topic – perhaps the myth – of gay 'style'. How willing are gay consumers to be seen in/with items bought from certain catalogues which have 'naff' reputations? Do they *want* to be, or to look, 'homely'? (How many self-respecting scene queens could survive the discovery that they buy their shoes from Argos or their maquillage from Avon?) On the other hand, it is not insignificant that shopping by catalogue may be the safest way for cross-dressers of either sex to stock up their closets. The drag queen does not have to be up to date. Indeed, she is more or less obliged not to be. Her nostalgia for pre-feminist styles, whether heartfelt or bogus, is adequately fed by the unassuming range of the catalogues – though she may well have to add sequins to taste.

Whether expressed as personality or sensibility, Camp is in need of both costumes and props. In general, its theatricality is not simply performed; it has to be staged. Male-as-female drag, in particular, has always been commodity-based in so far as it obviously relies on clothing, make-up and other accessories of constructed femininity. Men who cannot bring themselves either to outstare impertinent shop assistants and fellow customers, or to pretend they are shopping on behalf of non-existent wives with suspiciously large shoe sizes, may have recourse to mail order. The fact remains, though, that such customers know they are not included in the dreams promoted by the straight catalogues. It is only the lack of an alternative that forces people to go on supporting commercial organisations which do not acknowledge their existence. Imagine what a fabulous text a glossy catalogue for drag queens might be!

The recent development of gay catalogues has attempted to redress the balance. They address the (male) gay consumer directly. While most of these display only erotic items – or items with a more immediate erotic cachet than that of a duvet cover or a three-piece suite – the manner of their display often suggests a lifestyle which, though established in the bedroom, can be extended into social life. For a good idea of how mail order catalogues might cater for lesbian and gay customers, one has the example of *Shocking Gray*, based in San Antonio, Texas ('The Catalog for the Other 25 Million People'). Advertising a relatively narrow range of goods, most of them decorative rather than strictly practical, this catalogue achieves its effect as much by virtue of its gentle good humour as with the intrinsic merit of the items on sale. Some items, indeed, bear no relation to the sexuality of the buyer (a wall-mounted, swivel-armed shaving mirror or a patterned doormat); some are displayed in ways designed to attract the gay buyer (a purple leather picture frame contains a photo of a shirtless young man); certain items are promoted as bearers of a particular style (the description above a photo of a 'Pink Flamingo Oil Lamp' is intended to appeal to the lesbian and gay reader alike: 'We crave the absurd, anything kitsch. And our Flamingo Oil Lamp is just that – *with attitude*, honey'); in yet others that oddity of style is implicit (a leaded crystal 'Cocktail Napkin Holder'). Many items are apparently job lots brought in from sources not necessarily gay, but have been relabelled or rearranged to appeal to the gay market. Thus, on a male-oriented page we find 'His & His Pillowcases' ('Sweet dreams are made of this') and later, on a female-oriented page – sure enough – we find the rest of the batch: 'Hers & Hers Pillowcases'.

The Fall 1992 issue of *Shocking Gray* persuasively quotes endorsements from satisfied customers. These range from generalised expressions of approval of the catalogue's upbeat approach to lesbian and gay lifestyles ('Hi! You guys and gals are doing a super job. Quality stuff that makes the statement that we are proud of our lifestyle') to thanks for sensitive attention to the detail of customers' lives ('With my busy schedule, I'm thrilled to find such service from a mail order catalog. In addition, I appreciate the concern of your staff who called me to ensure it was OK to receive SG catalogs at my office'). Perhaps the most touching and yet the most revealing of these endorsements is the following: 'To the folks at *Shocking Gray*: my friend gave me your catalog today. I have never read a catalog with as much excitement as I read yours. For the first time in my life, the pictures I saw in a catalog had something to do with me. A picture of two men hugging is all the persuasion I need: I have enclosed an order form and a check. Thank you.'

The pictures mentioned by this customer are, indeed, crucial in making the catalogue gay-friendly. The lead-in photograph in the Summer 1992 edition shows a policewoman holding hands with her girlfriend across a cafe table; outside the window behind them, a male couple are kissing across their outdoor table; standing immediately beyond them, a matron in hair-curlers is reacting in evident disgust. Later in the same edition, a young man is shown placing his hand on his friend's shoulder. This is, of course, the classic our-models-aren't-faggots catalogue pose; but *Shocking Gray* disrupt it by showing in the middle distance a straight couple – complete with baby buggy – spectating in dismay. On the back page, leather luggage is advertised with a photo of two men cruising each other in some kind of transit lounge.

The New York lesbian and gay bookshop *A Different Light* also publishes an impressive catalogue, friendly to its target customers. Comfortably balancing a broad range of materials for both women and men, often illustrating them with items from the books themselves or with photographs of the books' authors, each issue of this catalogue is itself an affirmation of the strength and health of contemporary lesbian and gay cultures. To have read the catalogue is to have kept oneself informed. As an indication of how differently British gay men relate to the dominant culture, it is worth noting that the books catalogue of the *Clone Zone* chain of gay stores, although it contains very little more sexually explicit material than *A Different Light*'s catalogue, bears on its cover the following note: 'Warning by their very nature some of the products shown are sexually explicit do not peruse further if you think that you may be offended. Please note all items in this catalogue are sold for their novelty value only' (*sic*). It is difficult to imagine how one is expected to read David Feinberg's novels or Harold Norse's autobiography 'for their novelty value only'; but the fact is that before one even opens this catalogue, the damage has been done. One is less resentful of such front cover warnings – like the one on the *Male Xpress* cover: 'WARNING Sexual material for adult gay men only' – when the advertised material is indeed 'sexual'.

When the specifically gay market and the specifically sexual range of goods coincide, the resulting catalogue may well be a lavish production on glossy paper, no less efficient as soft porn than as a window for buyable goods. It is no mere chance that the *BodyTech* and *Zipperstore* catalogues are produced by Millivres Limited, Britain's largest publisher of erotic magazines for gay men. Lavishly illustrated with photography by Colin Clarke of named models (Michael, Joe, Philip; Darren, Mark), both catalogues promote a solidly visible fantasy of carnality before the customer can draw breath to consider whether actually to purchase the clothing or sex toys on display.

On the other hand, it is often the case that the most purely functional of the sexual catalogues are the most cheaply produced. They make no concessions to the mere browser, who is likely to be satisfied to keep his sexy catalogues in a bedside drawer and never order any of the goods on sale. Some catalogues, therefore, do not bother with distractingly erotic photographs or drawings, and confine themselves to the very barest of functional descriptions. The *Fantasy Erotique* collection, for instance, although it has a drawing of a leather man on the front cover, contains a strictly businesslike list of items and prices: 'American sling with thigh restraints and pillow', 'Boomerang stretcher divider with D ring', 'Briefs with front sheath and rear plug', 'Executioner's mask' and so on. Not in itself an erotic experience, the catalogue is produced on the understanding that customers will be left unsatisfied by the mere list of names. They will have to order the items themselves. *Eagle Leathers*, too, provide unillustrated interim 'updates' to their main catalogue.

While considering the relationship between sexuality and mail order goods, one should also take into account the rear pages or pull-out centre pages of gay newspapers, where advertisements for erotic phone-lines and (in the USA and on the continent) pornographic magazines and videos sit comfortably alongside Personal Ads – which is to say, advertisements for persons. Both sexual fanasy and sexual intercourse itself – not to mention love – are thus subjected to the skills and prejudices of the advertising copywriter. The perfect orgasm becomes as routinely shoppable – something to be sent for, postage and packing extra – but as elusive as the harassed housewife's perfect wash.

Considering that one of capitalism's principal means of inveigling individuals into the cycle of production and consumption is the commercialisation of identity, one has to recognise that there is a seamless logic to the process by which, within a capitalist economy, identity politics likewise become commercialised and commodified. One key example of this must be the way in which London's annual Gay Pride march, a political demonstration, has turned into the Pride Parade, a leisurely walk from a tube station to an outdoor market.

Similarly, health education materials promoted by the Health Education Authority, or by private charitable organisations like the Terrence Higgins Trust, have since early in the crisis justifiably relied on the slick stratagems of the advertising agency and market research. Nor should it come as a surprise that the tendency of the HIV crisis to generate publicity for just about anything except health care and human rights has led, not only to such opportunistic advertising campaigns as Benetton's notorious use of a photograph of a man dying 'of AIDS', but also to the commodification of prophylaxis: condom shops, condom ads, condom pouches and pockets, and so on. The relative 'stylistic' success of the promotion of this definitively phallocentric object is worth contrasting with the perceived 'tastelessness' of recent television campaigns to sell women's sanitary towels. Of all complaints received by the Independent Television Commission during January and February 1992, a third were related to commercials for 'sanitary protection' items. Of the complainants, between 70 and 80 per cent were women, reportedly from all age groups (Hunt 1992).

The recession of the early 1990s has had a depressive effect on the mail order economy. The clearest sign of this effect was the decision by the most famous of the mail order companies, Sears Roebuck, to discontinue publication of its catalogues, and to axe 50,000 jobs (Tran 1993). On the day that this announcement was made in Chicago, 25 January 1993, the Littlewoods company in Britain announced a more modest cut in its mail order operations: 350 jobs were to be axed at its Sunderland and Preston sites (Cowe 1993). As with shops, so with catalogues. The survival of gay companies is all the more remarkable, therefore.

As a cultural document, the mail order catalogue is fully involved in the values of the dominant culture – which is capitalist first, and heterosexual only second. The lesbian or gay consumer is welcome to participate in the catalogue to the extent that she or he subscribes (literally) to the values of capitalism. This is true whether the catalogue is straight or gay. As purchasers we are included, even while as sexual beings the straight catalogues exclude us. Though we may view these texts, as it were, from the outside, our commodified identities are sufficiently in tune with the ethos of the whole culture – shop till you drop – to recognise the consuming aspect of ourselves in even the heterosexual fantasies the catalogues purvey.

On the other hand, viewed from a gay perspective, such catalogues do create an overwhelming impression of the heterosexual household as a locus of neurotic acquisitiveness, founded and maintained on gaudily material values and an anxiety about potential otherness. At their heart lie two conflicting impulses: the desire to outshine one's neighbour and his (*sic*) family, and the fear of building a home which is sigificantly different from his. This is a world of consumerist individualism policed by conformity.

NOTE

I owe a debt of thanks to David Shenton, who gave me the idea, and to the following, who gave me their catalogues: Susan Fischer, Liz Morrish, Kathleen O'Mara, Cedric Rawlings, Paul Roebuck, David Shenton, Freda Sketchley, George Smith, Alan Spooner and Ben Taylor.

CATALOGRAPHY

* denotes US catalogues.

General catalogues

Ace: Original Cards and Gifts (Christmas 1992).
Argos Superstore Catalogue (Autumn/Winter 1991).
Argos Superstore Catalogue (Spring/Summer 1992).
Avon Campaign 9 (1992).
Avon Campaign 13 (1992).
L. L. Bean (Summer 1992).*
L. L. Bean (Fall 1992).*
L. L. Bean (Christmas 1992).*
L. L. Bean (Spring 1993).*
Best of Together! (Spring 1992).
Body Aware (1992).
Body Aware: The Inspirational Guide to Men's Underfashion (no date).
Brainwaves: Science Museum (1992/1993).
The Bronson Collection (no date).
Burlington: Home Shopping at its Very Best (Autumn/Winter 1991/92).
Burlington: A World of Ideas in Fashion and the Home (Spring/Summer 1992).
Burlington: A World of Ideas in Fashion and the Home (Autumn/Winter 1992/93).
Choice: A World of Fashion (Spring/Summer 1992).
Choice: A World of Fashion (Autumn/Winter 1992).
Ciro Citterio, Stilista Italiano: Menswear (Autumn/Winter 1992/93).
Complete Essentials 14 (Summer 1992).
Complete Essentials: Summer Review 15 (Summer 1992).
Cost Cutters (no date).
Cotton Traders Directory (Spring 1993).
J. Crew (Summer 1992).*

Damart Colourways (May 1992).
Designs in Leather (no date).
Direct Collection (Spring/Summer 1992).
The Esso Collection (April 1991).
Family Album (Autumn/Winter 1992).
Fantasy Erotique (no date).
Grattan Big Book (no date).
Grattan Looking Great (Spring/Summer 1992).
Green Shield A2 (no date).
Heather Valley (Spring/Summer 1992).
High Lights (no date).
Home Free Christmas Catalogue (Christmas 1992).
Index: The Catalogue Shop (Spring/Summer 1992).
The Innovations Report: A Buyer's Guide XVIII, 3 (Christmas 1992).
Innovations: The Report (Spring 1993).
International Buyers Guide from Innovations (Autumn/Winter 1992).
International Male (1992).*
Janet Frazer: Your Fashion, Your Style (Spring/Summer 1992).
John Moores: Classic Lines in Fashion and Style (Autumn/Winter 1992/93).
Kays (Autumn/Winter 1991).
Kays: A Better Style of Shopping (Autumn/Winter 1992).
Kays Fashion Extra Collection (no date).
Kiniki: Designer Briefs, Sun, Swim & Sportswear (no date).
Lands' End Direct Merchants (January 1992).*
Lands' End Direct Merchants (June/July 1992).*
Look Again (Spring/Summer 1992).
Milletts: The Camping Store. First Choice for the Great Outdoors (March 1992).
Modern Originals: the catalogue of new ideas from around the world (Winter 1992).
The National Trust Magazine 66 (Summer 1992).
The Natural History Museum Collection: Catalogue of the Unusual (1992/93).
Next Directory 9 (Spring/Summer 1992).
Racing Green (Summer 1992).
Racing Green (Autumn 1992).
Racing Green: Classic Casuals (Christmas and New Year 1992).
Racing Green (Spring 1993).
Reader Offers from the Observer: An Innovations Publication (Spring 1992).
The Royal Society for the Protection of Birds: Catalogue for Christmas (1992).
Sanders & Kays Mail Mart 292 (no date).
Self Care: The Catalogue for Better Living (no date).
The Selfridge Selection (Summer 1992).
The Shamian Collection III (1990).
The Terrence Higgins Trust: The First Catalogue (Summer 1992).
Victoria's Secret 10 (Summer 1992).
J. D. Williams (Spring/Summer 1992).
You Magazine 14 (Summer 1992).
You Magazine 34 (Summer 1992).
You Magazine: Summer Sensations (Summer 1992).

Gay catalogues

BodyTech at Zipper (Winter/Spring 1992).
BodyTech Summer Style (Summer 1992).

Clone Zone (no date).
Clone Zone (Christmas 1992).
Clone Zone: Spring Book Catalogue (Spring 1993).
A Different Light Review: A Catalog of Gay and Lesbian Literature, vol.3, no.1 (Summer 1992).*
A Different Light Review: A Catalog of Gay and Lesbian Literature, vol.3, no.3 (Winter 1992).*
The Essential Eagle Leathers Catalogue (1990).
The Essential Eagle Leathers Update (Autumn 1990).
The Essential Eagle Leathers Update 2 (1992).
Expectations . . . (no date).
Male Xpress (no date).
Shocking Gray: The Catalog for the Other 25 Million People (Summer 1992).*
Shocking Gray: The Catalog for the Other 25 Million People (Fall/Holiday Wish Book 1992).*
Zipperstore: The Catalogue (1992).
Zipper, The Store: Catalogue '91 (1991).

REFERENCES

Blanchard, T. (1992) 'Will there be a G-string in your Stocking?', *The Independent*, 17 December 1992: 15.
Cowe, R. (1993) 'Cuts at Littlewoods show British Mail Order is on Downward Slope', *Guardian*, 26 January 1993: 13.
David, H. (1992) 'In the Pink', *The Times Saturday Review*, 13 June 1992: 10–11.
Dyer, R. (1989) 'Old Briefs for New', *New Statesman and Society*, 22 March 1989: 43–4.
Ferguson, H. (1992) 'Watching the World Go Round: Atrium Culture and the Psychology of Shopping', in R. Shields (ed.) *Lifestyle Shopping: The Subject of Consumption*, London: Routledge: 2–39.
Hunt, L. (1992) 'Woman object to Sanitary Towel Adverts', *The Independent*, 14 March 1992: 6.
Mort, F. (1988), 'Boy's Own? Masculinity, Style and Popular Culture', in R. Chapman and J. Rutherford (eds) *Male Order: Unwrapping Masculinity*, London: Lawrence & Wishart: 193–224.
Mort, F. and Green, N. (1988) 'You've Never Had It So Good – Again!', *Marxism Today*, May: 30–3.
Short, B. (1992) 'Queers, Beers and Shopping', *Gay Times* 170 (November): 18–20.
Tran, M. (1993) '50,000 Jobs to Go as Sears Axes "Big Book" Catalogues', *Guardian*, 26 January 1993: 13.

Part IV

THE VIEW FROM
THE OTHER SIDE

8

MONIKA TREUT:
AN OUTLAW AT HOME

Colin Richardson

Monika Treut has a fondness for hyenas; you could almost call it a fellow-feeling. After all, in hyena society, the female is dominant and, moreover, these are beasts which survive by scavenging for scraps, fearlessly standing up to larger predators for a share of the spoils. Such is the life of an independent film-maker. When, in 1984, Treut and Elfi Mikesch, one of Germany's leading cinematographers and directors, decided to set up their own film production company, what else could they call it but 'Hyena Films'?

In truth, though Treut has a fearsome reputation, she hasn't quite grown a full set of canine teeth. Indeed, she is much more the survivor than the tearer of flesh. For ten years, she has worked to the point of exhaustion to carve out a niche as an international film-maker, writing and directing all her films, raising the production finance herself, editing, promoting and even, on occasion, distributing the finished product. As a result, she is perhaps the only lesbian film-maker whose work has crossed over from art house to the mainstream while consistently dealing with the more controversial and 'incorrect' aspects of female sexuality – what Treut refers to as 'female misbehaviour'. Treut's women are often confused about their sexual orientation but they are united in their search for unconventional, unexpected, often confrontational and 'difficult' ways of being a woman. The title of her very first feature film (co-directed and written with Elfi Mikesch and with Mikesch as cinematographer) seems to say it all: *Seduction: The Cruel Woman*.[1]

Released in 1985, *Seduction* tells the story of Wanda, a dominatrix who runs a waterfront gallery in Hamburg where audiences pay to watch the enactment of various sado-masochistic fantasies. Wanda also delights in playing games with her entourage of female and male lovers. At the film's heart is the humiliation of the man who first encouraged Wanda to express her 'cruelty', only to lose control of his creation. It also includes two scenes which have at times got the film into all kinds of trouble. In one, a male journalist grovels at Wanda's feet, begging her to use him as her toilet. Then there is a short fantasy scene in which one of Wanda's lovers, the shoe fetishist Caren, imagines tying one of her customers up and forcing her to watch her 12-year-old daughter pose like a pin-up girl.

16 Female to Male: Monika Treut (Elfi Mikesch, 1990)

Seduction has been compared by Richard Dyer to *Querelle*[2] which is not entirely surprising since, apart from being German films, both are set on the waterfront, both examine power and role-playing in sexual relationships and both are beautifully lit and shot, prompting Marcia Pally of *Film Comment* to remark: '*Seduction* is a stunner. This is s/m by Avedon, outfits by Dior.' However, as Dyer points out, where *Querelle* is a hellish red, *Seduction*'s primary colour is an icy blue.

Three years after this striking debut, Treut (again with Mikesch on camera) followed up with *Virgin Machine (Die Jungfrauenmaschine)* in which journalist, Dorothee Müller, to quote the official synopsis,

> leaves Germany for the Oz of San Francisco, searching for her long-lost mother and a cure to the malady of love. Installed in the Tenderloin, she peeps in on neighbours' bizarre sex rituals, as well as doing sight-seeing of a more traditional kind. But encounters with male impersonator Ramona, charming Hungarian bohemian Dominique and Susie Sexpert, barker for an all-girl strip show, lead to exploratory adventures of self-discovery and fun. When Dorothee surfaces like a dazzled tourist on the wilder shore of the city's lesbian community, she's discovered her true sexuality. And left some illusions behind.

Filmed this time in black and white, *Virgin Machine* expresses Treut's disdain for the notion of romantic love and her delight in discovering the United

17 'Here's one I prepared earlier.' Susie Sexpert (Susie Bright) shows Dorothee (Ina Blum) her dildo collection in *Virgin Machine* (Monika Treut, 1988, © Hyena Films)

States. The first half of the film, set in Hamburg, has a brooding, melancholic, dissatisfied quality, harking back to German expressionist cinema. But when Dorothee hits San Francisco, the atmosphere lightens and the film becomes funnier, if rougher around the edges. Some of the American scenes were clearly shot on the run in one take to save money, giving them an almost documentary feel.

Treut's third feature, released in 1991, was shot entirely in New York. *My Father Is Coming* – working title, *Success* – marked a return to colour and is perhaps Treut's most conventional film in terms of form. A sweet, 'polysexual comedy of manners', it takes up the story of Vicky, a sexually confused German at large in the Big Apple. Struggling to hold down a job as a waitress, she dreams of becoming an actress yet fails even an audition for a commercial where she is required to play a German tourist. When her father arrives from small town Germany, lured by her tales of success, she desperately tries to live up to expectations. Naturally, things soon spin out of control when papa discovers his daughter in bed with another woman. However, the interventions variously of a transsexual, a porn queen and a fakir who is heavily into body-piercing and mysticism ultimately effect a reconciliation.

Treut's films are low budget films but, unlike Norma Desmond's, they are getting bigger. In early 1993, Treut was approached by Group 1 Films in Los Angeles to contribute to their new project, *Erotique*, a package of four short

18 Publicity for *Virgin Machine* (Monika Treut, 1988, © Hyena Films)

films by women directors from around the world.[3] *Taboo Parlour* was shot in Hamburg, Treut's adopted home town, in August 1993 with an international cast, and completed by the end of September.[4] Though only half an hour long, it is Treut's biggest budget film to date, costing around DM600,000 (about £240,000). However, even this will soon be surpassed when she returns to a project she has been working on for some years – a film based on Robert Merle's futuristic novel, *The Virility Factor*, which will have a budget in excess of $3 million.

19 Publicity for *My Father Is Coming* (Monika Treut, 1990, © Hyena Films)

As well as Fassbinder, Monika Treut has been compared to Jean-Luc Godard and John Waters,[5] among others. New York's *Village Voice* magazine has called her 'an agile, intelligent director' and an 'art-film outlaw' while *The Mirror/The Entertainer* in Toronto commented, 'Treut is her own woman in an industry dominated by men and her films reflect that independent sensibility. The next German Cinema Wave might just look to her for inspiration.'[6] In a round-up of cult directors from around the world, Jonathan Romney wrote in the British national newspaper, the *Guardian*: 'In Europe,

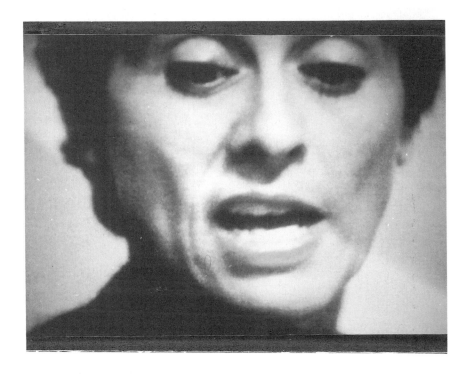

20 The art of the soundbite – Camille Paglia shows how (*Dr Paglia*, part of *Female Misbehaviour*, Monika Treut, 1992, © Hyena Films)

where cult independent work seems largely to be a male preserve, Monika Treut stands out for her films combining lesbian sex-pol with Teutonic jollity. . . . Even Almodóvar[7] fans find her a touch too risqué.'

Monika Treut is also a friend. I got to know her when I worked for Out on a Limb[8], the lesbian and gay film and video distribution company which distributes her films in the UK. She agreed to write an essay for this book but then *Taboo Parlour* got in the way. So instead, I interviewed her at her home in Hamburg in February 1993, immediately following the Berlin Film Festival where she launched her two documentary shorts, *Max* and *Dr Paglia*.[9]

Monika Treut was born in Mönchengladbach in 1954. She became a film-maker by accident. In 1972 when she went to university in Marburg/Lahn to study German literature, 'I had no idea of ever becoming a film-maker.' However, Marburg is a small town 'in the middle of nowhere' and the only entertainment was going to see films. 'So I sometimes went to see two movies a day.' Later, when she and her friends began to organise screenings of European art house films she had, by her own admission, become a 'movie maniac'.

172

21 How to win friends and influence people (*Female Misbehaviour*, Monika Treut, 1992, © Hyena Films)

While a student, Treut began to make super-8 films. Then, when the first video equipment came out, she trained herself to use it and taught herself how to edit. When she graduated, in 1978, she could not face the prospect of becoming a teacher so, instead, she went to work in a media centre in Berlin: 'It was all men and I had problems; I just could not get along with these macho media types.' In 1979, therefore, she accepted an invitation to work in a new women's media centre in Hamburg.[10]

'We worked as a collective of ten women. We had a photo lab, a video library, video equipment, and a small movie theatre. I was in charge of organising screenings of 16mm films made by women and I also made a few video documentaries. It was the time of hard-core lesbian feminism in Germany and I was enjoying my period of separatism then. But since I'm not an ideal group person, I didn't last more than a year and a half there.'

In 1980, Treut returned to academic work to take a Ph.D. 'I had this thing in my mind that I wanted to do something about evil women, I was always interested in evil women and women who broke the rules. I called it *The Cruel Woman* and I just tried to research the image of the cruel woman in films made by women but I only found bits and pieces here and there so then after researching all kinds of movies I thought, ach!, I had better go back to the real sources, go back to de Sade[11] and I'll go back to Sacher-Masoch.[12]

'I still worked a little in the media centre but then I used to take all my books in the car and go to Italy and stay there for three months to write a chapter of my thesis. I had funny experiences on the way because at the German/Italian border they said, "What are all these books?" So I had to get every single book out and put it on the street, on the road at the border. So, imagine having a street full of Marquis de Sade because they thought I was bringing pornography into Italy. I had to explain to them that this was a scientific project, for the university, but I don't think they believed me.'

Then the accident happened – Monika met Elfi Mikesch and found herself becoming a full-time film-maker. 'I met Elfi whose work I adored. She was – and still is – my favourite German film-maker and cinematographer. When I told her about this book[13] I was writing, this thesis, Elfi got really interested in it and she said she would love to make a movie about sado-masochism. So I sent her chapters of the thesis and over the years we became very friendly and finally became lovers.'

In 1983, Mikesch and Treut wrote the screenplay which was to become *Seduction: The Cruel Woman*. Though it was ahead of its time in its depiction of sado-masochism from a female perspective, the script was none the less well received by the (then) West German government film funding panel, composed of fellow film-makers and artists, and at the end of 1983 an award of a quarter of a million marks was made. But then the politicians stepped in. Within months the money was withdrawn on the orders of the new, and far right, Minister of the Interior, Friedrich Zimmermann. Apparently, he objected to the 'I want to be your toilet' scene.

But all was not lost. Indeed, the publicity generated by the Minister's decision backfired when the social democratic regional government of North Rhine–Westphalia and the film house in Hamburg stepped into the breach and together came up with 400,000 German marks, more than had been lost. However, all this pre-publicity was not entirely welcomed by Treut and Mikesch 'because the film was already in the papers before we even shot one frame. You know how that is for artists and everybody had expectations beforehand – this cruel, hot movie made by two women. We shot the movie in the harbour at Hamburg in late Fall, 1984. Because the budget was very tight, we had to be fast. Almost on the day we got the first print back from the lab, we went to the Berlin Film Festival [in February 1985] to premiere it there and we ran into the next scandal. So my welcoming into the film community was by two wonderful scandals . . .'

The Berlin screening was packed with people expecting to be shocked, hoping to be outraged. Some walked out before the end but most stayed for the discussion with Treut, Mikesch and two of the leading actors. As Treut describes it, men queued up to denounce the film. She was enraged and, much to the discomfort of the festival director, harangued back. Only Elfi stayed calm. When someone asked her about the two nuns who appear at the end of the film, she quietly said with a wry smile, 'Oh, they represent the women's movement.'

The film is based on Sacher-Masoch's novel, *Venus in Furs (Venus im Pelz)*. 'It's one of his most kitschy novels from the late nineteenth century. It's a very basic story about an aristocrat (Gregor) who one day sees a woman (Wanda) and falls for her. She's just an ordinary woman and in the course of the novel he educates her to become a dominatrix and to fulfil his dreams. The most interesting parts of the novel are the descriptions of architecture, interior design, costumes, colours and so on. The masochistic mind needs to over-indulge in the history of the art; that's as important as the dominatrix herself. Parts of the novel are almost written like a screenplay. We did change one important thing, though: we changed the roles. We made Wanda much stronger from the very beginning. In the novel it takes her almost two years to take over and turn Gregor into her slave.'

Of the two – de Sade and Sacher-Masoch – the Marquis is probably the better known. Can you explain a little about Masoch and his attitude towards women?

'People have named this behaviour masochistic after Sacher-Masoch which is a weird thing to do when you research his life. Because in life he was not a masochist at all, he was a macho man. Also, he wrote more than a hundred novels between 1860 and 1892 – two or three a year – and the way he describes masochism in these novels is very boring. His style is very kitschy and artsy. He always talks about the same phenomenon which is a strong, dominating woman and a man who looks up to her, a man who wishes to be dominated by this woman. But the interesting thing with Sacher-Masoch is that his masochism, his so-called masochism, in his books as well as in his life, is a trick. The masochistic man in fact dominates the woman because he acts like a director on stage, he tells the woman exactly what to do. So the woman is not a dominating woman by herself she just *looks* dominating and the man is the one who gives her all the attributes of being a dominant woman – he asks her to wear boots and fur and leather and whips and everything.'

So she's only powerful as long as he allows her to be: he can take it away?

'Yes, exactly. I found that very, very interesting because we see that a lot in this society – that women are not powerful by themselves but they just stand on a pedestal somewhere which only makes them powerful for a second, it's just a glimpse of what they could be but it could be taken away quite easily. I began to see the masochistic universe as a very different universe to the de Sade universe because I think de Sade has a much more avant-garde mind, is much more feminist than Sacher-Masoch who just pretended. Also Masoch was sentimental and I do not like sentimental people; he's a dreamer, forever dreaming about ancient matriarchal societies yet he is pretty much aware that he is the dominant person even being the masochistic male, that he still holds the power. Whereas de Sade is really interested in transforming the rules of society and is really an anarchist in that he really analyses *this* is the structure of society and *this* is the way the women can escape. Masoch, on the other hand, just holds them in this double bind situation of being mothers and lovers and slaves but giving them for a moment a chance to dominate.'

Despite the initial reaction to *Seduction*, Monika and Elfi continued to attend screenings. At the Montreal Film Festival, they began to have fun. 'Elfi and I greeted the audience before the screening and then went and sat outside the theatre. After ten minutes a woman came out, screaming at us, "You are the makers of this movie, this is the worst movie I've seen in my life . . ." She was hysterical, a woman film critic, and I just said OK why don't you just sit here and calm down, what is this, what is bothering you? And then she said, all of a sudden it burst out of her, "That film is my life, that is how I feel" and all her life, her psychological problems came out. We talked to her for a bit which made her change her mind completely about the movie. She grabbed our hands, thanking us, and rushed right back into the movie. I love it when people have such strong reactions, I love it.' [Laughs]

Then, through the summer of 1985, the whole circuit of West Coast US festivals: 'I really enjoyed it; the lesbian and gay festivals were the most pleasurable. In Los Angeles we had a wonderful audience response despite the fact that they began by screening it at the wrong ratio: I remember because Wanda's (Mechtild Grossmann) head was cut off and I had to throw a fit and the projectionist almost broke his leg running up and down the stairs in the theatre.[14]

'But the audience still enjoyed it and afterwards people came up to me to tell me so. An SM couple came up to me and said, "This film is amazing, it's just like our marriage." I met a woman park ranger from California, a lesbian, who adored it and offered me hundreds of dollars for a video cassette. Leather guys offered me their handkerchiefs which I really loved, it was very personal. In fact, the whole gay SM community loved *Seduction*.

'At the San Francisco lesbian and gay festival, I was a bit worried at first since some European producers had warned me about audience expectations there. Like Dieter Schidor, the producer of Fassbinder's *Querelle*, who had said to me: "Monika be careful, San Francisco gay people do not appreciate art, they booed and hissed at *Querelle*."

'I remember experiencing a kind of culture shock at first in San Francisco. On the opening night of the festival, the audience seemed to enjoy most sentimental films with lesbian or gay heroes so I was ready to take the print and run. But then I met all these exciting women at the opening night party: Susie Bright, Nan Kinney and Debi Sundahl, the publishers of *On Our Backs*,[15] the lesbian SM scene and the Hungarian sisters, Dominique and Flora.[16] Finally, *Seduction* itself was well received.

'During this first visit to San Francisco, I stayed in the *On Our Backs* office and my new friends took me to lesbian strip shows and I was in wonderland. That's when I had the idea to turn my experiences into a script which later became *Virgin Machine*.

'Then in the Fall were the Canadian festivals. In Toronto, *Seduction* got banned by the board of censorship, the only film out of the 180 that were screened that year. Apparently, the board objected to the scene where the 12-year-old girl is dressed up like a pin-up girl and her mother is forced to watch her pose – this was accused of being the exhibition of a minor in a sexual context. The members of the board were mostly housewives.

'Elfi and I were shocked by this decision because we considered our movie to be relatively timid: no genitals, no sexual intercourse, everything in it probably a fantasy, happening in the minds of the spectators. The festival seized the opportunity to fight the board's decision. Kay Armatage, one of the programmers, a professor of film and a film-maker herself, wrote what was almost a thesis in defence of *Seduction*. So the board had a second screening and finally, reluctantly, allowed it to be screened in the festival. Elfi and I got so much publicity out of this that the festival was able to get rid of the board altogether.

'I spent the rest of the year working on getting distributors for *Seduction* and doing publicity for the openings. In 1986 I worked on the script for *Virgin Machine* and I went back to San Francisco to scout for locations. But it was not until 1987 that I got the financing going. Germany is thought of as being a place where it is relatively easy for film-makers to get funding – but it's a different story in my case. The agencies here think that I am this man-hating SM lesbian with scissors in her pants, ready to cut off their penises – the majority of funders are male in Germany. The agencies in Hamburg, my home town, and one television producer for NDR[17] are the only exceptions. These two sources combined still only make for small budgets but this is pretty much all I can rely on.

'And so we shot *Virgin Machine* in 1987 in the summer, first in Hamburg then in San Francisco for another ridiculous budget. We had two different crews, a German crew and an American crew. Then we came back from San Francisco in early November to edit the film.

'I had a sneak preview at the Gay and Lesbian Film Festival in San Francisco. Industry people tell you never have a world premiere at a gay film festival because then it is marked and branded, just look for like a big film festival first and so I thought, ach!, I don't give a shit, San Francisco helped me to make the movie, I mean the lesbian and gay community, and I used all kinds of bars and I had connections through the community. This film was my way of saying thank you.

'It was a very interesting screening, I could tell by the way the audience reacted very directly, spontaneously that they didn't like the parts where the main character, Dorothee, is in touch with her big boyfriend or when the Pope was on screen they would hiss – every time some hateful object appears on screen they hissed like in the Punch and Judy show. So I could tell exactly what parts they had problems with and they effectively wrote a script for another movie, you know by reacting, a script for a film they would have loved. This one, they had to work to get along with but in the end they liked it so that was fine.'

You said that you could have rewritten the film from the audience reaction into the film they would have liked. Tell me about what kind of reactions you've had to your work, particularly from lesbians, as to what they expect from you as a lesbian director, what they expect from a lesbian film?

'That is my ongoing discussion with lesbian audiences, especially the San Francisco lesbian audience. They are very explicit in what they want to see, though it's changed a bit since the mid-1980s. My nasty take on it is this: they want to see lesbian love scenes on screen, they want to see attractive girls on screen, they want to see girl meets girl, girl has romance with another girl, girl has wonderful sex with another girl and maybe the highlight would be at the end mom and dad approve and they all live happily ever after.'

In *My Father Is Coming* and even in *Virgin Machine* the main character is uncertain about her identity to start with. Do you think the lesbian audience wants all the lesbian characters to be lesbians through and through and there never to be any doubt?

'It's not only that. A huge part of the lesbian audience wants to see some kind of a heroine, somebody who is bigger than they are, bigger than life which, for me, is a kind of a caricature thing. *Virgin Machine* and *My Father Is Coming* are about real people and real experiences and real life situations and when I make a film like that I just tend to portray people as they are in real life. That girl, Vicky, in *My Father Is Coming* was a typical person of the time, just somebody who does not really know who she is.

'I do not believe in these identity concepts – that people can completely tell you this is what I am, this is what I want to become, these are the people I want to meet, this is the career I want and this is how it will go for me – ten years from now I will be there and will have done this and this work and whatever. I don't see people that way, I see that people in the late twentieth century are creatures very much influenced by their time, by their surroundings, by their jobs, by their friends, by their economic situation, by lots and lots of things and to say *this is my identity* to me is just a lie or it's a dream or a nightmare.

'I see the chance for people to accept that there is not just one core source of identity but that you can have different identities at the same time. That's probably something that puts me in opposition to the queer or lesbian and gay self-consciousness, whatever, because I'm also an artist and that also puts me directly in opposition to all kinds of movements or politically correct concepts because I have to play several different roles in my life all the time. When I'm with actors and actresses, I have to be the ringmaster, the mother, the shrink, the dominatrix. When I'm talking to money people, to funders, I'm a different person – not that I'm a different person but I do have to play different music. I'm a business person with funders or co-producers and, say, half an hour later I'm playing the "mother" with actors, playing the partner with editors and so on. And even that can change – I can be a good mother, I can be an evil mother. I'm a different person with lovers and with friends and, of course, I'm another person when I'm by myself writing a script: I just feel like a machine driven by my hormones. So it just depends on what you do. I always doubt it when people have the urge to present themselves as the same kind of being everywhere in every situation – I don't think it is possible.'

So do you feel that lesbians and gay men who are out, who are part of a movement and have acquired this identity, this lesbian or gay identity, are expecting from you to reflect that identity in a fairly unproblematic way but nothing else? That they want you to show the kind of people that they think of themselves as being in a kind of fixed and yet positive and fully formed way? Is it because partly we want to see reflected back at ourselves what we feel about ourselves, to be reinforced? Is it also because we're thinking about straight people who watch these films and we want them to think well of us when they see them. Do you think that is part of it?

'Darling, I have to say that I deeply hate this expectation. Who are we as poor, struggling lesbian or gay film-makers to reassure lesbian and gay identities? Of course, cerebrally, I can understand these wishes; but I think the screen gets abused as a shrink and eight bucks is not enough to get the full treatment. One goes to a shrink to hear – oh you're a good person, I love you and your one and only problem is that your parents didn't love you and therefore you have to get a new perception of yourself and you have to love yourself. This is basically what therapy is about – many years and thousands of pounds or dollars or marks later, you come to accept yourself no matter whether you are gay or lesbian or whatever.

'I'm not in favour of the old habit of using the screen as an ersatz shrink – psychoanalysis for poor people which is indeed an historic concept of cinema in the early part of the twentieth century. People went to the movies to feel good about themselves, to identify with the huge hero or heroine on screen in order to reassure themselves.'

What do you think of the idea of the male gaze, the notion that mainstream Hollywood cinema assumes that the spectator is male so that

179

the object of a film is a woman, the woman represents sex and so the
female spectator has no easy way in?

'I don't think that's true. We had actresses like Marlene Dietrich, Greta
Garbo, Joan Crawford, Barbara Stanwyck and so on in the 1930s and 1940s,
playing absolutely strong female characters, *femmes fatales*, in the *film noir* –
lots of female characters for straight and lesbian women to identify with.'

But you've had that thrown at you – that your films somehow fail to cater
to the female spectator and to legitimate the female gaze . . .

'Well, I do question this whole theory about the so-called female gaze. When
I see a movie I never identify with a female victim. If I identify at all, I
identify with the character I like and that can be a man or a woman or an
animal. Lots of female friends of mine share the same experience. Also, I
don't think this is thrown at me – my experience is that lots of women are
indeed amused about the adventures of Dorothee Müller in *Virgin Machine*
or Vicky in *My Father Is Coming*.'

There was an item on the British lesbian and gay TV series, *Out*, in 1991
which suggested that one of the most popular films with lesbians was
Aliens[18] where Sigourney Weaver totes a gun throughout but she's also
the mother to the little girl.

'So phallic but motherly. The mother with a phallus, isn't that what we're all
looking for?'

Do you feel that you have an expectation upon you that a lot of women
and maybe some lesbian women come to your films with the expectation
that the women in your films will fulfil that heroic role? And even if you
do feel that how do you respond to them?

'Well I'm glad that there are films out like *Aliens* so they can fulfil their
wishes. I myself am unable to cater to these expectations. It's all about
fulfilling the Hollywood studio formula. I don't see cinema, as I tried to point
out earlier, as a representative or stand-in for real life experiences.

'My movies do not consciously set out to create a big following, they're
just original pieces. But I'm not trying to torture audiences, unlike other
independent film-makers. I try to make it fun to watch my films. But then the
audience also gets to see things that they have to combine in their heads and
work a little.'

What is your kind of cinema then?

180

'I like challenge in movies, I like challenge a lot. Again, I cannot say my taste is in one drawer. I do like experimental movies a lot; for example, I love Kenneth Anger's[19] films and Maya Deren's[20] work. But then at the same time I adore ancient Hollywood movies like Billy Wilder's work. He's my favourite Hollywood director of all time. Then, of course, as a German I adore Fassbinder. For me, he's the most interesting German film-maker after World War II. Though I don't really relate to his melodramatic touch, his films have been and still are a *big* source of inspiration to me.'

Do you think films can make the world a better place?

'No!'

In 1992 after a screening of *Virgin Machine* at the Goethe-Institut in London, you were talking to Julia Knight[21] and what you basically said was, 'I make my films, they're released, I say bye, bye, in terms of what they mean. That's it I've said it. It's up to the audience what they make of it.' Do you really feel that or do you actively try and shape people's interpretations of your films?

'My story is: after a film is finished, I have to come to terms with it and this has always been like making peace with it. I know that I did my best under the specific circumstances – the budget, the time, etc. Then when we do the sound mix, I always get goose pimples, meaning I love this movie, no matter what. But of course it's a never-ending learning experience. I know exactly what we could have done better on each movie but that's another story to remember for the next one.'

But you don't care if somebody reads it differently from you – you know, there is some huge cultural study of it, reinterpreting what you meant. You don't care if people get completely the wrong idea?

'I'm amused when I read such things. After I've given birth to a movie, it's no longer mine and people can do with it whatever they please.

'This is not the smart American way of promoting your work but I'm sick and tired of pushing my own films. That is the work of distributors and agents, publicists and so on. I'm probably a stupid person because most of the other film-makers put as much effort into promoting their films as making them but that's not really my cup of tea. When I've finished one movie, I'm already thinking of the next one and that is pretty much the end of the love affair.'

Many directors get very upset if people 'misunderstand' their films.

'I don't. I like strong reactions.'

What if people don't talk about your films a lot, they don't talk about them at all – that must be the worst part?

'Luckily enough I've never experienced that. If they don't talk about my work in one country, they do in another. So I have never suffered from not enough feedback. Of course, feedback is important to me when it is smart – it helps you for your next movie.'

One of the favoured strategies in marketing is to categorise a film within a particular genre – something which is not particularly easy with your work. One of the genres that's come under particular study in our book is the vampire film and there has been a lot of interest in that lately with Coppola's *Dracula*[22] coming out and ideas of vampires being a *fin de siècle* phenomenon and so on. Have you any particular interest in expressing any ideas through any genre?

'No. I've never been very much attracted to the vampire genre because to me it's all about repressed sexuality – very bourgeois. There's the yuppie person on the outside and then comes the night and they fall victim to something or turn into a monster. To me, it's a dated, Victorian fantasy which is alien to me. It's a nice fairy tale but I cannot relate to it emotionally.

'Or, the same thing, I could never relate to that lesbian movie *Mädchen in Uniform*[23] which is another repressed thing – I see millions of lesbians crying at this movie: "I had a teacher like that and I was in love with her . . ." It's repressed sexuality to me. I've seen it twice out of historical interest, this typical teacher/pupil story, but that was it and so I analysed it – fine, but I could not watch it with a bunch of lesbian girlfriends and go, like, "my mathematics teacher, I fell for her when I was in 3rd grade . . ."'

But if genre is not the way to express yourself . . .

'I'm a marketing failure!' [Laughs]

. . . . If critics have a problem fitting you into a genre then they try to compare your work with another film or film-maker. So, for example, you may be compared with Percy Adlon, with *My Father Is Coming* being compared to *Baghdad Cafe*. Both of you are German, both films are a German take on America and, of course, Adlon also has lesbianism involved in an unlikely way. How do you respond to comparisons of your films with other sort of films like that?

'I don't give a shit!'

It's a question that you were asked by Jenni Murray on the *Woman's Hour*[24] interview – you were asked about whether you saw yourself as a German film-maker, as a woman film-maker – she didn't actually say it but the subtext was as a lesbian film-maker. Do you think in those terms yourself?

'Of course I'm all of that. But as I tried to express earlier in my pidgin English, I am not too fond of these labels. As a film-maker I see myself as a loner, an outlaw. Whether it is the art film community, whether it is the lesbian and gay film community, or the commercial film community or the B-movie, trash film community.

'Sometimes, of course, I do have this human desire to look around for relatives in this cruel world of movie-making. And then I see that the people I like are all either busy or unable to communicate. To name a few – Jean-Luc Godard who has been in splendid isolation for many years now; or Liliana Cavani[25] whose work I really love. *The Night Porter*[26] is still one of my favourite movies. I feel close to her though I've never met her. She does documentaries as well as features and she loves to touch taboo subjects: sado-masochism in combination with the Nazi Terror. But I have little hope that there will be a meeting soon of all the loners in this business.

'I am everywhere and nowhere with my work and as long as I can raise enough money to make my next film, I'm happy.'

NOTES

1 *Verführung: Die Grausame Frau*, Monika Treut/Elfi Mikesch, Germany, 1985.
2 *Querelle* (1982), based on Jean Genet's 1947 novel, *Querelle of Brest*, was the last film of the German director, Rainer Werner Fassbinder (1944–82).
3 The other directors are Lizzie Borden (USA), Clara Law (Hong Kong) and Ana Maria Magalhaes (Brazil).
4 *Taboo Parlour* includes in its cast, Marianne Sagebrecht, a leading German actress and star of, among others, *Baghdad Cafe* (Percy Adlon, Germany/USA, 1987), and features songs from British singer-songwriter, Tanita Tikaram.
5 Jean-Luc Godard (b.1930), French director associated with *nouvelle vague* (new wave) of French cinema (films include *A Bout de Souffle*, *Vivre Sa Vie*); John Waters (b.1946), cult US director, self-styled 'Pope of Trash', famed for his films starring Divine (including *Pink Flamingos*, *Female Trouble*, *Desperate Living*).
6 For more about Treut's relationship to German cinema, see Julia Knight, *Women and the New German Cinema*, Verso, London, 1992.
7 Pedro Almodóvar (b.1951), Spanish film-director and writer. Films include the explicitly gay *Law of Desire* and camp cult classics such as *Matador*, *What Have I Done To Deserve This?*, *Pepi, Luci, Bom . . .*, and *Women on the Edge of a Nervous Breakdown*.
8 *Out on a Limb*, Britain's first exclusively lesbian and gay film and video distribution company, was set up in June 1991 by Val Martin. I worked there from the beginning until October 1993.
9 *Max*, a portrait of a native American, female-to-male transsexual, and *Dr Paglia*,

a barely controlled explosion occasioned by the trenchantly outspoken US academic, Camille Paglia, form part of a feature-length collection of Treut's documentaries which span the years 1983 to 1992 and which rejoices in the title, *Female Misbehaviour*.

10 The Bildweschel – which is still active today.

11 Donatien Alphonse François, Marquis de Sade (1740–1814), French aristocrat, soldier, writer, debaucher and debauchee.

12 Leopold von Sacher-Masoch (1835–95), Austrian writer.

13 Monika completed her thesis – becoming Dr Treut in the process – in 1982. It was published in book form in Germany in 1984 with the title, *Die Grausame Frau (The Cruel Woman)*, and it is now in its second edition. An English edition will be published in the UK and the USA in 1994, funnily enough by Routledge.

14 The screening ratio determines the dimensions of the rectangle of light projected onto the screen – obviously, if this differs from the ratio adopted when the film was made, parts of the image will be cut off. Monika Treut uses the ratio 1:1.37 when shooting her films, a ratio which has gone out of fashion somewhat. It is closer to a square than the most commonly used modern ratios – for example, wide screen movies adopt a ratio of 1:2.35 which produces a wide, but narrow strip. If the projectionist does not check, then incidents similar to that described here will occur: the top and bottom of the image will be cut off. In fact, I've seen it happen myself at a London screening of *Virgin Machine*. On this occasion, I was the one making the projectionist run up and down stairs until heads were restored.

15 *On Our Backs* is a US lesbian sex magazine which has attracted much criticism, particularly from lesbian feminist anti-pornography campaigners some of whom have launched a direct action campaign against the magazine. Susie Bright, *aka* Susie Sexpert, writer, sex educator, performer and editor of *On Our Backs*, plays a leading role in *Virgin Machine*.

16 Dominique and Flora Gaspar. Dominique is in *Virgin Machine*; both sisters feature in *My Father Is Coming*.

17 The NDR (Nord Deutscher Rundfunk) is a North German TV station, a subdivision of the First Programme.

18 *Aliens* (James Cameron, USA, 1986), second film in the *Alien* trilogy.

19 Kenneth Anger (b.1929), US underground film-maker, celebrated for the homo-erotic appeal of his work. Author of the *Hollywood Babylon* books which dished the dirt on numerous Hollywood stars.

20 Maya Deren (1908–61), Russian-born US film-maker (films include *Meshes of the Afternoon, Meditation on Violence*).

21 In June 1992, the Goethe-Institut in London organised a season of screenings, entitled *Women and the New German Cinema*, to coincide with the publication of Julia Knight's book of the same title (op. cit.). Following a screening of *Virgin Machine*, Treut talked to Knight and answered questions from the audience.

22 *Bram Stoker's 'Dracula'* (Francis Ford Coppola, USA, 1993).

23 *Mädchen in Uniform (Maidens in Uniform)* (Leontine Sagan, Germany, 1931) – described by *Time Out* as: 'A key early German talkie: a powerful melodrama about life in a Prussian boarding school for the daughters of the bourgeoisie – a bastion of the ideology of "strength through suffering".'

24 Jenni Murray interviewed Monika Treut and Julia Knight for the BBC Radio 4 programme, *Woman's Hour*. The interview, which was broadcast on 11 June 1992, coincided with the publication of Knight's book, *Women and the New German Cinema*, op. cit.

25 Liliana Cavani (b.1937), Italian film-maker.

26 *The Night Porter (Il Portiere di Notte)* (Liliana Cavani, Italy, 1973) – Dirk Bogarde and Charlotte Rampling star as, respectively, a former SS guard and a one-time child inmate of his concentration camp who, years later, meet in a hotel to take up sexually where they left off.

9

THE WILD, WILD WORLD
OF FANZINES

Notes from a reluctant pornographer

Bruce LaBruce

We hate it when our friends become successful.
(Morrissey)

Every fag's a jury. Twelve angry men in one.
(Buddy Cole)

It's not all autographs and sunglasses.
(Morgan Fairchild)

So I wake up one day with a hangover, as usual, and I remember that a chapter I'm supposed to write about fanzines for this book called *A Queer Romance* is due in about a week, and I hate the word 'queer', and I'm just getting over a three-year relationship so I don't even want to think about the concept of romance, and I practically don't even read fanzines anymore. I'm not exactly motivated, i.e. So I drag myself out of bed and light up the first of too many cigarettes of the day and sit with my legs crossed and arms akimbo like I'm in a straitjacket or something and stare down into a cup of coffee and wonder what I can possibly say about a movement that no longer seems to be moving. I mean, isn't that why they call it a movement, because it's supposed to move?

'Queercore' is dead. I know, because I say it is. Our son is dead. I killed him. (It could be daughter, mind you, but that's not the way Edward Albee wrote it.) *Who's Afraid of Virginia Woolf?*[1] was on television last night, and although I've seen it about a hundred times, it was the first time I really understood it – how you can create something out of a desperate need, and make it so convincing that not only you but others around you start believing it too. But, well, when it becomes an international phenomenon or something, and people start referring to your imaginary creation as 'legendary' and 'important', it's time to deliver the telegram proclaiming that your blonde-eyed, blue-haired son is dead. It's time to move on to the next game.

Welcome to the wild, wild world of 'queercore', née homocore, the cut-rate, cut-throat, cutting edge of the homosexual underworld. Enter at your

22 A hitch in time: eat your heart out Madonna. Bruce LaBruce in *Super 8½*, 1994
(Publicity still courtesy of Dirty Pillows and Candyland Productions)

own risk . . . I'm not going to act as some kind of authority on the subject,
or a goddamn tour guide (my name is not Dita[2]), because I'm not sure I quite
understand it myself – always a good sign. I'm not going to tell you how to
pronounce 'fanzine', or how to gain access to this exclusive little sub-
terranean queer cartel. Some people say it's as simple as stapling together a
few xeroxed pages of naked boys or disembodied vaginas and dropping it in
the mail, but I don't think so. You have to be a keen propagandist, a dedicated
pornographer, a shameless self-promoter, and an inveterate shape-changer to
exist in this ambitious little cosmology. Of course it wasn't this way in the
beginning, or maybe it was and I never noticed, but where did this desperate
need to create an alternative to the extant gay community come from, and
where do I go from here?

These questions burn like an STD as I prance through the aisles of my
favourite bookstore, shopping for my thirty dollar weekly fix of glossy
magazines. I rarely read a fanzine these days, but I feel compelled to keep in
touch with what's going on in *Vanity Fair*, *Vogue*, *Spin*, *Sassy* (and *Dirt*,
when available), *Celebrity Sleuth*, *Spy*, and a host of others. Lately I've come
across more controversial material in *Entertainment Weekly* than in any
'queercore' fanzine I've been sent, and you can quote me wildly on that. Since

187

its co-option by established gay literary figures and 'legitimate' publications such as *Artforum*, *i.D.*, the *Village Voice*, and others, 'queercore' has been simultaneously demystified and glorified, diluted and trumped up into something it can't sustain. It's like when ACTUP[3] became a big celebrity and got its picture in *Vanity Fair* – it exhausted its star potential, and in effect, the dog and pony show was over. The media will only tolerate its bad children as long as they entertain and perform within the limitations it dictates; when it is no longer amused, or gets bored, you have to be savvy enough to transform yourself into something else or risk having your head chopped off.

Speaking of severed heads, I've recently been compared to Jayne Mansfield in the *Village Voice*, and, as the Prince of the Homosexuals, let me tell you, it's not easy to keep the crown on your head when it's been wrenched from your body in a gruesome car accident. But at least Jayne did it her way, before Hollywood and the media machine did it to her. It was the ultimate career move, and an important lesson to anyone like myself who has become an international sex star: don't let the bastards fuck with your head – do it yourself (or DIY, as they say in punk circles).

No Skin Off My Ass, my first porno, was a logical progression from *J.D.s*, the original homocore fanzine. With *J.D.s*, I and my former partner in sexual revolution introduced homosexual pornography to the punk fanzine formula, and like naughty kids in the basement with a chemistry set, created an explosion heard around the world, or at least half way down the block. Not only did we unabashedly steal punk images from dirty, glossy gay magazines (which had, incidentally, already begun, at this early stage, to co-opt punk – fags are always so up on the latest trends!), but we also began to exploit – gently, always very gently – our friends and various passers-by, politely requesting, after getting them drunk, to remove their garments and pose for us. I was always as loaded as my camera, and spent as much time in front of it as behind; I quickly learned a good rule of thumb for budding pornographers: never ask anyone to do anything you wouldn't do yourself. (Unfortunately, after a certain point in your career, this strategy doesn't always seem to work, but that's another story.) The super-8 movies that accompanied our fanzines became more and more graphic, each of us spurring on the other to go further and further, and sometimes we got a little over-enthusiastic, we'd go just a little too far. But when you go a little too far over and over again, suddenly you wake up late one afternoon and you realise that you've gone *really* far, and there's no turning back. It was all so romantic in the beginning, crashing through the world, not remembering how you got that latest tattoo, not caring whose bathroom door you kicked in, or tiled floor you woke up on, not giving a damn how your wrist got slashed (as long as you got it on film), or how you got such a bruised ass, a crumpled Polaroid in your back pocket the only clue as to who accommodated you the night before. Of course, this particular style of 'queer romance' can only go on so long before it kills you. But what the hell, I've always been a sucker

*J.D.s and Associates
in association with
The New Lavender Panthers
and Jurgen Bruning
present*

NO

SKIN

OFF

MY

ASS

"being a fag

is a definite

plus"

ONE OF THE BEST
FILMS OF 1991!

J. Hoberman
Amy Taubin
and
Manohla Dargis
THE VILLAGE VOICE

*a movie by Bruce LaBruce
'starring'*
*G.B. Jones • Bruce LaBruce
and introducing
Klaus Von Brucker
as the skinhead.*

23 Publicity shots for *No Skin Off My Ass*, featuring Bruce LaBruce as the
Hairdresser, Klaus von Brücker as the Skinhead and Gloria B. Jones as his
Sister, 1991
(Courtesy of Bruce LaBruce and Candyland Productions)

for self-destructive impulses and damaged personalities, especially my own. I am not now nor have I ever been a likely candidate for the position of GLAAD[4] poster child.

Years later, the exciting gay long that once constituted Toronto homocore is no more. Disputes over affairs personal and financial – and credit, always credit with fags and dykes: who thought of which idea first, who contributed more, who deserved to become more famous – tore asunder the terrible triumvirate that started it all. New alliances and allegiances have been formed, different strategies developed, but the bitterness remains like the bad aftertaste of an imprudent blow-job that is momentarily savoured but immediately regretted. After the 'modest' international cult success of *No Skin Off My Ass* (believe me, modesty had nothing to do with it), I became the pariah, the sell-out, the Judas, the Amy Fisher[5] of 'queercore'. No one is particularly interested in hearing that I've yet to make any monetary profit from my little movie – unfortunately it's a lot easier to get famous than rich in this world. No one cares to hear that despite all outward appearances, I'm really not that much different than I was before I became a household – or rather, bathroom – word. I'm comforted by my favourite Madonna quote: 'Everyone always talks about how fame changes you, but no one ever

24 Comings and (must be) goings. Bruce LaBruce and friend in *Super 8½*, 1994 (Publicity still courtesy of Dirty Pillows and Candyland Productions)

mentions how it changes the people around you.' Although I remain the lowest form of celebrity, my fellow 'queercore' alumni choose to believe that I have sold my soul to the devil. Well, after all, Jayne Mansfield *was* a devout disciple of Anton LaVey, as was Tuesday Weld, whom I play in *Super 8½*, a loose remake of *Play It As It Lays*.[6] Perhaps now you can begin to see how it all connects.

After poring over my new stash of magazines, I mince over to the local repair shop to pick up my busted VCR. The East Indian man who owns the place is obviously quite taken with me; after studying several of my fashion flourishes, he comments conspiratorially, 'Oh, I like your outfit. It's very fancy. *Very* fancy', significantly raising his bushy eyebrows. Of course he's trying to tell me that he understands I'm a fag and would be interested in getting to know me a little better, perhaps in the back room, but being the shy, self-conscious pornographer that I am, I merely blush, mumble thank you, grab the VCR, and swish out of the store. On the way home I think of how I sometimes wish the homosexual world were still like this – the furtive signals, the hidden signs, the unanalysed affectations that suggest rather than proclaim deviation. I suppose I'm an anachronism, a throwback, but at times I imagine myself more at home in the thirties or forties, surreptitiously, or perhaps brazenly entering a movie theatre with my special friend to watch a Cocteau movie, our flamboyant style alone causing people on the street outside to speak in hushed tones. Or sitting around languidly in cafes with companions drawn together only by an aesthetic, arguing feverishly about the importance of sexual revolution without actually revealing the exact nature of our own sordid sex lives. I picture myself in the sixties, when even your parents were swingers, and everyone had to work harder to distinguish homosexual style from the general frenzy of mod fashion. There was no need to identify yourself as gay then, because everyone was having an identity crisis anyway, and sexual experimentation was hip. All the girls looked like Jean Shrimpton, the boys like Christopher Jones, and Max Frost didn't care if his male followers liked other boys – in fact, he flirted with the idea himself. If you look at seventies homosexual pornography today, none of the actors look particularly gay – they could be any man on the street who happened to stumble into a dirty movie career. Something about that excites me.

Later in the evening I meet for dinner with a friend who is just as alienated from the gay community as I am, if that's possible. There is nothing about his style or mannerisms or the subjects he chooses to talk about that might indicate that he is a homosexual; in fact, whenever I talk to him I always forget he's one of us. He says he envies me because although my arms are covered with gnarly sailor and punk tattoos and I'm wearing a huge bondage dog collar and tight butch black clothes and knee-high motorcycle boots, I can still sit with my legs demurely crossed at the knee and smoke a cigarette in a holder and be a total fag. I guess it is a talent of mine. He tells me I should direct the marketing for my new movie towards a 'regular' audience,

25 The Prince of the Homosexuals (Bruce LaBruce)

and steer clear of the ghettoisation of the gay and lesbian film festival circuit. I'm at a bit of a loss to think how an explicit movie about a washed-up gay porno star who is shown sucking a lot of cocks and getting fucked up the ass could appeal to a heterosexual crowd, but I guess you can market anything these days. And you know, somehow I think he's right.

Here, then, is my dilemma. I, Bruce LaBruce, the Prince of the Homosexuals, one of the most famous fags in the world, do not now, nor have I ever felt part of any gay community. Don't get me wrong – I love being gay, and if I had a choice, I wouldn't be any other way. But there's something about gay society as it exists today that really goads me. When I first came to the big city as a naive, virgin farmboy, desperate to lose my cherry, it offered me no solace. Yes, I cruised the bars then, unsuccessfully, ineptly, but I always found it a cruel, impenetrable world, as impenetrable, it seemed, as I was, though not for lack of trying. I never quite understood why everyone

192

tried to look like everybody else, and why if you didn't conform to the precise uniform, and the Pavlovian behavioural patterns, and the doctrinaire politics, you were treated with a contempt that you might expect to be reserved for some kind of enemy. To me, it was as cold and uninviting a country as the straight world that loathed me. I began to work the streets, not because I needed the money, particularly, but because it felt like a warm exile by comparison. I hung out in front of the French Embassy with the hustlers (although never really feeling like a member of their community, either), getting picked up by lonely, married men in family cars with photos of their wives and kids taped to the speedometer, and listened to their problems after blow-jobs in seedy lakefront motels. It was oddly comforting for a while, but then it started to get sad, so I stopped.

Eventually, I fell in with a bunch of punks. The gay underworld used to be the refuge for misfits and malcontents, a meeting place not only for the sexually adventurous, but for anyone who didn't fit in, or resisted being programmed, or was rejected or ostracised by the heterosexual system. But now punk had become the repository of lost souls, and all the excesses and conceits of style and political radicalism and the pure anarchic melodrama that had once been the crowning glory of homosexual disenfranchisement suddenly belonged to a mob of snot-nosed, fucked-up kids. The gay scene must have been kind of like this once: rebellious and wild and impulsive, full of individuals who knew how to become part of a movement without sacrificing their own style and temperament and ideas. That's what punk was, for a while. But today, political correctness has even brought punk to its knees, everyone adhering to the party line. It almost makes me long for the days when my girlfriends would have to protect me from getting beat up at the hard-core show.

I'm not going to be a fucking sentimentalist now, and I'm not going to write about punk, because whenever anybody tries to, they come off sounding really stupid. Punk isn't supposed to be written about, just like 'queercore' fanzines aren't supposed to be catalogued and historicised and analysed to death, for Christsake. They're supposed to be disposable. That's the whole point. Throw your fanzines away right now. Go ahead. Xeroxed material doesn't last forever anyway, you know. It fades. I'm not going to write about punk because sometimes to explain is to weaken. All I can say is that once again, I became disillusioned. Oh, it was a dangerous, edgy, intense milieu, and I lived in a dilapidated household of militant women who taught me everything I know, but the scene itself didn't exactly put out the welcome mat for a raving queen like myself. In fact I was beat up on more than one occasion simply for being me: for showing super-8 movies with brash homosexual content, or appearing in bands with a decidedly fruity demeanour. I even fell in love with a skinhead hustler who hated fags, and, during our tempestuous relationship, got the shit beat out of me on more than one occasion. It was entertaining at the time (sort of), but I longed for something better. That's how we came up with the idea of homocore: the bastard child of two once exciting, volatile underground movements, gay and punk (now failed and spent), the little bugger who knew how to boost the best from both worlds.

Homocore had its day, I suppose, but utopian ideologies hatched in cold basement apartments on long, lonely nights never really stand up to the light of day. You have to understand that fanzine editors live in an imaginary world of ideas protected by the anonymity of the mail. We invent ourselves on paper however we choose, create an ideal version of ourselves, or a monstrous one, give it a name and an identity, and drop it off at the post office, waiting patiently for it to take on a life of its own.

At least that's what I did. Bruce LaBruce was, originally, a fiction, a character that I longed to be. At first I tried to maintain a certain distance between myself and my pseudonym – I even interviewed myself in more than one periodical – but the day came when I had to venture out into the real world and live the part. You don't know how terrifying it was. For years I felt like I could never live up to the image I had created, but not so long ago I suddenly realised that reality and fiction had become indistinguishable, and as in a bad ventriloquist dummy movie, the puppet had finally taken over the act.

Things are different now, and the world can never be the same after Kim Gordon's[7] Gap ad. (I'm sure I meant that as a compliment, particularly considering how amazing she looks in it.) Apparently I have become some kind of spokesmodel for a movement called 'queercore', a word that I cannot even write without putting quotation marks around it. I have also been lumped in with something called 'The New Queer Cinema', which to me is equally meaningless. You see, I don't feel I have a lot in common with a bunch of rich kids with degrees in semiotic theory who make dry, academic films with overdetermined AIDS metaphors and Advocate Men in them. I've never felt comfortable with the new 'queer' movement, never attended a Queer Nation meeting or participated in any marches or protests or actions. Some people may think that's irresponsible, but what can I say? I've never been able to surrender my mind to prefabricated dogma, or reduce my politics to a slogan, or even situate myself in a fixed position on the political spectrum. No, I'm not 'queer', and I don't know why they had to go and ruin a perfectly good word, either. They are so gay.

What I am, I think, is the reluctant pornographer. I've had to ask myself lately how it is that an innocent farmboy who didn't lose his virginity until he was twenty-three, who had a perfectly healthy, wholesome Waltons childhood, has come to the point of disseminating pornography on a global scale. There is no pornography industry in Canada – I mean, essentially, I'm it. So why do I put myself in the position of having film labs call the cops on me, of having people pull morality trips on me, of driving directors of photography into the nut house, with me not far behind? I don't really have an answer to that question, except to say that I seem to be at my happiest flat on my back with my legs in the air in front of a whirring camera. I guess that's my way of asking the world to love me.

NOTES

1 *Who's Afraid of Virginia Woolf?* (Mike Nichols, USA, 1966), the brilliant film version of Albee's play, starred Elizabeth Taylor, Richard Burton, Sandy Dennis and George Segal as two married couples who, one evening, get together to play intense psychological games and shout a lot. The film was nominated for nine Oscars and won three: Taylor, in one of her best performances on film, won her second Best Actress Oscar; Dennis won Best Supporting Actress; and Haskell Weskler was awarded the Best Cinematographer gong. Some have speculated, though he denies it, that Albee intended the play to depict two gay couples.

2 Dita is the name of the character adopted by Madonna in her role as guide to the sleazy side of life in her book, *Sex*.

3 AIDS Coalition To Unleash Power – direct action, AIDS campaigning organisation. ACTUP began in the US but there are now local groups in Canada, Australia, the UK and several other European countries.

4 Gay and Lesbian Alliance Against Defamation – US campaigning group which attempts to promote 'positive images' of homosexuality in the mainstream media – and to banish 'negative' ones.

5 Amy Fisher shot to fame in the US in 1993 by shooting her lover's wife. US TV companies fought to be the first to make a mini-series out of her life and several conflicting versions – either siding with Fisher or with her errant partner – were screened. Fisher went to jail for ten to fifteen years; her lover was given a suspended sentence for abusing Fisher.

6 *Play It As It Lays* was directed in 1972 by Frank Perry for Universal Studios. It was adapted by Joan Didion and John Gregory Dunne from Didion's novel. Starring Anthony Perkins and Tuesday Weld, it is described in *Halliwell's Film Guide* (Paladin, London, 1988, p.816) thus: 'An unsuccessful actress takes stock of her wrecked life. With-it melodrama which audiences preferred to be without.'

7 Kim Gordon is a member of indie-band, Sonic Youth, the mothers and fathers of grunge/noise music. Kim herself is also seen as the mother of the 'riot grrrl' movement, riot girls being a continuation of Minnie the Minx by other means: punk attitude with a feminist twist. Gap is a US clothing company, specialising in quality casual wear mainly consisting of variations on the theme of jeans and T-shirt. They have run for several years a highly effective ad. campaign featuring a number of celebrities, photographed in black and white by fashionable photographers such as Herb Ritts.

Part V
THE MIRROR IMAGE

10

'BY WOMEN, FOR WOMEN AND ABOUT WOMEN' RULES OK?

The impossibility of visual soliloquy

Anna Marie Smith

The defence of 'alternative' sexually explicit imagery has become an urgent task for feminists. These images, which range from the low budget lesbian 'zines to feminist-oriented safer sex material, are playing an important role in interrupting sexist discourse, heterosexism and AIDS demonisations. Feminists are, of course, divided on the question of censorship; for the most part, anti-censorship feminists have to defend these alternative discourses from attacks by both the state and other feminists. Although the anti-censorship feminists' political work is extremely valuable, they often reproduce traditional arguments about representation. Viewed in terms of this traditional framework, the defence of alternative images often becomes self-contradictory

THE PORNOGRAPHIC IMAGE: TOTALLY OMNIPOTENT OR ABSOLUTELY HARMLESS?

Many feminists, for example, reject the pro-censorship feminists' claim that pornographic images directly cause the viewer to engage in violent acts against women. In other words, they reject the claim that there is absolutely no gap between the misogynist essence of sexually explicit material and the misogynist practices of sexual harassment and rape. Feminists who oppose censorship insist on the responsibility of all social agents: even if individual men are influenced by sexist images, they must nevertheless bear the responsibility for the very real choices that they make, especially when these choices contribute to the oppression of women. With post-structuralist critics, they also argue that no text has an 'essential' meaning; even the most explicit *sexual* image may or may not have a *sexist* connotation. The connotation of a sexual image depends on the ways in which multiple codes are intertwined together in that particular instance. As such, we cannot define sexist elements in abstraction. The distinction between non-sexist sexually explicit material and sexist sexually explicit material must always be established with respect to particular texts, and these texts must be evaluated in terms of their specific contexts.

The pro-censorship feminists rule this contextualisation out of order (Smith 1993). They define sexist images in abstraction – by virtually equating sexual explicitness with sexism. They further claim that sexist images have an omnipotent effect on both female and male subjects. Women supposedly suffer a direct loss of self-esteem after exposure to this imagery. Indeed, pro-censorship feminists allege that minority women – women of colour and poor women – are especially vulnerable to induction into the sex trade industry, and they claim that it is pornography's self-enclosed cycle of sexist images/ sexual abuse which causes these women's disproportionate participation in the sex trade – rather than complex socio-economic relations of oppression. Men supposedly increase their misogynistic behaviour, including discriminatory acts and violence, towards women after viewing pornographic imagery. These claims legitimate further state intervention in the already over-policed terrain of consensual adult sexuality and disempower women in that they reduce women to helpless victims of both sexism and sexuality.

Pro-censorship feminists attempt to support their claims by presenting a profoundly distorted description of pornography which places an extreme emphasis on sado-masochistic materials. Given their narrow agenda, pro-censorship feminists fail to focus on the real problem. Female desire *is* depicted in a sexist manner in much of soft-core and hard-core pornography. We should not, however, give further licence to popular anxieties and demonisations around sexuality and sexual minorities in advancing this critique of sexist pornography. The conflation of *sexuality* and *sexism* only invites extremely dangerous appropriations of the feminist critique by agents who are hardly motivated by genuine feminist concerns. Right-wing religious fundamentalists such as the American Family Association and right-wing extremists such as Senator Jesse Helms claim that they are truly concerned about defending women from violent sexist crimes. However, their censorship campaign has targeted Robert Mapplethorpe's explicit photographs of gay male s/m sex and Karen Finley's performance art which actually deals with the sexual abuse of women.

Against these distortions of feminist politics, we have to insist on the fact that sexism is not extraordinarily located within sexually explicit representations. Any representation which naturalises the strategic claim that women are inherently inferior to men is a sexist representation. It could be found in a religious text, a literary classic, a silence in a corporate boardroom, a popular television show, a rock, opera or rap lyric, an insult traded between two gay men, or a government bill. A sexist representation may suggest that women are not the moral equals of men, or that women are not equal participants in the public sphere and hence cannot be treated like equal citizens, or that women ought to be barred from certain military positions because of their natural feminine dispositions, or that women are inherently unsuited to senior corporate and government decision-making positions, or that women are naturally at home with repetitive piece work and that it is therefore just that women are disproportionately concentrated in the most exploitative manufacturing occupations. A sexually explicit sexist representation simply takes this basic theme and recodes it around sexual imagery: it disempowers women by legitimating the notion that women are, by nature, not equal to men within sexual relationships.

Against the religious fundamentalists, we have to insist that the problem with sexist pornography is not that it is explicit, kinky, anti-family, anti-Christian or pro-queer. Sexist pornography is sexist because, like other sexist representations which can be found throughout our social spaces, it erases alternative representations – representations which empower women by depicting us as fully choosing subjects, actively *choosing* our lesbianism or heterosexuality, traditional sex practices or kinkiness, from a wide range of possibilities – in so far as it renders these alternatives unthinkable. Ultimately, there is very little difference between sexist pornography and religious fundamentalism; both of these discourses naturalise women's subordination and attempt to disempower women by erasing our challenges to patriarchal oppression and compulsory heterosexuality.

The continuities between the pro-censorship feminists' discourse and that of the supporters of Section 28 in Britain are also striking. Section 28 of the Local Government Act 1987–8 prohibits local governments from promoting homosexuality. The entire 'promotion of homosexuality' crisis was manufactured by right-wing bigots who took the few modest initiatives of a small number of local governments totally out of context. Policy proposals around curriculum review and equal opportunities were exaggerated, linked with gay liberation slogans from the early 1970s, supported by distortions and untruths about the availability of sexual education material, and verified through sheer repetition. The Tories who drafted the Section claimed an omnipotent status for 'positive images' of homosexuals. They argued that everyone is open to corruption of their 'true' heterosexuality, to the extent that the mere exposure of school children to an openly lesbian or gay teacher, or to non-judgemental teaching materials on homosexuality, was supposed to be a sufficient means for this corruption. Images in the classroom on their own – rather than relationships within the family, identifications, fantasies and desires – were supposed to have this tremendous power to determine sexual identities. Some feminist and lesbian and gay critics of Section 28 located this legislation in terms of the broader anxiety around the unfixity of identity in British New Right discourse. These critics of Section 28 have much in common with the anti-censorship feminists. Both groups argue that identity formation is an extremely complex process which cannot be reduced to a causal model – that children cannot be made homosexual, and men cannot be made into rapists, through their mere exposure to certain images. Both groups also share a similar political strategy: they object to the official regulation of consensual sexual practices by the state, and they defend the rights of lesbians, gays and feminists to produce radically pro-queer and pro-feminist representations.

While I would agree that children cannot be made homosexual and men cannot be made into rapists by images alone, it is not at all clear where we go from here in our understanding of the political role of representations. If sexual images do not by their nature install an identity in the consumer which corresponds exactly to the supposed essence of the image, they also do not remain purely external to the viewer's identity. A return to the traditional conception of the viewer as a fully constituted subject, as a substance already there before discourse, is hardly a promising alternative to the pro-censorship model of causality. Even among the feminists who oppose censorship, there are many different approaches to this problem. Some argue that fantasy is an entirely autonomous realm: they say that fantasies do not cause any particular behaviour to take place and that fantasies are therefore blameless. These feminists quite rightly reject the conception that women who have 'politically incorrect' fantasies should feel guilty about them and are merely perpetuating their own oppression through their own desires. However, they attempt to reject the causal model of the pro-censorship camp by proposing its exact opposite, namely that fantasies have absolutely no effect whatsoever on practices and identities.

In the recent debates within Feminists Against Censorship in London, for example, some members have argued that sexual fantasies in particular occupy a purely separate realm which stands apart from 'reality'. They say that while it is problematic and undesirable for some people to entertain deeply racist fantasies, such as those of Enoch Powell or David Duke, sexual fantasies are above criticism by definition, since they have no material effect. While the theoretical problems with this special autonomous status of sexual fantasies are enormous, this model also presents various practical problems. Safer sex campaigns, for example, are located on the terrain of sexual fantasies, and seek to rescript those fantasies as a way of promoting different sexual practices. The effects of these campaigns demonstrate quite clearly that although images do not cause certain behaviours, they certainly do influence desire. As Slavoj Žižek argues, desire is constituted through fantasy; it is through fantasy that we 'learn how to desire' (Zizek 1990: 118). If fantasies did indeed have no effect whatsoever on practices and identities, then the entire project of producing feminist sexual imagery to displace sexist sexual imagery would become merely an interesting amusement rather than an intensely political intervention.

Other anti-censorship feminists accept that fantasies do contribute to the complex process of identity formation and contestation, and argue that we must pay close attention to the effects of specific sexual images. One of the many approaches to reading these images centres on contextual analysis. When pro-censorship feminists present their usual lists of images which they believe should be restricted, anti-censorship feminists argue that radically different representations, some with sexist and some with non-sexist effects, are illegitimately grouped together in this *a priori* list. In Britain, pro-censorship feminists have reproduced the McKinnon/Dworkin by-law terminology verbatim. Both the pamphlet of the Campaign Against Censorship and Pornography and Dawn Primarolo's Private Member's Bill, which would restrict the display of pornographic material, define pornography as representations which 'objectify women' or 'depict body parts for the purposes of sexual arousal'. Like the McKinnon/Dworkin approach, pornography is defined without any attention whatsoever to context. Given these proposals for new pornography laws, the demand for a contextual approach is more than an academic issue. The new laws on pornography would virtually grant the police and the magistrates a licence to single out feminist and lesbian and gay images for regulation in the name of feminism.

In the United States, the anti-pornography lobbies which were organised around the MacKinnon–Dworkin initiatives faced strong criticism from feminists, lesbians and gays, booksellers, and artists on the grounds that these initiatives constituted a threat to civil liberties. Similar concerns about the appropriation of feminist anti-pornography initiatives by anti-lesbian and anti-gay police forces and judicial systems have arisen in Canada. In February 1992, the Canadian Supreme Court redefined obscene material as sexual representations which 'cause harm' through 'degrading' and 'dehumanising' portrayals, including bondage and s/m. Kathleen Mahoney, the lawyer who represented the Women's Legal Education and Action Fund in court, explained the strategy behind their 'victory'.

> We showed them the porn – and among the seized videos were some horrifically violent and degrading gay movies. We made the point that the abused men in these films were being treated like women – and the judges got it. Otherwise, men can't put themselves in our shoes. Porn makes women's subordination look sexy and appealing; it doesn't threaten men's jobs, safety, rights or credibility.
>
> (Landsberg 1992)

In other words, LEAF did not ask the court to make the crucial distinction between sexism and sexual explicitness, two distinct elements which may or may not coincide with one another. It made no attempt to place graphic sexual materials in their various contexts. Finally, it gave free rein to the classic anti-gay male trope: men being dominated and penetrated by other men are 'abused' and 'degraded' because they are being 'treated like women'. Their initiative had its origin in feminist intentions, succeeded because of the anti-gay male bigotry of the courts, and had the effect of censoring lesbian sexuality. A lesbian sex magazine, which was on sale at a lesbian and gay bookshop, was targeted in the first obscenity prosecution following this decision. Glad Day bookshop in Toronto was charged for selling the American lesbian sex magazine, *Bad Attitude*, because it contained images of lesbian s/m sex.

ANNA MARIE SMITH

THE 'BY WOMEN, FOR WOMEN, ABOUT WOMEN' CRITERIA

Although I would agree that contextualisation of images is exactly where we should start in the discussion of their effects, it has become apparent that many of us are working with different conceptions of contextualisation. Some anti-censorship feminists argue that it is the images which are 'by women, for women and about women' which we ought to defend, as if these images are, by definition, not sexist, and as if this description adequately captures all the images which we ought to defend. Paying attention to the context of the image is understood in terms of an analysis of the subject-position of the producer, her intended audience and her intended effects. The possibility of a radical contextualisation of the image – in which the intentions and identity of the producer are bracketed, and the meaning or effects of the image are analysed in terms of the place of the image within a broader text; the relations between that text and other texts; the specificity of the image as a unique fabric, constructed through the weaving together of many different codes; the ways in which these codes run through the image and other images; the absences, moments of interruption and self-contradiction in the image; and so on – is simply ruled out.

By placing their faith in the images which are 'by women, for women and about women', these anti-censorship feminists, like the pro-censorship feminists, are actually reproducing many traditional conceptions of representation. This argument presupposes that women are, in their essential nature, inherently endowed with a privileged knowledge of the distinction between sexist and non-sexist images, and possess some special faculty for producing non-sexist images. It is in this sense that this feminist argument closely resembles the highly problematic conception of truth and representation which can be found, for example, in Plato's *Republic* (Plato 1968: 377c–379a).

The 'for women only' aspect also resembles traditional models. By women – for women – about women : the guarantee here is that nothing which is not 'womanly' is involved in the production/consumption process. In this case, the production/consumption process is supposed to be completely purified of any element of otherness, the not-womanly. This is, in other words, supposed to be a perfectly 'safe' space because of its perfectly self-enclosed character. Within this enclave, communication is supposed to be free from any impediment or distortion. Thanks to the absence of otherness, the images produced are supposed to be nothing but the pure reflection of the 'truth' about women's sexuality. Absolutely nothing is added or taken away from this truth, since male-defined images and the imperatives of external interests are wholly excluded. We would do nothing but speak the truths about ourselves, by ourselves and for ourselves, as the absence of otherness would transform our discourse into the ideal form of soliloquy. In other words, the 'by women, for women and about women' guarantee is just as ideal as, for example, Husserl's conception of soliloquy in his *Logical Investigations*

(Husserl 1970). Feminist separatist dreams are hardly original; in this case, the form of the argument has been borrowed from texts which are central to the philosophical tradition. As such, the 'by women, for women and about women' guarantee is just as vulnerable to deconstruction as any other text.[1]

As an idealisation of soliloquy, the logic of this guarantee is self-contradictory. If we could indeed construct a woman-only space for 'our own' communication, then there would be no need to talk to ourselves, to represent ourselves to ourselves, for we would already know the truth about ourselves before a single word was uttered, before a single line was drawn. Instead of this absence of womanly signification, however, we are confronted with excess: a virtual explosion of discourse about representation between/for/by women. It is this excess itself which shows the impossibility of a womanly soliloquy. Many texts nevertheless claim to occupy this impossible space. Other texts explicitly refuse the universal and neutral claims of the woman-only project, drawing attention instead to the ways in which the fantasy of a singular woman-only space can only be constructed through the exclusion of the not-white, the not-middle class, the not-heterosexual, the not-normal, and so on (Butler 1990: 5–6).

The 'by women, for women and about women' phrase has nevertheless become a kind of marketing slogan or a feminist seal of approval. On the back cover of a 1985 issue of the lesbian magazine *On Our Backs: The Magazine for the Adventurous Lesbian*,[2] an advertisement for the three video tapes, *Private Pleasures*, *Fun With a Sausage*, and *Shadows*, features the sales pitch: 'Order Now Page 43: Lesbian acted, directed, produced and filmed.' An advertisement for the lesbian sex tape, *Shadows*, in the January/February 1991 issue includes a text which states that the two models in the tape are a 'real life' lesbian couple. I do not want to undermine the defence of these materials. I also do not want to ignore the material effects of impossible space-claims: even if a woman-only space is impossible, there are strategic situations in which it can be extremely useful to demand affirmative action for women and to organise woman-only caucuses, housing, services, sex clubs and so on. It would be highly illegitimate to deploy the tools of psychoanalysis and deconstruction to dismiss the importance of these kinds of arguments; even if they are sometimes buttressed by problematic invocations of separate spaces and essentialist subjects (and perhaps these invocations are indeed inevitable in every case), they must be defended.

I think that it would nevertheless be useful to ask two questions about this 'seal of approval': does it really work as a guarantee of the non-sexist effects of images which meet these criteria, and is the 'by women, for women and about women' ideal an actual possibility?

There are many examples of images which both meet these criteria and nevertheless have sexist effects. For example, representations of women as unthinking pawns of the patriarchal system who need to be rescued from their false consciousness by other women who have somehow achieved a true

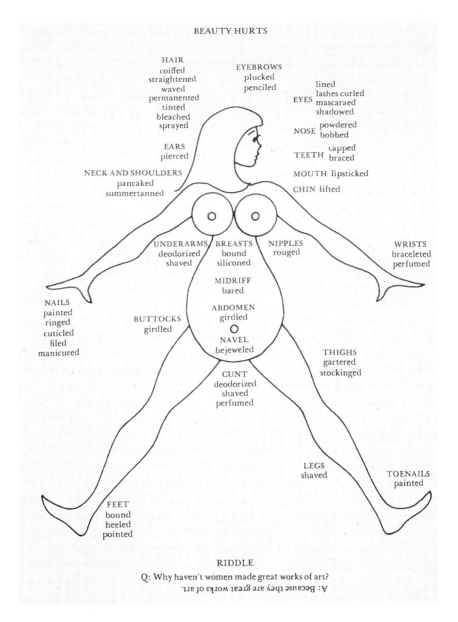

26 From Andrea Dworkin, *Women-Hating* (Dutton, New York, 1974, p.117)

grasp of their real interests are common in the pro-censorship feminist arguments around sex trade workers. In this image, femininity, make-up, fashion, piercing and jewellery are equated with the 'bimbo' stereotype, as if virtually any feminine identity game were, by definition, a total capitulation to the all-powerful demands of the patriarchy. It is one thing to criticise the oppressive aspects of the fashion industry, but it is quite another to argue that feminine identity games signify nothing but victimisation. Instead of em-powering women, this representation erases alternative texts as unthinkable. It suggests that there is absolutely no possibility of subverting and redefining the feminine body, and that women who engage in these practices are at best brainless dupes, and at worst, traitors of the worst kind. The stylisation of the breasts, the spread-open limbs and the facial expression all contribute to the erasure of this figure's subjectivity; she is reduced to a depersonalised specimen whose formalised surfaces allow us to observe the effects of her total subjection to the omnipotent patriarchal forces. We supposedly do not need to consider a particular image of a specific feminine body, since the patriarchal imperative produces an endless monotony of quiescent feminine clones. In this particular case, the 'by women, for women, and about women' guarantee has failed us. In its erasure of women's subjectivity, the effects of this image are quite sexist, and yet, as an illustration from Andrea Dworkin's *Women-Hating*, it was produced by women, for women and about women.

Other sexual images fail the 'by women, for women and about women' test and yet still have non-sexist and even anti-sexist connotations. The Madonna video, *Justify My Love* (1990), directed by the French photographer Jean Baptiste Mondino, is a case in point. The video borrows a typical narrative from heterosexual male pornography, namely the male figure watching two women touching and kissing each other. In this version of the narrative, however, it is the female figure who is scripting the scene. In her body language and her spoken lyrics, she seductively invites the male figure to have sex with her, but when he takes the initiative, she stops him and says, 'No, not like that.' Through a series of editing manoeuvres, the viewer then becomes confused about the gender of her partner: we are shown an androgynous facial profile of the figure who is kissing Madonna and a pan down the figure's back reveals a glimpse of lingerie. In the next shot, the point of view is reversed, and it becomes clear that the male figure from the original scene is watching rather than participating in the scene. There is a sense, however, that rather than reducing lesbian sexuality to the demands of a narrowly defined set of male heterosexual interests, this scene has been set up by the female figures: the male figure seems to occupy the position of the voyeur only in so far as he has been placed there by the female figures as a support for their exhibitionism.

The dominant role of women as determining the gaze of the viewer is reinforced in the following sequence. A male figure wearing the gear of a submissive s/m fetishist is seated on a chair, looking in the direction of the two female figures on the bed. He is approached by a third female figure who sports the cap and facial expression of a dominatrix. In one fluid movement, she grasps his chin and firmly turns his head towards her own, obliging him to focus his gaze on the exact point of her own choosing. In another gender game, two androgynous figures are shown drawing stylised pencil-moustaches on each other's faces. They part to reveal Madonna, sitting on the bed behind them, laughing. At the end of the video, it is the original male figure who is left behind in a dishevelled state, reaching out and wanting more, while Madonna walks down the hotel corridor, laughing once again. With these various subversive interventions in a typical pornographic narrative, the *Justify My Love* video playfully redefines heterosexual male codes and creates instead a valuable representation of female sexuality in terms of sex-positive imagery and freely chosen practices. This video should in this sense be categorised as an alternative to sexist pornography, even though it fails the 'by women, for women and about women' guarantee.

I am nevertheless quite reluctant to position the *Justify* video as an exemplary text, for it depends upon a problematic articulation of racial codes. What, for example, should we make of the way in which Madonna's whiteness is heightened in contrast to the black dancing figure and her Latino/Latina sexual partners? To what extent does Madonna occupy the privileged position of the choosing subject – she is the only figure who enters and exits the hotel room, and we must therefore assume that the others remain locked within the sexual tableaux – through her whiteness? Her whiteness becomes the passport for her subjectivity, in the sense that it is through her occupation of the universal position of whiteness that she becomes permitted to take a 'walk on the wild side', just like the boys do.

The racial tradition which is reactivated through these images is as old as the West's encounter with the 'Orient'. White Europeans have classified the Oriental other as the earthy, sensual, passionate, irrational and sexually promiscuous counterpart to the rational and civilised Westerner (Said 1985). The myth of racial superiority has always been twinned with a theory of sexual liberation through racial otherness. Where white Europeans have recognised that the pursuit of rational civilisation has necessitated alienation and repression, they/we have always imagined that figures of racial otherness are completely available to them/us as the sensual medium for the recovery of an integrated self. Where Madonna turns to specifically black and Latino/Latina figures for her night of sexual freedom, she is treading the same path as countless whites who have similarly used racial difference as a doorway into their own sexual 'hearts of darkness'. Fanon quotes an African-American teacher who states, '"The presence of Negroes beside the whites is in a way an insurance policy on humanness. When the whites feel that they have become too mechanised, they turn to the men of colour and ask them for a little human sustenance."' Fanon then comments, 'At last I had been recognised, I was no longer a zero' (Fanon 1986: 129). The racial codes in

208

the *Justify* video, then, are far from innocent, for they become coherent only in so far as they reinvoke the racist Orientalist tradition. Alternatives to sexist pornography ought to empower women as choosing subjects, but our subjectivity should not be constructed through the fetishistic containment of black bodies within racist phantasmatic frames.

'TO BE REAL': DYKES DO FAG DRAG

The 'by women, for women and about women' 'seal of approval' is, actually, false advertising on two counts. Not only does it fail to guarantee the effects of the image, it also promises conditions of production and consumption which are virtually unobtainable. Frontiers never actually operate like the ideal boundaries in the soliloquy model: boundaries always fail to protect a separate space from the constitutive effects of otherness. Even the attempt to exclude 'male-defined' interests from the woman-only space ultimately constructs the woman-only space as the not-male-defined space. Frontiers also never reduce each of the two divided spheres to pure homogeneity. As soon as two chains of equivalence are constructed, such as the opposition, all 'womanly' elements versus all male-defined elements, these equivalences are interrupted by differences. In different contexts, different male-defined elements will take on different values, depending on the specific ways in which they are linked together with other elements in particular contexts.

Lesbians, for example, have drawn extensively on 'male' texts in creating sexual scripts and role-playing. Sex toys, videos, magazines and fine art images have been borrowed, refitted, redesigned and redefined. In two recently published lesbian photographic collections, *Love Bites* (Grace 1991) and *Stolen Glances* (Boffin and Fraser 1991), these appropriations have been explored in particularly subversive ways. The accusation that this presence of male-ness, in what is supposed to be a womanly image, necessarily defines that image as nothing but male-defined and anti-woman, is far too simplistic. It should be noted that lesbians tend to draw on not just any so-called male texts, but on those texts which have already begun to subvert gender roles and heterosexism. As Julia Creet puts it, 'Lesbian male-ness may be a "gay maleness" – not a re-enactment of fixed gender roles, but an exploration of the very signs, "male" and "female"' (Creet 1991: 33). This is not to say that gay male texts are inherently non-sexist; there is no such thing as an essential gay male text, and gay male-ness is all too often intertwined with sexist codes. However, because some gay male codes are structured in terms of a parody of sexist and heterosexist definitions of gender roles, they are in a sense already prepared for a further subversive redefinition for lesbians.

This borrowing and subversive redefining is becoming more explicit in contemporary lesbian imagery. A sex 'zine in San Francisco, *A Taste of Latex: The 'Zine for the Sexually Disenfranchised*,[3] caters to both lesbians and gay men, heterosexual perverts and queers, traditionally gendered people

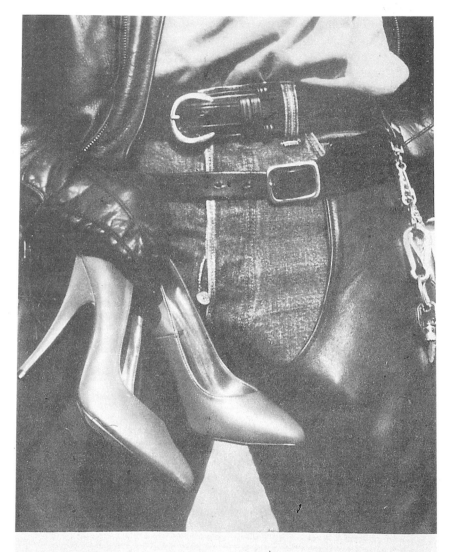

"Straight boys don't know how to give me what I want."

27 From *Taste of Latex* (Winter 1990–1; photograph by L.B.)

and transsexuals and transvestites. In the Winter 1990–1 issue, 'Carol Queen' offers a story about one of her sexual encounters with gay men. She dresses to pass as a gay man herself, and is picked up by an older gay man in leathers, a typical gay male 'daddy'. She begins to suck his cock, but then he discovers that she is actually a woman. He says that she must be bisexual, she insists that she identifies as a lesbian. He asks, 'Why waste this on gay men? Straight boys must fall for you.' Again, she insists on the uniquely queer character of her desire in her reply. 'Straight boys don't know how to give me what I want. Besides, your cock says I'm not wasting this on you.' She changes into lesbian-femme clothing, and encourages him to dominate her. At the end of the story, with the daddy figure wondering aloud how he himself is going to be dominated and penetrated in this scene, she reaches into her bag for her strap-on dildo.

'Carol Queen''s story is not, of course, an isolated text. In a photo essay on relationships for the Valentine's Day issue of *Outweek* in February 1991, a butch-femme lesbian couple are captured sharing a passionate kiss. The photograph remains faithful to lesbian traditions; the motorcycles, the lace of the femme, the tattoo of the butch, and the short hairstyles are all signifiers of lesbian culture. The texts which accompany the photographs of lovers and

ALISTAIR FATE & DIANE MELE

DIANE: I have a big dick, and so does Alistair. And we both
consider ourselves faggots.

ALISTAIR: It's true. We've had long conversations about that.

28 From *Outweek* (February 1991; photograph by Michael Wakefield)

friends in the photo essay are written testimonies by the models about their relationships. In this case, however, the text interrupts the codes in the photograph. Diane says, 'I have a big dick, and so does Alistair. And we both consider ourselves faggots.'

These two women are not kidding. Many lesbians are going beyond the tentative appropriations from gay male culture to take up explicitly gay male-identified positions. In Los Angeles and San Francisco, some lesbians are playing in what they call the 'daddy–boy' scene: they go out in groups, wearing gay male masculine drag, 'packing' strap-on dildoes, using male names, partying in gay male spaces, participating in sex scenes with other gay male-identified lesbians and, in some cases, doing s/m scenes and penetrative sex with gay men. This portrait from the LA lesbian 'zine, *Screambox*[4] refers specifically to this scene. Lesbian photographer Cathy Opie has produced a series of photographic portraits of women who are either involved in or heavily influenced by the 'daddy–boy' scene (Smith 1991). References to lesbian 'daddy–boy' play are also prominent in this personal advertisement from the January/February 1991 issue of *On Our Backs*.

Dyke Needs Daddy
Butch Dyke/Boy looking for Top/Daddy for heavy S/M, TT, bondage, elec., if you're crazy enough to think it, I'm crazy enough to do it. I need to be pushed. No Wimps, No Femmes.

In the 1980s, many lesbians erred on the side of caution when it came to dildoes. They tended to reassure each other that their new-found phallic toys, their dildoes, were actually women-identified sex aids which had absolutely nothing to do with gender roles. Put on the defensive after the decades of normalising readings of Freud's conception of female penis envy, they wanted to refuse the suggestion that lesbians, like all women, actually did want to have a penis in their sex lives. Pat Califia, for example, wrote in *Sapphistry*,

> The dildoes available in sex shops are usually phallic in appearance, so many lesbians prefer to carve or cast their own. . . . A real lesbian who wants to play with a dildo has motives that would be incomprehensible to the makers of commercial erotica or to clinical psychologists. . . . She knows that women don't need men to be sexual. . . . Using a dildo puts the mythology about them into perspective. It is, after all, just a piece of plastic. Whatever symbolic meaning it has is assigned by our culture.
>
> (Califia 1983: 50–1)

The 'daddy–boy' lesbians of the 1990s may be less concerned about becoming 'real lesbians', but they are following Califia and other lesbian pioneers in the exploration of the infinite plasticity of 'male' roles, images and sex toys. In this discourse, dildoes are not substitute penises which don't quite make up for the lack of the 'real thing'; for these lesbians, their dildoes

Your parents should be happy that you have such a man for a girlfriend.

29 From *Screambox* (November 1990; portrait and text by Pam Gregg)

are the 'real thing': gay male cocks. They are saying that lesbians can put on or take off these gay male cocks at will, without ever abandoning or weakening their claim to their own lesbian identities. Indeed, the gay male cock, in the context of these self-described lesbian representations, can be a finger, a dildo, a nipple, a clit, a tongue or even an idea. Instead of marking a retreat to the already well-worn conception of bisexuality, these appropriations constitute a subversion of the entire lesbian/gay male distinction.

The lesbian 'daddy–boy' discourse, like Madonna's *Justify My Love* video, utterly fails the 'by women, for women and about women' criteria, but nevertheless has the potential to interrupt sexist discourse. These two examples, however, should not be regarded as exceptions to the rule. The conception that discourses can be categorised in terms of the simple typology, woman-identified versus male-identified, is an essentialist myth. The lesbian daddy–boy discourse is only exceptional in that it explicitly shows that which essentialist discourse on gender and sexuality wants to conceal, namely the constant appropriations and redefinitions which take place across gender distinctions, the already differentiated character of 'woman-identified' and 'male-identified' discourses, and the possibilities of creating new genders and sexualities which at least partially escape the sexist and heterosexist containment of female sexuality.

'I CAN PLAY, BUT YOU'VE GOT TO BE REAL': RACISM AND GENDER GAMES

Sexual gender subversion, however, is not in itself subversive. Gay male drag has often become the site of both vicious misogyny and an internal critique of masculine norms. The racial dimension of many of our apparently 'subversive' texts is also highly problematic. Many white lesbians borrow the clothing, jewellery, body decoration, language and gestures of native people, Latinos/Latinas and blacks. These appropriations are creative strategies of empowerment, but at what point do they lose their innocence and become colonising and racist? Lesbian 'visibility' has often depended on racial representations. In stereotypical readings of butch/femme imagery, for example, it is usually argued that the femme 'passes' as straight, and that the butch performs the subversive role of visibly opposing heterosexual codes. Where the butch/femme couple is cross-racial, it is often assumed that the black woman is, by nature, the butch. Indeed, stereotypes of butches as working class and as racially 'other', in contrast to their whiter and more privileged femme counterparts, are common in lesbian texts.[5] The 'new' lesbian identity games of the 1990s may in fact reproduce some very old codes, and racial otherness may yet again be pressed into service by white women in an oppressive manner. While some queers of colour are actively exploring the role of racial difference in gender subversion,[6] white queers ought to devote far more attention to this crucial problem.

NOTES

This essay is a somewhat revised version of a paper which I presented at the Outspoken Differences Conference, Institute of the Contemporary Arts, London, on 13 April 1991. I would like to thank Sunil Gupta in particular for his contribution to our panel.

1 I am borrowing Derrida's critique of soliloquy in Husserl's phenomenological account of spoken communication (Derrida 1973: 32–47). I am adding two new twists to the argument: first, I am applying it to visual imagery – hence the almost nonsensical phrase, visual soliloquy – and second, I am exploring the political implications of the privileging of soliloquy over other forms of representation.
2 *On Our Backs* is a bimonthly magazine published by Blush Entertainment, 526 Castro Street, San Francisco, CA 94114, USA.
3 *Taste of Latex* is published quarterly by Tastefull Productions, PO Box 460122, San Francisco, CA 94146–0122, USA.
4 *Screambox* can be contacted at 7985 Santa Monica Boulevard, Suite 109–51, Los Angeles, CA 90046, USA.
5 My thanks to Biddy Martin who has raised this issue in several presentations at Cornell University.
6 See, for example, the self portrait photography of Lyle Ashton Harris (Harris 1991).

REFERENCES

Boffin, T. and Fraser, J. (1991) *Stolen Glances: Lesbians Take Photographs*, London: Pandora.
Butler, J. (1990) *Gender Trouble*, New York: Routledge.
Califia, P. (1983) *Sapphistry: The Book of Lesbian Sexuality*, Tallahassee: The Naiad Press.
Creet, J. (1991) 'Lesbian Sex/Gay Sex: What's the Difference', *Outlook*, no.11, Winter.
Derrida, J. (1973) *Speech and Phenomena*, trans. David B. Allison, Evanston: Northwestern University Press.
Fanon, F. (1986) *Black Skin, White Masks*, London: Pluto.
Grace, D. (1991) *Love Bites*, London: Gay Men's Press.
Harris, L. A. (1991) 'Revenge of a Snow Queen', *Outlook*, no.13, Summer: 8–13.
Husserl, E. (1970) *Logical Investigations*, trans. J. N. Findlay, London: Routledge & Kegan Paul.
Landsberg, M. (1992) 'Canada: Antipornography Breakthrough in the Law', *Ms*, May/June 1992: 14–15.
Plato (1968) *The Republic of Plato*, trans. Allan Bloom, New York: Basic Books.
Said, E. (1985) *Orientalism*, London: Penguin.
Smith, A. M. (1991) 'The Feminine Gaze: A Profile of Cathy Opie', *The Advocate*, 19 November 1991: 82–3.
Smith, A. M. (1993) '"What is Pornography?" The Rhetoric of the Campaign Against Pornography and Censorship', *Feminist Review*, no.43: 71–87.
Smith, A. M. (1994) *Representing the Enemies Within: British New Right Discourse on Race and Sexuality*, Cambridge: Cambridge University Press.
Žižek, S. (1990) *The Sublime Object of Ideology*, London: Verso.

11

TVOD:
THE NEVER-BENDING STORY

Colin Richardson

Mary Ann: Mom, he's not a strange man, he's a homosexual. I know
you've heard of it. They have them on TV now.
(Tales of the City, Channel 4, 28 September 1993)

Some stories simply have to be told. And where better to tell them than on
TV? For, to adapt Sarah Kozloff's observation, television is now 'the
principal storyteller' in contemporary Western society (Allen 1992: 67). It
occupies such a central and dominant position in our culture that the stories
which television tells have a strange power, the power to shape, even to
define reality: if it hasn't been on TV, it hasn't really happened. In the
1980s, British television started telling a new story, the lesbian and gay
story, and reality shifted a little though not necessarily in predictable
directions.[1]

Just before 11pm on Tuesday, 14 February 1989 – Valentine's Day, no less
– the sense of excitement that had been building for some time, a feeling that
television would never be the same again, took on a tangible form. Channel
4's continuity announcer took a deep breath: 'And now, a lesbian and gay
weekly magazine that invites you to come *Out on Tuesday*.'

Out on Tuesday started as an eight-week series of hour-long episodes.
In 1990, the second series extended to ten weekly episodes, now starting at
the earlier time of 9pm, and this is the format it stuck to – except for one
further change. In 1991, the series moved to Wednesday night and it changed
its name to plain *Out*.[2] In 1992, as the fourth series was staggering to a
close, *Out* was axed. But the story continues, for in 1993 a summer season
of lesbian and gay programmes was broadcast on Channel 4 under the generic
title, *Summer's Out*. At the same time, the channel announced a change of
heart. Director of programmes, John Willis, declared that due to 'widespread
protest', *Out* would be revived in 1994, thus proving that fairy stories do
have happy endings (for the time being, at least).[3]

IN THE BEGINNING: THE CHANNEL 4 STORY

Dorothy: Honey, I didn't even know if you'd know what a lesbian is.
Rose: I could've looked it up!

(The Golden Girls)

Sarah Kozloff argues that every story told on television has three layers of narration. The innermost layer is the *story* itself ('what happens to whom'); then, moving outwards, there is the *discourse* ('how the story is told'); and finally, there is the *schedule* ('how the story and discourse are affected by the text's placement within the larger discourse of the station's schedule') (Allen 1992: 69). The story of *Out* and the stories it told – and, for all I know, will continue to tell – is first and foremost the story of Channel 4. Unless you first understand the channel, you cannot begin to get to grips with *Out*.

Britain's fourth national channel began broadcasting on 2 November 1982, though it is as much a product of 1970s social democratic consensus politics as of 1980s right-wing, free market dogma. The idea of a new channel to complement the existing public service stations, BBC1 and BBC2, and the commercial network, ITV, was first mooted in the late 1970s by James Callaghan's Labour government. However, by the time the enabling legislation was introduced to Parliament in February 1980, there had been a change of government. Mrs Thatcher's Conservative Party had swept to power in May 1979 on a radical right programme of deregulation, tax-cutting and free enterprise. The fourth channel which finally emerged was thus a peculiar mixture of left-wing cultural concerns and right-wing anti-statist obsessions.

The 1980 Broadcasting Act established Channel 4 not as a fully independent company but as a branch of the Independent Broadcasting Authority (IBA).[4] Advertising space was to be sold on the new channel's behalf by the other independent TV companies who, in turn, would remit a set proportion of their total advertising revenues to the channel. In this way, Channel 4 was guaranteed a certain level of income which, to a considerable extent, freed it from the tyranny of the ratings. In addition, as the formal creation of the Conservative government, the channel gained a certain immunity from right-wing criticism which afforded it the room for manoeuvre necessary (if not always sufficient) for the fulfilment of its statutory obligations.

The 1980 Broadcasting Act lays a duty on the IBA with regard to the fourth channel:

(a) to ensure that the programmes contain a suitable proportion of matter calculated to appeal to tastes and interests not generally catered for by ITV;

(b) to ensure that a suitable proportion of the programmes are of an educational nature;

(c) to encourage innovation and experiment in the form and content of programmes, and generally to give the Fourth Channel a distinctive character of its own.

(Broadcasting Act, 1980, section 3(i))

The new channel set out to achieve these aims by adopting a distinctive structure, one unique in British broadcasting. Channel 4 does not make any television programmes, with the exception of the weekly viewer response programme, *Right to Reply*. Instead, it commissions independent production companies to make them and buys in ready-made films and programmes from home and away.

Channel 4's 'appeal to tastes and interests not generally catered for by ITV' has, from the beginning, been very much informed by the politics of identity which sprang up in the 1970s and took root in the 1980s as the continuing political triumph of the right led the left to lose faith in the old verities of the class struggle. As pundits discussed the decline of the working class and prophesied the end of history, an increasingly desperate left identified 'new' oppressed social classes – women, black people, the disabled, lesbians and gay men – which might provide that elusive electoral majority. Though the 'rainbow coalition' turned out to be a political pipe dream, the equal opportunities philosophy which it spawned retains an influential hold upon the cultural imagination – as Channel 4's early pitch for viewers demonstrated.

A commissioning editor for multicultural programmes was an early appointment, for example. The channel also worked closely with the main independent broadcasting union, the ACTT, to support new, community-based production companies (or workshops as they were called) in an effort to give a voice to the culturally disenfranchised, to create a rainbow coalition of the airwaves. Companies run by women and by black people were among those so favoured. In 1984, a lesbian and gay production company, Converse Pictures,[5] was given money to develop two scripts; though, in the event, the company was not awarded workshop status (which would have guaranteed it some broadcast commissions) and the scripts never made it to production.

The programmes that began to emerge from all this, though they only formed part of the channel's output, came to be seen as typical Channel 4 fare. The black sitcom, *No Problem*, was an early and not unsuccessful experiment which ran for several seasons. The fortnightly magazine programmes, *Eastern Eye* and *Black on Black*, which alternated with one another, were also proudly showcased by the new channel as evidence of its commitment to groups hitherto marginalised by mainstream broadcasting. As time went on, the range of programmes 'by and for' various 'minority' groups broadened. There was, for example, *Club Mix*, a live black music show; *Watch the Woman*, an unintentionally hilarious feminist-inclined magazine programme; and *Bandung File*, a current affairs programme which was a harder-edged successor to the earlier black and Asian magazines.

Despite the fact that these programmes were of mixed quality, they held a strange fascination for many lesbian and gay activists. The fact that 'we' didn't have 'our' own show could only be construed as an insult, suggesting that unlike, say, women and black people, lesbians and gay men did not constitute a valid social group deserving of attention. So Peter Tatchell[6] and others, through the pages of the gay press, encouraged a letter-writing campaign to put pressure on Channel 4. In May 1985, ten Labour MPs joined in, sending a letter which urged the channel to produce a new series which 'as well as meeting the needs of the lesbian and gay community ... could also potentially have a far broader appeal and educative function in relation to the heterosexual population'.[7]

Then, in the Autumn of 1985, a research project – *Gays and Broadcasting* – recruited volunteers to monitor a week's output of British TV and radio. The findings were published in February 1986 as a report which concluded that lesbians and gay men were unacknowledged by the broadcasters except in wholly negative contexts.[8] The report didn't throw its weight behind the campaign for a series on Channel 4 so much as call for more and better representations on all the channels.

This was also the approach of the lesbian and gay group of the Campaign for Press and Broadcasting Freedom (of which I was a member) which, in June 1986, organised a conference specifically to formulate a series of demands upon Channel 4[9] which, some months later, we took to a meeting with the channel's then boss, Jeremy Isaacs, and most of the senior commissioning editors.[10] Our general presentation was against a single series – largely on the grounds that it risked ghettoisation – and in favour of more programming across the board.

In fact, Channel 4 was not unaware of the pressures upon it and had been broadcasting some programmes made by or featuring lesbians and gay men since at least 1985. Films such as Jan Oxenburg's 1973 short, *Home Movie*, and Derek Jarman's (homo)sexually explicit feature, *Sebastiane* (1976), were given a welcome airing. Indeed, the latter broadcast provoked considerable right-wing outrage.[11] The channel, however, weathered the storm and in September 1986, it launched *In the Pink*, an eight week season of lesbian and/ or gay films in the late night *Eleventh Hour* strand. Two months later, it followed up with a weekly documentary series, *Six of Hearts*, six quirky portraits of assorted gay 'characters'. Finally, to round off the year, the *Eleventh Hour* kicked off its four-week youth season, *Turn it Up*, with *Framed Youth: Revenge of the Teenage Perverts*, a documentary by the Lesbian and Gay Youth Video group.[12]

Early in 1987, Channel 4 broadcast another controversial feature film which it had itself part-financed. *My Beautiful Laundrette* (Stephen Frears, 1985), the archetypal *Film on Four*, married rainbow politics wish-fulfilment with neo-Thatcherite individualism, in the story of a rising young Asian entrepreneur who forms a sexual and business relationship with his one-time tormentor, a white youth with a fascistic past. Shortly after, the channel tried to play it for laughs with a sitcom set in a right-on, alternative café, *The Corner House*. Excruciatingly 'correct', each character a 'cause', it was an unfunny disaster which sank without trace.[13] Returning to first principles, Channel 4 rounded off the year with a second series of *In the Pink*.

For all this, somehow there was a feeling that Channel 4 wasn't doing enough. A lesbian and gay series, along the lines suggested by Peter Tatchell and his fellow letter-writers, seemed to have attained an almost iconic status – a kind of holy grail. Which is why when, in the autumn of 1988 the channel announced that it had finally decided to commission a full-blown lesbian and gay series, there was a tremendous sense of achievement and excitement.

ONCE UPON A TIME . . .

Roseanne: . . . OK, I'm just going to come out and tell you this, OK? Marla and Nancy are lesbians.

Bev: Of course they are! Any fool could see that. I guess I'm supposed to walk up and say, 'oh hello, you nice lesbians', hmm? Or something equally embarrassing and then everyone gets a good laugh at the expense of the stupid old lady. Sure they're lesbians! I'm a lesbian! You're a lesbian! We're all lesbians! I'm not falling for it, Roseanne. I'm not that old.

(Roseanne)

By the time *Out* came along, then, Channel 4 had established a distinct identity. Having realised its ambition to capture around 10 per cent of total viewing figures, it was clearly positioned as a minority channel: political, liberal, vaguely left of centre, community-oriented, experimental, even arty, and willing to tackle 'difficult' 'adult' themes, notably sex and sexuality. The channel thus ushered in a new and definitive tradition of programming from which *Out* sprang fully formed. This was equal opportunities TV; television made by a minority, for a minority on the minorities' channel. The concern was not necessarily with producing *good* television so much as the *right* television.

Caroline Spry, assistant commissioning editor for independent programmes at Channel 4, was assigned the task of overseeing *Out*'s transition from drawing board to small screen. As a result she became the channel's *de facto* commissioning editor for lesbian and gay programmes (but that's another story). On the eve of *Out on Tuesday*'s launch, Spry told *The Pink Paper* what she wanted from the new series and who she hoped would be tuning in. 'There is an identifiable gay culture with interests and issues quite separate from that of the dominant culture,' she said. 'We're not creating a gay ghetto. There's not an absolute division and I'd be very surprised, for example, if many of the items in the series didn't have an appeal for straight audiences' (*The Pink Paper*, 11 February 1989: 7). Meanwhile series producer Clare

Beavan outlined her plans for representing this 'identifiable gay culture'. 'We want', she told the *Guardian*, 'to show gay people not agreeing with each other: 'til now on TV, it's usually been "gays are like this," a homogenous group. This series will challenge the idea that there's one kind of gay person, politics or sensibility' (*Guardian*, 6 February 1989). Mandy Merck, the series editor, elaborated: 'We've tried to avoid victimology. These programmes are much more exuberant, cheeky and much less self-pitying than most TV programmes on gays have been' (*Guardian*, 6 February 1989).

So, as far as its creators were concerned, *Out* was very much a Channel 4 series. It was clearly supposed to be read as a positive, assertive representation of lesbians and gay men in all their cheeky, uncomplaining diversity. It would be different, alternative, yet with a strong cross-over potential; it would validate and affirm *us* without making *them* too uncomfortable.

Such narrative expectations were confirmed by the reception accorded the series in the lesbian and gay press. 'It's finally out!' cried Jonathan Sanders in his first review of the series for *Gay Times*, 'C4's long-mooted mag may be in the traditional 11pm ghetto but, unlike most of its previous efforts at lesbian and gay programming, *Out on Tuesday* is worth staying up for. Wise and witty, eloquent and eclectic, it splinters the monolithic TV image that usually represents us' (*Gay Times*, March 1989).

Six weeks into the first series, Peter Tatchell, writing in *Capital Gay* went even further over the top. 'Channel Four's lesbian and gay community programme, *Out on Tuesday*', he wrote, 'is a landmark in the history of television. As the world's first nationally televised series by and for lesbians and gay men, it represents a major breakthrough in terms of media access and visibility.' He concluded rather breathlessly: 'Congratulations and thanks to *everyone*, including *Capital Gay* and its readers, who helped make it possible' (*Capital Gay*, 24 March 1989). Interestingly, though six episodes had already been broadcast by the time his article appeared in print, Tatchell did not reveal what he thought of them. He seemed to be saying that the important thing was that the series was *there*; what it was *like* did not matter.

Whether this excitement was shared by the viewers is a matter of interpretation. The ratings for the first series averaged out at 1,045,000[14] viewers per episode, making *Out on Tuesday* the eighth most popular programme on Channel 4 each Tuesday. This viewing figure, in turn, represents approximately 2 per cent of the national viewing audience,[15] not particularly startling, but, then again not bad for a series broadcast on a weekday evening at 11pm on the minority channel. This generous view is underscored to some extent when you consider that ratings for the second series, though it was now broadcast at the earlier time of 9pm, dipped alarmingly to an average of 914,000[16] viewers per episode. Drastic measures were taken. Abseil Productions, the independent production company in overall charge of the series for the first two years, was quietly dropped and Channel 4, in the person of Caroline Spry, took a more hands-on approach.

The series was given a new image and a shorter name, it was moved to Wednesday nights and the channel took out weekly adverts in the lesbian and gay press during the run of the series, trailing forthcoming attractions. The third series responded to the treatment, attracting on average 983,700 viewers each week, not quite a return to the levels of the first. But the fourth series made up for that, soaring to an average of 1,181,000,[17] the best-ever average score; whereupon, of course, *Out* was axed.

THE LOOK OF *OUT:* ARE YOU SITTING COMFORTABLY?

> But need alone is not enough to set power free: there must be knowledge.
>
> (Ursula Le Guin 1979)

Perhaps the reason that the first two series went up and down so in the estimation of the viewing public – the series recorded both the highest and the lowest ratings for a single episode during this period[18] – was that *Out on Tuesday* gave off such conflicting and ambiguous signals. Abseil, the production company, was so named in recognition of the lesbians who abseiled from the public gallery onto the floor of the House of Lords in 1988 during the debate on Section 28 of the Local Government Bill (which forbade the 'intentional promotion of homosexuality' by local authorities and grant maintained schools and which became law shortly afterwards). Section 28, though in practice it changed little, was a symbolic gesture of great importance, the first measure intended to diminish the rights of homosexuals passed into British law in almost a hundred years. For the first two years, each episode of *Out on Tuesday* ended with a credit sequence which concluded with Abseil's animated corporate logo, the silhouetted image of a woman sliding down a rope. By aligning itself with this particular protest, Abseil seemed to be saying something about the new series: that it would be political, feminist, daring, risky and confrontational.

However, the opening credits sequence set a somewhat different scene. Against a swimmy blue and white background – like a raging sea or a sky smothered with rolling clouds – various images float across the screen as the theme tune starts up. A satiny-red heart flies by (romance?); a champagne cork pops (decadence? ejaculation?); a dove flies from a gilded cage as a soprano's voice soars on the soundtrack (liberation?); a black cat is picked up in a woman's arms and is put out of shot through a computer-generated catflap (cosy domesticity?); Martina Navratilova serves, a linesman cries 'out!' (coming out? role models?); a bare-chested hunk bursts from a cake (camp? sex?); the hunk puts his hand on his crotch (explicit sex?); but the camera zooms in teasingly on the rose tattoo on his forearm (no sex after all?); dissolve to a real rose whose petals blow away in the wind (the passage

222

of time? ageing?); enter a barbie doll holding a bow and arrow (Diana, the huntress?), a green fig leaf on its crotch (Eve?), the fig leaf flies off revealing the word 'OUT' (??) which also spins off to fill the screen as the words 'ON TUESDAY' appear, running vertically at its side.

This juxtaposition of unconnected images, each more or less ambiguous, suggested trendy post-modernism. This would be a pick 'n' mix show, a jumble of bits and pieces which would not attempt to construct some totalising world-view but would allow the viewer almost complete freedom to make whatever meanings they wanted (or even none at all). It wasn't to be taken too seriously; rather it would be light, bright and frothy. Or as Mandy Merck put it: 'exuberant, cheeky and much less self-pitying' than the average gay show.

The transition from *Out on Tuesday* to *Out* implied a slimming-down, a tighter focus, a more direct message. The new opening sequence reflected this. It starts with an old-fashioned one-armed bandit, standing alone in the dark. Then lights!, music! and the gleaming metal machine crackles to life, the new theme tune featuring the distinctive tones of an organ, suggestive of old-time movie houses, or fairgrounds. The handle of the fruit machine cranks down by itself and the counters whirl. As the fruits whizz by, the tumblers click into their final position from left to right: W–9–4. Or, Wednesday, 9pm, Channel 4. The music reaches a crescendo and triangular, golden tokens, each stamped with the word OUT, spew forth. The message of this sequence is less ambiguous than that of the earlier one – and a lot more self-congratulatory. It was saying: you've hit the jackpot, your luck is in, you (we?)'ve made it!

Not everything about *Out*'s self-presentation was confused; it was always quite clear about its own genre. *Out* proclaimed itself a magazine programme and most critics seemed to agree. But it wasn't. Typically, television magazines are like many of their counterparts on the news-stands: crammed with lots of short, unrelated items which don't, on the whole, require a lot of attention. In addition, TV magazines are invariably introduced by a regular presenter or presenters, usually from a specially dressed studio, maybe in front of an audience, and they're often broadcast live. In virtually every respect, *Out* differed significantly from these specifications.

There was no *Out* studio (and no studio audience) though series two and series three each devoted all or most of an entire episode to a studio discussion (outing and coming out in programme ten of series two; love and marriage in the second programme of the third series). The entire series was pre-recorded, the individual items commissioned months ahead. For the first two series, as *Out on Tuesday*, each episode was introduced by a presenter, but a different one each time 'to avoid', as Mandy Merck put it, 'having a presenter who's meant to stand for all gays, male and female, young and old, black and white' (*Guardian*, 6 February 1989). For the last two years this idea was dispensed with altogether. Furthermore, very few of the items were reporter-led, that is to say introduced and narrated by an individual who

30 The changing face of lesbian and gay TV. From trendy post-modernism . . .
(*Out on Tuesday*, © Channel 4/Abseil Productions)

31 . . . to establishment triumphalism (*Out*, © Alfalfa Entertainments)

would appear on screen from time to time, either addressing the viewer directly or visibly conducting interviews. Beatrix Campbell's report from the former USSR in the second series (*Sex 121 and the Gulag*) and Chris Woods' report on the Obscene Publications Squad of the Metropolitan Police (*Blue Boys*) in the last series are almost the only examples of this kind of item.

As a result, *Out* was a somewhat impersonal series. Almost every other long-running TV series – even the News – relies upon familiar characters to create a rapport with the viewer, to establish a point of identification and involvement and to generate viewer loyalty. Perhaps because *Out* took its viewers for granted, it was so ready to dispense with such niceties. Yet, if *Out* had no face, it none the less had a distinctive voice. The series evolved a house-style which essentially consisted of a series of interviews cut together in such a way as to remove all traces of the interviewer. It is a fairly common TV technique – interviews are conducted so that the interviewees respond by including the question (or prompt) in their response. Thus we never hear the interviewer asking the questions, there are no two-shots (also known as 'noddy shots' as the interviewer is often seen nodding her/his head in exaggerated accord) to show us the questioner reacting to the interviewee's words of wisdom, no actual dialogue. Instead, dialogue is fashioned by cutting back and forth between interviewees as they give their apparently unprompted, unmediated thoughts. In other words, *Out* tended to serve up an almost endless sequence of talking heads which, as I will suggest later, made for disconcerting viewing.

But what really set *Out* apart from the traditional TV magazine and gave it its distinctive feel was the length of each item and, as a consequence, the number of items per episode. Overall, including repeats and not counting the *Out Bulletins* (see p.227), 90 separate items were broadcast under the *Out* banner, an average of around 2.25 items per episode. But this global average, it must be pointed out, is misleading. The first series contained 26 items spread over eight episodes, an average of 3.25 per episode; the second 25 spread over ten episodes, an average of 2.5 per episode. There were no repeats in the first two years. In the third and fourth years, the averages fell significantly. Series three had 20 items, including one repeat, making an average per episode of 2. The final series comprised 19 items of which four were repeats: an average of 1.9 items per episode.

So even in the first series, the average item was more than a quarter of a television hour long.[19] By the end, items were over half a TV hour long. This was very noticeable from the armchair without recourse to a stopwatch and calculator. *Out* simply didn't view like a magazine programme.

Television has developed a style of presentation which is in keeping with the ways in which it is watched. Television is a domestic medium, quite literally part of the furniture. It is so much a part of the vast majority of homes in Britain and the USA that its presence is noted less than its absence ('there's nothing on the box tonight'). Although some people do still treat it in much the same way they would a good book – putting it on only for the purpose of watching a specific programme and then turning it off again – most of us switch it on for no particular reason and leave it on, regardless of whether we are at any one moment watching it. And when we do, we'll most likely flick from channel to channel as the fancy takes us. In other words, as John Ellis puts it, 'TV's regime of vision is less intense than cinema's; it is a regime of the glance rather than the gaze' (Ellis 1992: 137).

However, although the bulk of television's output can be characterised in this way, Ellis reminds us that 'TV can, at particular moments, adopt a form that corresponds much more closely to that of cinema' (Ellis 1992: 116). He points to the transmission of feature films made originally for the cinema and to such phenomena as the 'made-for-TV film' and the 'one-off play'. He concludes, 'It is significant that these productions are increasingly cinema films in all but name; they rely upon cinematic techniques, and they invite the audiences to try to view them with the attitudes and concentration that is more characteristic of cinema. For broadcast TV, the culturally respectable is increasingly equated with the cinematic' (Ellis 1992: 116). *Out* leaned heavily in this direction with a number of episodes consisting of one long piece, taking up most of the hour, accompanied by one or two short supporting items. Half a dozen episodes were given over entirely to just one 'film'.[20] In this way, *Out* seemed to be positioning itself not as popular or trash TV but more as serious, respectable, highbrow television. It was therefore more interested in *issues* than in news, gossip or current affairs.

And what issues did *Out* have on its mind? It is perhaps unfair to summarise nearly 40 hours of television in a few lines; but, on the other hand, it would be foolish to assume that the reader watched all 38 episodes. So, in an attempt to convey something of the flavour of the series, allowing for overlap, and picking some examples (this is not an exhaustive list), I will take the plunge and roughly categorise *Out*'s items as follows:

Personal and Identity Politics (representing around a quarter of the total items)
- *I Am What I Am* – lesbians and the politics of sex; inter-racial relationships; lesbians and gay men and disability; Jewish lesbians and gay men; South Asian lesbians and gay men; luppies (lesbian yuppies); working-class lesbians; gay skinheads; lesbian and gay Tories; bisexuality; older lesbians; Australian aborigines; outing and coming out; marriage.

Lesbian and Gay Rights (also about a quarter of the total)
- *I Will Survive* – homophobia in Hollywood; the Obscene Publications Squad, gay porn and s/m; AIDS activism in the US; immigration law; British law on homosexuality; adoption and fostering; housing; AIDS drugs trials.
- *Abroad is Another Country (or is it?)* – lesbian and gay life in India,

the US, New Zealand, the former USSR, Poland, post-revolutionary Nicaragua, Eire, Greece and the EC as a whole.

Lifestyle (closer to a third of the total)
- *'Lesbians and Gays and . . .'* – pets, sport (twice in the same episode), opera, coupledom, hair and dinner parties
- *Read the Book! See the Film!* – lesbians and gay men as producers and consumers of cultural artefacts. There were book plugs and/or celebrity profiles (lesbian detective novels; guns 'n' lipstick lesbian thriller, *After Dolores*; artist Alan de Souza; poet and novelist, Suniti Namjoshi; photographer, Rotimi Fani-Kayode; singer/musician, Rita Lynch) along with items on music (punk, disco, country), cinema (lesbian and gay roles played by straights, lesbian and gay actors forced to play straight), TV (lesbian and gay characters on British and US TV), and the British film industry ('white flannel' films such as *Maurice* (James Ivory, 1987) and *Another Country* (Marek Kaniev- ska, 1984) and made-for-TV movies).

History (less than a tenth of the total items but, since these were among the longer items, more than a tenth of the total screen time)
- *The Good Old Gays (or not)* – scenes from lesbian and gay life from 1910 to the present day including, British lesbian and gay life before law reform and since, lesbians and gay men in the Second World War, sexuality in Germany 1910–45.

Fiction (also less than a tenth of the total)
- Six short films, five directed by gay men (*Looking for Langston, Alfalfa, Fasten Your Seatbelts, Flames of Passion, Caught Looking*), one by a lesbian (*Rosebud*).

News
- In the fourth and last series, an additional element was introduced – the topical news report or *Out Bulletin*. Each bulletin was less than five minutes long and did not appear in every episode so they cannot be said to constitute a definitive feature of the series as a whole.

It is not immediately obvious, from this admittedly partial list,[21] to which televisual genre *Out* belonged. It cannot accurately be called a current affairs series. Investigative reporting, with one exception (*Blue Boys*), was absent and political enquiry was mainly carried out at one remove – either in other countries or in the past. The cumulative, subliminal impression this created was of a lesbian and gay Britain which has reached some sunny upland from which it can look *back* at past struggles and difficulties overcome or *down* upon other societies less fortunate than our own. Thus, *Out* seemed to say, the main problems left for British lesbians and gay men to deal with are concerned less with pressures from *without* (such as the law) and more with difficulties from *within*; those arising from the relationships between ourselves (for example, racism, sexual politics, body culture and bisexuality). Certainly the balance of items reflected this bias which is why I think Sally Munt is closer to the mark when she characterises *Out* as an 'anthropological/lifestyle series' ('Sex and Sexuality', in Hargreave 1992: 119).

In essence, *Out's* characteristic appearance was that of the *educational programme*. Raymond Williams defined such programmes as 'Education as seeing':

> there are many examples of what can best be called educational practice: the language 'lesson' which is simply half an hour in a foreign town, listening to people speak while we watch them doing things and meeting each other, in a whole social context; the natural history or geography 'lesson' which is in effect a televisual visit to some place where we can see as if for ourselves; *the presentation of some other way of life*, or some work process, or some social condition.
>
> (Williams 1975: 74; my italics)

But, as I shall argue, the way of life being presented was not so much a *real* way of life as an *ideal* one. In order to understand why that might have been so, I need first to answer the question: who was being educated and why?[22]

IDENTITY PARADE

Sophia: Dorothy, I never understood why your brother liked to wear women's clothes – unless he was queer.
Blanche: Sophia, people don't say queer any more. They say gay.
Sophia: They say gay if a guy can sing the entire score of *Gigi*. But a six foot three, two hundred pound married man with kids who likes to dress up as Dorothy Lamour, I think you have to go with queer.

(The Golden Girls)

The answer to the question, 'who was *Out* for?' seems clear enough. Despite Caroline Spry's professed desire for the series to 'cross-over', the audience for *Out* was almost overwhelmingly, if not exclusively, lesbian and gay. It is impossible to prove this as the official ratings are not compiled according to sexuality; however, several factors would seem to support this contention.

To begin with, *Out* expended most of its promotional energy wooing viewers with a decided lesbian or gay identity and lifestyle. As has already been mentioned, Channel 4 advertised the series in the lesbian and gay press. However, the channel ran very few trailers for the series on screen, suggesting both that it neither wanted to draw attention to what it was doing lest it attract criticism nor that it had much interest in courting – converting? – a straight audience. Besides, although *Out* was not uncomfortable viewing for heterosexuals in that it was not addressed out at them (challenging) but inwards at

32 The Village People school of gay sociology: putting working-class 'types' on a sexual pedestal (*Skin Complex*, *Out*, programme 6, series 4, an item which examined the fascination some gay men have with the image of the skinhead; photograph by Nicky Johnston)

us (questioning), it was, all the same, not easy for them actually to tune in. To do so might imply that they were in some way *identifying* with us; to do so regularly would risk *becoming* us. It would be like a straight person going regularly to a lesbian or gay club; questions would be asked, not least by the individual concerned: 'Why am I here?'

For similar reasons, anyone who was unsure of their sexuality – assuming they were even aware of the programme's existence, given how little publicity it attracted outside lesbian and gay circles – would be unlikely to have formed a significant proportion of *Out*'s viewing public. In the case of young people still living at home with their parents, to watch *Out* would mostly have been out of the question, it being hard in such circumstances to watch television furtively without the possibility of discovery. Its timing – after the 9 o'clock watershed – further limited *Out*'s reach, marking it as adult television.[23]

So was *Out* queer? In the sense of odd, undoubtedly. But in the postmodern, 1990s sense where queer speaks for the fluiditiy of sexual barriers and encourages a promiscuity of sexual identification, clearly not. *Out* was not TV for those yet to come out, or for those who refuse labels, but TV for the already out. Indeed, its very choice of name reveals its utter lack of interest in those without a definite and decided identity. The word 'out' is a code word understood as such only by those who apply it to themselves. As the title for a lesbian and gay series, it was only calling to those in the know, to the converted. While taking a break from writing this, I switched on the TV to see a trailer for a new series called *Out and About*. It turned out to be a holiday programme.

Out, in short, was not aimed at people who are sexually attracted to people of the same sex, an attraction which they may indulge physically from time to time. For as Jeffrey Weeks has remarked, 'One difficulty is that not all homosexually inclined people want to identify their minority status – or even see themselves as homosexual' (Weeks 1989: 196) No, *Out* was for people whose sexual proclivities have led them to adopt a lifestyle and an identity as either a lesbian or gay man and who, further, are assumed to have a great deal in common because of this shared identity.

Sally Munt has argued that *Out* succeeded in 'affirming existing lesbian and gay identities, and it has also appealed to the "sympathetic straight" viewer in "explaining" homosexuality in terms more of its own making. . . . Its lifestyle magazine format has utilised an anthropological viewpoint which serves a crucial function of reflecting a subculture back on itself, enhancing a group identity and the sense of a community of viewers' ('Sex and Sexuality', in Hargreave 1992: 119). But has it? What is this 'group identity', how real this sense of 'community', and can television bolster either?

LESBIAN *AND* GAY?

. . . no thing can have two true names . . .
(Ursula Le Guin, *A Wizard of Earthsea*)

The first thing people notice about us is not that we're gay, it's what sex we are.
(Della Grace, photographer, *Sex Wars*: *Out*, 12 August 1992)

Lesbian and gay identities – never mind lesbian and gay communities – are very recent inventions. Or, as many others have noted, such identities are fictions, albeit necessary ones, which provide a flag of convenience under which sexual minorities have been able to rally and fight for political rights. They also serve a function in providing a beacon to those who are in the dark about their sexuality and a frame of reference for those who are attempting to break from the straitjacket of heterosexual expectations. But there is always a problem in seeking to go beyond that to some kind of essential lesbian or gay identity, a danger of swapping one straitjacket for another. For one thing, if there is any kind of identifiable lesbian or gay sensibility, then it is surely an outsider's view of the world which is not exactly what *Out* was about. More than this, though, as Chantal Mouffe has remarked in another context, 'The problem is the very idea of the unitary subject. . . . [W]e are in fact always multiple and contradictory subjects, inhabitants of a diversity of communities . . . constructed by a variety of discourses and precariously and temporarily sutured at the intersection of those subject positions' (cited in Allen 1992: 337). Not only do the words lesbian and gay mean different things to different people, or even different things to the same person at different times, but the stitching which binds lesbians to gay men is very loose and apt to unpick itself.

Wisely, *Out* refused to face up to this until almost the last minute. For when, in programme eight of the last series in an item entitled *Sex Wars* (12 August 1992), it dared to ask lesbians and gay men what they thought of each other, the limits of 'lesbian and gay unity' were cruelly exposed. To be meaningful, to be other than a ritual incantation, *lesbianandgay* needs a common cause other than same sex attraction to hold it together . In 1987 and 1988 in Britain, Section 28 provided such a cause, bringing lesbians and gay men onto the streets together in numbers never seen before.[24] In the US, AIDS activism helped forge a political alliance between lesbians and gay men which, in the 1992 Presidential campaign, raised more than a million dollars for Bill Clinton and which, in November of that year, was apparently translated into an almost solid block of anti-Bush votes. However, even the gravity of the AIDS crisis cannot disguise the fragility of lesbian and gay unity.

Take these two contributions to *Sex Wars*. Natasha Gray, a US journalist (introduced earlier in the item as author of an article entitled, 'Bored with the Boys: Cracks in the Queer Coalition') suggested that lesbians experienced 'an envy that comes when you've been working in AIDS activism a long time that's very difficult to talk about and feels very shameful. It's very like the feeling that a well child has when a sick sibling is getting all the attention. At some point, you're gonna have to ask, "well what about *me*?"' Then we cut to writer and AIDS activist, Simon Watney, who earlier on had said that lesbians who demanded safer sex material from AIDS organisations were 'trivialising' gay men's experience of the AIDS epidemic. He now said: 'Gay men can't, shouldn't, I think, expect all lesbians automatically to understand everything about AIDS, that we've been living through. But by the same token, lesbians shouldn't, I think, imagine that gay men can necessarily always have the time to be, as it were, you know, assuaging tender vulnerabilities and sensibilities and drying tears, as it were.'

This contestation of experiences and feelings as either exclusively *lesbian* or exclusively *gay* property is all too depressingly familiar. What, essentially, both Gray and Watney were saying is this: whenever *they* get anything, *we* lose out. Many of *Out*'s viewers seemed to think the same way. Catherine Treasure, previewing the third series in *Capital Gay* wrote: 'As to the lesbian/gay balance, there *is* more lesbian material now, but it doesn't seem to matter how the balance is altered; women will always complain there is too much about men and men will never see enough men.' She then quoted Caroline Spry's give-away remark: 'They phone up to complain and I sometimes wonder if we've been watching the same programme' (*Capital Gay*, 28 June 1991).

In the end, it is precisely television's openness to a multiplicity of readings that thwarted *Out*'s attempts to position and direct its viewers. As Sandy Flitterman-Lewis argues,

> The television viewer is a *distracted* viewer, one whose varied and intermittent attention calls for more complex and dispersed forms of identification. . . . Television's fractured viewing situation explodes the singular vision of the cinema, offering instead numerous partial identifications, not with characters but with 'views'. The desire to see and the desire to know, wedded in the cinema by the spectator's guided gaze, find themselves liberated in TV and intensified because of this. Voyeuristic pleasure is not bound to a single object, but circulates in a constant exchange.
>
> ('Psychoanalysis, Film and Television', in Allen 1992: 219)

Likewise, Justin Lewis has argued that television facilitates a variety of readings which may diverge from or be in outright opposition to the 'preferred' readings of the programme-makers and broadcasters. In his study of *The Cosby Show* he demonstrates how the social positioning of the Huxtables, the black family around which this popular US sit-com revolves, in the affluent, upper middle class, allows white viewers to forget that they are looking at black people. Many white viewers testified to the fact that they considered the Huxtables not to be a black family but a 'regular American family'. However, for black viewers, the blackness of the Huxtables is a lot of the reason why they are watching the show in the first place; it is not something that ever ceases to register. Black viewers of *The Cosby Show*, in other words, see successful black people who are just like them only richer. Thus the show doesn't so much transmit positive images of black people to white society – still less challenge racism – as reinforce the myth of the 'American dream' – that anyone can make it, no matter where they come from.

Something like this operated with *Out*. There is what I have already characterised as the activist view of *Out* as a mark of the onward, upward progress of campaigns for lesbian and gay rights; it is another 'right' we have won. Jonathan Sanders made a related point at the end of the first series. Although, as we have seen, he acclaimed the series when it first appeared, he soon lost much of his enthusiasm but none the less retained the hope that it would do 'us' some good: 'Frustratingly directionless, garrulous and superficial at times, the series was also hearteningly eclectic, cheeky and concerned at others. Above all, it was *there*, and I hope its presence may have persuaded straight programme-makers to stop excluding or marginalising us' (*Gay Times*, May 1989: 63).

Catherine Treasure has identified a yearning quality to the series, a desperate striving to be liked. 'During the earlier series I often asked myself whether the programmes were for "us" or for "them",' she wrote; 'to what extent were they trying to show straight viewers that we were quite nice really?' (*Capital Gay*, 28 June 1991: 18) Indeed, the first series, for example, did include items which seemed designed to do for lesbians and gay men what *The Cosby Show* seems to have done for black people in the US: to suggest that with a little bit of effort we can make it, that perhaps we are already making it. Thus there were items on luppies, lesbian yuppies with six-figure salaries, opera queens, the society magazine *Tatler*, and lesbian and gay members of the Conservative Party.

Contrast this with the fact that there was only one half-hour item in four years – *Working Class Dykes from Hell* (series 4, programme 2, 1 July 1992) – which specifically set out to give a voice to the unfashionable working classes. Even then, the approach chosen was peculiar – working-class lesbians were presented as loners, representatives of a minority in a largely middle-class world, suffering the sleights of the snobbish and mannered majority. Thus class became nothing more than an issue of personal identity. There was no sense of the existence of communities of working-class dykes or queens; of pubs, clubs or other social networks of working-class perverts. Instead, this 'equal opportunities' view of class ended up reinforcing the hoary old stereotype that homosexuality is a middle-class affectation. As an unwitting metaphor for the class perspective of *Out* itself, however, it was spot-on.

For in *Out*'s sanitised and rather bourgeois world, there was no place for lesbian pimps, prostitutes or strippers, nor for rent boys, escorts or masseurs. Sex clubs, back rooms, bar room brawls, domestic violence, none of these belonged. *Out* was clean and bright, not down and dirty. Here men didn't go cruising at dead of night on windswept heaths and commons, nor did they look for sex in public toilets[25] – until the very last episode, that is, when Channel 4 obviously felt it could afford to let *Out* be a little naughty without in any way besmirching the reputation of the series as a whole.

So, at the special late time of 10.45pm, programme ten of the last series presented two films – Cheryl Farthing's *Rosebud* and Constantine Giannaris' *Caught Looking* – each of which contained explicit depictions of sexual desire. Of all thirty-eight episodes of *Out*, this was the only one which attracted the censure of the Broadcasting Standards Council (BSC), the statutory body which draws up guidelines on the portrayal of sex and violence on television. Responding to a viewer's complaint, the BSC judged that *Rosebud* was acceptable (effectively because it 'only' featured vanilla lesbian sex) but that *Caught Looking* overstepped the mark (notably in a scene set in a public toilet where a man spies on two other men having sex in the next cubicle).

It says a lot that *Out* caused remarkably little offence, creating almost no public controversy.[26] The BSC's 1992 Annual Review (*Sex and Sexuality in*

Broadcasting) is quite revealing in this respect. Chapter 4 of the review is entitled 'The Special Concerns of the Homosexual' wherein a sample group of lesbians and gay men from around the country[27] were asked what they wanted from television. The answer, broadly speaking, was more lesbian and gay characters in soap operas and dramas and less censorship of sexual matters. A larger sample, representative of all viewers, was also surveyed for their opinions on homosexual representations on television: 61 per cent of this group were opposed to banning 'programmes and films about gays and lesbians', but 71 per cent agreed that they 'would find it embarrassing to watch homosexual sex scenes with some of the people with whom I watch TV' and 58 per cent agreed that 'homosexuals should be able to see their own programmes.'

Interesting, that: 'their *own* programmes.' Because, of course, *Out* was just that. Unusually for a television series, it was cut off from the general flow. As Raymond Williams has argued convincingly (Williams 1975: 86–96), television programming operates less as a succession of discrete programmes, individual texts which can be isolated and studied as one may a film or a novel, but more as a continuous, open-ended flow of images and sounds. *Out*, however, was an enclosed narrative; a ring-fenced portion of the schedule. We were left talking to ourselves.

LOOKING AT OURSELVES

Ah! Je ris de me voir si belle en ce miroir.
(Ah! How I laugh to see how lovely I look in this mirror.)
('The Jewel Song' from Gounod's *Faust*)

Almost every other essay in this book has concentrated on the efforts of the lesbian or gay spectator to find in popular culture some indirect representation of themselves. With *Out*, however, there was no need to look between the lines; for there we were in the foreground for all to see. I want to suggest here that this is not necessarily a pleasurable or comfortable experience for the lesbian or gay viewer.

Watching a film in a cinema has been likened to dreaming. Sitting in a hushed, darkened auditorium, confined to one's seat in a way which minimises motor activity and heightens sensory awareness, one watches with rapt attention the giant images projected onto a screen many feet away. Some writers have gone so far as to suggest that the cinema spectator almost regresses to a state of infancy during a movie.[28]

The experience of watching television, however, is altogether different. Sandy Flitterman-Lewis points to the fact that:

A film is always distanced from us in time (whatever we see on the screen has always already occurred at a time when we weren't there), whereas television, with its capacity to record and display images

234

33 History as a little slap on the face (*Storm In a Teacup, Out*, programme 3, series 4, an item which excavated the history of London's lesbian and gay clubland from the 1920s to the 1970s; photograph by Tricia de Courcy Ling)

simultaneously with our viewing, offers a quality of *presentness*, of 'here and now' as distinct from cinema's 'there and then'. It is television's peculiar form of presentness – its implicit claim to be live – that founds the impression of immediacy.

('Psychoanalysis, Film and Television', in Allen 1992: 218)

This sense of immediacy is heightened by TV's mode of address. For, as John Ellis argues, 'direct address is recognised as a powerful effect of TV' (Ellis 1992: 134). The effect is particularly noticeable in news and current affairs programmes where everyone – interviewees, interviewers, reporters and newsreaders alike – makes it plain that they know they are being watched. They therefore appear to be talking directly to you, the viewer, from a box which is much closer-to than the cinema screen. In addition, Ellis notes, 'Close-ups are regularly used in TV, to a much greater extent than in cinema. They even have their own generic name: talking heads. The effect is very different from the cinema close-up. Whereas the cinema close-up accentuates the difference between screen-figure and any attainable human figure by drastically increasing its size, the broadcast TV close-up produces a face that approximates to normal size. Instead of an effect of distance and unattainability, the TV close-up generates an equality and even intimacy' (Ellis 1992: 131).

Television is also watched in small groups or by people on their own. The relationship of viewer to the figures on screen is thus more like one-to-many than cinema's many-to-few. In other words, there tend to be more people on the TV screen than in front of it; in the cinema, it is usually the other way around. To watch TV for any length of time is to be outnumbered.

The experience of watching *Out*, then, could be a disconcerting one. Every week a procession of talking heads trooped through the living room, talking (thanks to the apparent absence of an interviewer) directly to the viewer. Instead of the dreamworld of the cinema, this was real. It was like being transported to a consciousness-raising session or to the classroom. This wasn't entirely *Out*'s fault. To identify oneself as a member of a social minority, as the *Out* viewer was required to do, brings with it a certain self-conscious feeling of responsibility. It is that wish not to 'let the side down', that feeling that individual lesbians or gay men to some extent speak for all lesbians and gay men. In other words, the people on *Out* weren't *other* people; in a sense, they were me.[29]

Out had very strong memories of TV's previous attempts to picture homosexuality – programmes which took the (assumed) straight viewer on a whistle-stop tour of the 'twilight world of the homosexual', a place peopled by back-lit, silhouetted victims. As Mandy Merck had made it clear at the outset, it was this 'victimology' that *Out* was determined to avoid. But in banishing the twilight world, it created an alternative mythical universe – a land of heroes and heroines, plucky survivors all. Thus *Out* viewers could be forgiven for feeling that they had something to live up to. It is precisely this aspect of *Out* – this self-consciousness both on the part of the 'performers' and the 'spectators' – that prevented it – most of the time – from being a relaxed and pleasurable experience.

BREAKING CAMP

Dorothy: There's one other thing . . .
Sophia: . . . Jean thinks she's in love with Rose.
Blanche: [Horrified] Rose? Jean has the hots for Rose?
   (Dorothy and Sophia nod.)
Blanche: I do not believe it! *I do not believe it!*
Dorothy: I was pretty surprised myself.
Blanche: Well I'll bet! To think Jean would prefer Rose over me! That's
   ridiculous!

(The Golden Girls)

That *Out* embodied a kind of realism is not all that surprising for Channel 4 appears to have a problem with camp. According to John Dugdale,[30] when *Out* was replaced in 1993 with a hastily assembled season of films and documentaries, there was disagreement about its title: 'Channel 4's forthcoming fortnight of gay and lesbian films', he wrote, 'was originally called Summer Camp; after vigorous internal discussion, it now answers to the meaningless phrase, Summer's Out.'[31]

'Camp', argues Mark Finch in his discussion of the gay appeal of the classic 1980s US soap opera, *Dynasty*, 'is what the liberal gay discourse/modern gay movement represses' (Finch 1986: 80).[32] Finch shows how the camp discourse in *Dynasty* constantly disrupts and usurps any attempt at delineating a liberal discourse on homosexuality. Realism, rationality and balance are constantly threatened by camp which is why it was largely absent from *Out*. Camp is unruly and cannot easily be contained; as Finch points out, camp may not always be radical but it is never serious.

It is *Out*'s tragedy that it took itself too seriously. For in the end, it was only a television programme; and even in those terms, not a particularly successful one. It must have seemed a good idea at the time when, in 1991, Channel 4 scheduled *The Golden Girls*[33] to follow directly after *Out*. A programme generally accepted to be a camp classic and a queer favourite was probably thought of as the ideal choice, giving us a good laugh after an hour of 'heavy' viewing. So throughout the third and fourth series, *Out* played the part of warm-up act for the Miami matrons. During the summers of 1991 and 1992, every Wednesday at 10pm, Channel 4 gained an extra two-and-a-half to three million viewers as the ratings jumped from around one million to close on four million. By the end, it was just plain cruel.

Those extra viewers can't all have been heterosexual, surely? So what did

The Golden Girls have that *Out* didn't? Humour, obviously, since *Golden Girls* is a sit-com, and camp humour at that. But that wasn't all, as *Out* itself suggested when it tried to pin down the special appeal of *Golden Girls* for the lesbian or gay viewer. In an item entitled *Cruising the Channels* (programme 8, series 1), gay screen writer Howard Schuman offered this opinion: 'The appeal of *Golden Girls* for many homosexual men and women is that while it's not *literally* about a homosexual group of people, it has an affinity to the kinds of situations and communities that a lot of us find ourselves in.' Later, actress Betty White, who plays the part of Rose in *Golden Girls*, made a similar point: 'I think if we courted that kind of audience [a lesbian and gay audience], we wouldn't get them. It would be dishonest – we would be trying for something that suddenly goes away when you try too hard for it. By just going straightforwardly along with what we're doing, it's wonderful if we can pick up along the way, pick up a following.' In other words, *Golden Girls* was aware that its humour had a particular resonance for those of a camp inclination but it wasn't about to be so crude as to say so out loud. It was like the flirtatious person, full of sly come-ons, who would be horrified, just appalled, if anyone were so mistaken as to misread the signals, cut the crap and say, 'let's fuck'.

Thus, *Golden Girls* essentially adopted the age-old strategy, seen elsewhere in this book, of being simultaneously knowing and innocent. The lesbian or gay viewer can feel a special thrill by catching meanings that largely elude a heterosexual viewer. It is what lesbians and gay men are used to from popular culture – and, perhaps, is what we have become too comfortable with. *Out*'s directness, in contrast with the oblique approach of *Golden Girls*, was admirable but, regrettably, it wasn't half as much fun.

HAPPY ENDINGS

Out was not unaware of its role as a spinner of yarns, that it was telling us stories about our lives. The very last episode of the last series ended with an on-screen message which made this only too clear: 'There are at least 5 million lesbian and gay stories in this country. These have been only some of them . . .'[34] Presumably, this figure is based on the calculation, after Kinsey, that 10 per cent of the adult population have had sex with someone of their own sex. However, to claim this 10 per cent as either 'lesbian' or 'gay' is pure myth-making.

In more ways than one, *Out* was telling a fairy story.[35] The story was: we are everywhere and everybody. The moral was supposed to be: 'This time we're going to make it, after all.' But, just as that proto-yuppie, Mary Richards,[36] fumbled her main chance every week in the title sequence of *The Mary Tyler Moore Show*, dropping her hat feebly at her feet when she meant to fling it exuberantly into the air, *Out* didn't convince in its role as arriviste. The place it occupied in the schedule, far from being a bridgehead from which lesbians and gay men would move on to conquer the commanding heights of British broadcasting, became in fact a black hole into which every programme idea even remotely concerned with homosexuality disappeared. Besides, for a minority to make it on Channel 4 doesn't really count – that's what the channel is *for*.

And so we're back to where we started – with Channel 4, the puppet-master. In Sarah Kozloff's view, broadcasting networks act like *super-narrators*. 'Because they are the narrators of the outermost frame, these strange storytellers are in the position of the utmost power and knowledge. They sit outside and above all the embedded narratives, unaffected by them. And it is through their sufferance that all the other texts are brought to us: they can interrupt, delay, or pre-empt the other texts at will' ('Narrative Theory', in Allen 1992: 94). *Out* could not quite escape the story of Channel 4, a supernarrative which framed and contained any wider meanings the series strained to realise. I have often wondered what *Out* would look like if re-broadcast in another slot or even on another channel. I suspect it would become, as James Hay suggests, ' a different narrative . . . recoded and renarrated' ('Afterword', in Allen 1992: 359). Many of *Out*'s items have played successfully at lesbian and gay film festivals around the world where members of the audience have been heard to remark: 'You British are so lucky. We don't have anything like that on TV.' Nor – quite – do we.

Channel 4's big idea was that one series could give lesbians and gay men *everything* that we might want – and that what we most wanted was to see ourselves. Channel 4 seemed to think it could tell the *whole* story – but this was only one version. It may have been a story worth telling, but I worry that *Out* has colonised the televisual imagination in a way which is not entirely healthy. *Out* is in danger of becoming a generic convention – *this* is how you make lesbian and gay TV. When BBC2, which hitherto had cornered the market in quality lesbian and gay drama (*Oranges Are Not the Only Fruit*, *Portrait of a Marriage*, *The Lost Language of Cranes*), decided to have a stab at documentaries, it gave us *Saturday Night Out*, an entire evening of *Out* clones.[37] It is as if nothing came before *Out* – at least nothing of value – and that nothing can come after it.[38] Well, all good stories must come to an end; and as far as *Out* is concerned, it is perhaps time we closed the book.

A DIFFERENT *OUT*-LOOK?

'Identity', insists Jane Gallop, 'must be continually assumed and immediately called into question' (quoted in Weeks 1989: 185). It's a difficult trick to pull off and *Out* could only manage the assumption part. It assumed an identity for itself and for us, its viewers, and stuck to it. It held up a kind of Lacanian mirror in which was reflected an image of a whole, unified lesbian and gay entity. But whereas the Lacanian mirror stage marks the beginning of the formation of individual subjectivity, *Out* marked the end.

In its way, *Out* certainly helped us to see ourselves more clearly – or at least differently – but that is not, perhaps, what we want from television. For just as the Lacanian child is delighted to see an ideal image of itself for the first time, it is also dimly aware that its own experience of life is rather less wholesome than the perfection of its reflected ego ideal. In *Out*'s world, self-doubt and self-loathing were banished; the solitary struggle with a burgeoning and troublesome sexuality was but a distant memory. All that remained was to enjoy being lesbian and gay (in the 'correct' way, needless to say). In part, *Out* was asking us to be better people, thereby coming dangerously close to reducing the problems we face down to one: self-esteem. In so doing, it let the world at large off the hook.

The very first episode of *Out on Tuesday* seemed to promise something else. In an item entitled, *Advertisements for Ourselves*, the advertising agency, Saatchi & Saatchi, was asked to devise a campaign which would seek to 'promote homosexuality'. It was smart idea – and topical too. Section 28 had been enacted only months before. At the same time, the choice of Saatchi & Saatchi was not coincidental; for they were the agency employed by the Conservative Party in the 1979, 1983 and 1987 general elections. In the latter election, they had devised a poster for the Tories which suggested that the opposition Labour Party was 'promoting' homosexuality in British schools. None the less, they accepted their new brief with relish.

When Richard Myers, the agency's Creative Group Head, was asked how they set about it, he said: 'I think we needed to initially start to knock heterosexuality – find what the bad things are about heterosexuality – in order to come at it from a slightly different angle.' His colleague, copywriter Adam Kean elaborated: 'I mean, say you take a Rolls Royce. Because the perception is that that is the greatest car in the world of one kind, you can then sell it on envy. You can say, "wouldn't you like to have one of these?", because you've already done the first half of the argument – it's been done for you – that it's a great car. You haven't done the first half of the argument with homosexuality – you haven't convinced people that it's a wonderful thing – so you can't then say to people, "wouldn't you like to be like us?".'

Out had a crack at saying just that – but on its own it wasn't enough. What it forgot to ask for the rest of the series was the question dreamed up by Saatchi & Saatchi as their campaign slogan: 'What's so great about being straight?'

APPENDIX

Out on Tuesday/Out:
programme contents, 1989–92

Title	Subject	Series	Prog. No.	TX Date	Rating '000s
Advertisements for Ourselves	Ad agency asked to 'promote homosexuality'	1	1	14/2/89	1,137
	Presenter: Paul Gambaccini (Radio DJ)				
Outtake	AIDS/gay sex				
Playing Gay	Hollywood, Lesbians and gays in				
Crimes of Passion	Detective novel, Lesbian	1	2	21/2/89	850
	Presenter: Beatrix Campbell (Writer/Journalist)				
Out in Africa	South Africa, Lesbians and gay men in				
Outtake	Theatre performance preview				
Video Postcard	USA (Janice Perry, comedienne)				
Alfalfa	A gay alphabet (short film)	1	3	28/2/89	843
Disco's Revenge	Disco, Lesbian and gay roots of				
	Presenter: Richard Coles (Musician)				
Outtake	Blasphemy laws				
Untitled	Immigration laws				
Desire	Germany 1910–45	1	4	7/3/89	1,294
	Presenter: Ian McKellen (Actor)				
Fasten Your Seatbelts	Hollywood (short film)	1	5	14/3/89	1,115
In Pursuit of Prince/ss Charming	Coupledom				
	Presenters: Parker & Klein (Comedians)				
Outtake	Adoption & fostering				
Video Postcard	New Zealand				
Looking for Langston	Black gay identity (film)	1	6	21/3/89	476
Outtake	News: Section 28 in action in Essex				
Video Postcard	India				
	Presenter: Audre Lorde (Writer/Poet)				
After Stonewall	History, UK 1967–89	1	7	28/3/89	1,068
Empire of the Senses	Inter-racial lesbian/gay relationships				
	Presenter: Ritu (Club DJ)				
Lust and Liberation	Sexual politics, Lesbians and				
Cruising the Channels	TV, Lesbians and gay men on				
Girls in Boy Bars	Fag hags or female friends?	1	8	8/4/89	1,576
	Presenter: Julian Clary (Comedian)				

Title	Subject	Series	Prog. No.	TX Date	Rating '000s
Social insecurity	News: HIV/AIDS welfare benefits	2	1	6/3/90	954
Video Postcard	Reno, Nevada – gay rodeo				
Luppies	Lesbian yuppies				
Opera	Opera, Lesbians and gay men and				
Right Wing, Right Off, Right Hons, Right?	Tories, Lesbian and gay				
	Presenter: Beatrix Campbell				
Tatler	Society magazine	2	2	13/3/90	915
A Matter of Life and Death	Bereavement (AIDS)				
	Presenter: Richard Coles				
Prisoners of Conscience	Amnesty International				
Walk on Bi	Bisexuality				
Alan de Souza	Profile (artist)	2	3	20/3/90	797
	Presenter: Hufty (Comedian)				
Punk	Punk, Lesbian and gay roots of				
Sex 121 and the Gulag	USSR, Lesbians and gay in				
After Dolores	Book plug: lesbian thriller novel	2	4	27/3/90	753
	Presenter: Storme Weber (Poet)				
AIDS Medical	News: HIV/AIDS drug trials				
Polskiseks	Poland, Lesbians and gays in				
Flesh and Paper	Profile: Suniti Namjoshi (poet/novelist)	2	5	3/4/90	660
	Presenter: Simon Callow (Actor)				
White Flannel	Film/TV genre: Oxbridge/upper class gays	2	6	10/4/90	1,319
Women Like Us	Personal history (older lesbians)				
	Presenter: Pat Arrowsmith (Writer and Peace Campaigner)	2	7	17/4/90	1,100
Comix	Comic strips				
	Presenter: Julian Clary				
Let's Not Pretend	Parenting, Lesbian and gay				
Untitled	Tabloid press and homosexuality				
Untitled	Church of England and homosexuality				
A Song for Europe	Europe (EC), Age of Consent across	2	8	24/4/90	564
David Norris	Eire, Gay Senator's law reform campaign in				
	Presenter: Katie Boyle (TV Presenter/Personality)				
Greek Love and Sapphic Sophistication	Greece, Lesbians and gay in/and				

Title	Description	Series	Prog	Date	Figure
Comrades in Arms	Armed forces, Lesbians and gay men in (WW2)	2	9	1/5/90	1,017
		Presenter: Lily Savage (Drag Comic)			
Untitled	Outing/coming out (studio discussion)	2	10	8/5/90	1,065
		Presenter: Simon Fanshawe (Comedian)			
Huntley & Palmers	British law on homosexuality	3	1	26/6/91	1,057
Stand On Your Man	Country music, Lesbians and				
Love and Marriage	Marriage, Lesbians and gay men and	3	2	3/7/91	997
Pride '91	Pride parade and festival footage				
Personal Best	Sport/body culture, Lesbians, gay men and	3	3	10/7/91	1,226
Running Gay	Sport, Lesbians and gay men and				
Talking Hairs	Hair, Lesbians and gay men and				
Sex and the Sandinistas	Nicaragua, Lesbians and gay men in	3	4	17/7/91	1,014
This Is Dedicated	Bereavement				
Women Like Us	Repeat (see prog. 2, series 6, 10/4/90)	3	5	24/7/91	1,290
Double Trouble	Australian aborigines, Lesbian and gay	3	6	31/7/91	747
Women Like That	Update (see 10/4/90 and 24/7/91)				
Over Our Dead Bodies	AIDS activism (USA)	3	7	7/8/91	500
Khush	South Asian experience/racism	3	8	14/8/91	1,100
The Battle of Tuntenhaus	Radical gay/drag squat in East Berlin				
Flames of Passion	Film (gay reworking of _Brief Encounter_)	3	9	21/8/91	1,014
We've Been Framed	Cinema, Lesbians and				
Guess Who's Coming To Dinner?	Food/dinner parties, Lesbians, gay men and	3	10	28/8/91	892
Heavy Petting	Pets, Lesbians and gay men and their				
Home Sweet Homo	Housing, Lesbians and gay men and				
Blue Boys	Obscene Publications Squad and gay porn	4	1	24/6/92	1,426
Call Me Your Girlfriend	Profile: Rita Lynch (singer/musician)				
Homophobia in Hollywood	Hollywood, Homophobia in	4	2	1/7/92	1,292
Working-Class Dykes From Hell	Class, Lesbians and				
Storm in a Teacup	History (London, 1920s–70s)	4	3	8/7/92	1,567
Double the Trouble, Twice the Fun	Disability, Lesbians and gay men and (drama/documentary)	4	4	15/7/92	1,092
Stand On Your Man	Repeat (see prog. 1, series 3, 26/6/91)				

Title	Subject	Series	Prog. No.	TX Date	Rating '000s
Oy Gay!	Jewish lesbians and gay men	4	5	22/7/92	1,206
Rage and Desire	Profile: Rotimi Fani-Kayode (photographer)				
Gay Sera Sera	Homosexuality, causes of	4	6	29/7/92	1,236
Skin Complex	Skinheads, gay and straight				
A Matter of Life and Death	Repeat (see prog. 2, series 2, 13/3/90)	4	7	5/8/92	761
Actions Speak Louder	Deaf lesbians and gay men				
Sex Wars	Lesbians and gay men talk about each other	4	8	12/8/92	963
Talking Hairs	Repeat (see prog. 3, series 3, 10/7/91)				
The Battle of Tuntenhaus	Repeat (see prog. 8, series 3, 14/8/91)	4	9	17/8/92	977
Update on Tuntenhaus	Update (see above)				
Caught Looking	Virtual reality gay voyeurism (film)	4	10	26/8/92	1,287
Rosebud	Lesbian coming out story (film)				

Average ratings
Series 1:   1,045,000
Series 2:   914,000
Series 3:   983,700
Series 4:   1,181,000

Sources: **Title**, **Subject** and **Transmission Date** – details from Channel 4's Independent Film and Video Department; Fulcrum Productions; Alfalfa Entertainments; *TV Times*; *Radio Times*; author's and author's flatmates video collections. Descriptions under **Subject** are author's own. **Ratings** – Broadcasters' Audience Research Board (BARB) Weekly TV Audience Network Reports.

NOTES

1 Before proceeding any further, I feel I should place one small but salient fact in the public domain. I – like many others – submitted programme ideas to *Out on Tuesday* in its early days. However, none of my ideas were taken up and I didn't work on the series at any time. Make of that what you will.

2 From here on in, I shall refer to the whole series as *Out* unless there is a specific need to distinguish between one year's series and another's.

3 It *was* renewed in 1994, with a six-part series starting in August. The formula was much the same as before.

4 The 1990 Broadcasting Act replaced the IBA as regulator of independent broadcasting with the Independent Television Commission (ITC). At the same time, Channel 4 was cut loose from the ITC, becoming a fully independent company and selling its own advertising 'with only a limited protection if its income falls below a certain point' (*ITC Factfile, 1993*). Given that this change occurred in the teeth of a deep economic recession with its attendant decline in overall advertising revenues for all TV stations, Channel 4 entered the 1990s facing the need to make financial cutbacks.

5 See note 12 below.

6 Peter Tatchell, writer, lesbian and gay rights activist and prominent member of direct action group, *OutRage!*, shot to national prominence in 1981 when he was selected by the Bermondsey Labour Party to be their candidate in the next general election – the sitting Labour MP, Bob Mellish, a senior member of the party's national establishment, having announced his intention to retire. The choice of Tatchell was denounced in Parliament by the leader of the Labour Party, Michael Foot, after Tatchell had written his support for 'extra-parliamentary action' to unseat Mrs Thatcher's then highly unpopular government. Mellish was so incensed that Tatchell had been chosen as his successor that he decided to resign ahead of the general election, thus forcing a by-election in Bermondsey on 24 February 1983. One of Labour's safest seats, it was lost to the Liberal Party on one of the largest swings ever recorded (and the victorious candidate, Simon Hughes, has held the seat ever since). The campaign was one of the nastiest in recent memory with Tatchell being subjected to tremendous personal vilification in the pages of the tabloid press and on the streets. His sexuality, though he refused at the time to say whether or not he was gay, became one of the central subjects of attention and he received a number of death threats. For a full account see Peter Tatchell, *The Battle for Bermondsey*, Heretic Press/GMP, London, 1983.

7 Quoted in Tatchell, op. cit.

8 Philip Adams, Mark Finch and Lorraine Trenchard, *Are We Being Served?*, London, 1986.

9 *Screened Out* was held at the South Bank Polytechnic in London on a sweltering day. It was attended by several hundred people, including Caroline Spry, assistant commissioning editor at Channel 4 for independent programmes and later *Out* supremo, and Mandy Merck, then editor of *Screen* magazine, later to become series editor for *Out on Tuesday*, 1989–90.

10 Caroline Spry was present at this meeting too.

11 In 1986, Conservative MP, Winston Churchill, citing the broadcast of *Sebastiane*, sought to introduce legislation which would have extended the provisions of the Obscene Publications Act to television. Although this was in the heyday of the far right, his proposal was defeated in Parliament.

12 *Framed Youth* was made in 1983 with the aid of C4 development money and in 1984 it won the Grierson Award for Best Documentary. It still makes good viewing and the list of those involved in its production makes for interesting

reading. Among others were: pop star Jimmy Somerville, then making his TV singing debut; fellow-Communard, musician and later *Out on Tuesday* presenter, Richard Coles; film-maker, Isaac Julien (*Looking for Langston* was shown in the 1990 season); Constantine Giannaris, another film-maker whose *Caught Looking* was shown in the last-ever *Out* and who directed a number of other items for the series; Nicola Field, researcher on *Desire* and *Comrades in Arms*; and film-maker, Jeff Cole. Giannaris, Field and Cole – together with Clare Hodson – went on, again with the aid of C4 development money, to set up Converse Pictures, Britain's first lesbian and gay film and video production company (now defunct).

13 The channel tried out a number of other sit-coms in 1987, none of which was successful enough to warrant a second series. *Never Say Die* (starring Irene Handl) was set among a group of elderly people living in sheltered accommodation. *The Refuge* was based in the flat of a woman who, following a messy divorce, had transformed it into a women's refuge.

14 *Source*: Broadcasters' Audience Research Board (BARB) Weekly TV Audience Network Reports.

15 *Source*: Broadcasters' Audience Research Board (BARB) Weekly TV Audience Network Reports.

16 *Source*: Broadcasters' Audience Research Board (BARB) Weekly TV Audience Network Reports.

17 *Source*: Broadcasters' Audience Research Board (BARB) Weekly TV Audience Network Reports.

18 In the first year in fact. The low point came with the sixth programme of series one which won only 476,000 viewers while the high point came a mere two episodes later, the last programme of the series winning 1,576,000 viewers (*Source*: BARB).

19 The television hour is always less than a full hour because of the links between programmes – continuity announcements and trailers. On commercial television, the hour is even shorter because of advert breaks. As a rule of thumb, a commercial TV hour is 52 minutes long.

20 Three of which – *Desire*, *Comrades In Arms* and *Over Our Dead Bodies* – were made by film-maker, Stuart Marshall. The other hour-long pieces were *A Storm in a Teacup* and *Women Like Us* (shown twice).

21 For complete list of *Out* programmes, see Appendix.

22 In a particularly bizarre way, *Out* attempted to explain homosexuality to its fellow-homosexuals by making it appear strange. I even began to wonder about myself. Some time in 1991, as the third series was being put together, a producer from *Out* rang me at home to ask if I would be prepared to be interviewed for an item they were planning about hair (which was duly broadcast as *Talking Hairs*). 'Because', she explained, 'a lot of gay men have short hair and you have short hair and we thought you could explain why.' I made my excuses and hung up.

23 In August 1993, Radio 1 (or 1 FM as it is now likes to be known), the BBC's youth-oriented national radio station, launched a weekly lesbian and gay magazine, *Loud & Proud*, which seems more likely to get round this problem. Broadcast at 8.30pm, it is tailor-made for furtive, teenage bedroom listening.

24 Another reason, perhaps, why the first producers of *Out on Tuesday* consciously allied themselves with this protest.

25 See note 28 below.

26 Of course, Channel 4's Duty Office took many calls complaining that 'this sort of thing' should not be allowed on television. But the tabloid press, the clean-up TV campaigners and the political/moral right in general more or less ignored the series, perhaps believing that to create controversy would merely boost *Out*'s

ratings or perhaps because there was so little to which they could seriously object (or maybe they simply didn't watch it because it bored them silly . . .).

27 'It was considered important to recruit homosexuals who were not considered "activists" and might not normally be asked for their opinions, as homosexuals, about matters' (Hargreave 1992: 130).

28 See particularly the seminal work by Christian Metz, 'The Imaginary Signifier', in *Screen* 16, no.2, 1975, pp.14–76, reprinted in a collection of essays by Metz, *The Imaginary Spectator: Psychoanalysis and the Cinema*, Indiana University Press, Bloomington, 1982, pp.3–87. See also Sandy Flitterman-Lewis's discussion of Metz's theories and their relevance to television in Allen, 1992, pp.203–39.

29 The attitude of *Out* towards cottaging is instructive in this regard. By ignoring the subject altogether – except for the scene referred to above in *Caught Looking* – *Out* implicitly conveyed its disapproval. Every year, thousands of men are prosecuted for a variety of sexual offences, real or imagined by the police, which take place in or around public toilets. These 'offences' have no victim except the 'perpetrator' who, in addition to the sentence he receives (usually a fine; sometimes a spell in prison), is forever branded a sex offender, his 'crime' categorised alongside rape. Many men lose their jobs as a result; some, unable to bear the shame, kill themselves. This would seem to be a prime issue for a programme interested in lesbian and gay rights. But, in fact, it was passed over for fear of its effect upon the reputation of the series. I remember an argument I had some years ago with a prominent gay rights campaigner who strongly believed that the police were right to want to close cottages down. 'Cottaging is the Achilles' heel of the gay movement,' he contended. 'It makes straight people think that we're all dirty cocksuckers.' My reply was: 'But we are, we are.'

30 John Dugdale, 'The Season Ticket', *Guardian*, 31 July 1993.

31 Since this was written, the channel has had what seems to be a change of heart. Christmas 1993 was notable for three programmes aimed at lesbians and gay men: *RuPaul's Christmas Ball*, *Camp Christmas* and *The Alternative Queen's Speech*. They caused a national outcry; which is to say, certain tabloid newspapers created a fuss and several bored Conservative backbench MPs put their names to an Early Day Motion in the House of Commons, a traditional way for frustrated politicians to grab the headlines. Interestingly, this minor and rather silly 'storm' prompted Channel 4's Director of Programmes, John Willis, to pen a half page *apologia* in the *Guardian* ('Seasonal cheer but not for bigots', 20 December 1993). Complaining of the 'typhoon of bigotry and homophobia' unleashed by the announcement of the three programmes, he gave the game away somewhat when he plaintively pointed out: 'Channel 4 is transmitting 250 hours of programmes over Christmas. Just 2½ hours will be gay and lesbian programming.'

32 Page references for the Finch article refer to the version reprinted in *The Media Reader* (see References).

33 *The Golden Girls*, in case you don't know, is a US sit-com set in Miami where four women share a house; three are over 50, one is over 80, and their husbands are either dead or divorced. Dorothy is a blunt-speaking teacher; Sophia, her mother, is even more outspoken since a stroke left her unable to stop herself saying whatever is on her mind; Rose, from a Norwegian farming community in Minnesota, is the archetypal dumb blonde with a heart of gold; and Blanche, whose house they occupy, is the classic Southern belle (and slut).

34 *Out*, programme 10, series 4, 20 August 1992.

35 Hence programme five of the first series (14 March 1989), which looked at coupledom, was entitled *In Pursuit of Prince/ss Charming*.

36 . . . and possibly the first female TV character to think that 'this time' she was going to 'make it after all'.

37 The evening in question was 16 November 1991. The similarity to *Out* – including the adoption of *that* word – was not coincidental. The production team included many of those involved in *Out on Tuesday* – ultimately rejected by C4, they thereby enjoyed a kind of revenge.
38 Researcher Stephen Bourne, by curating at the National Film Theatre two seasons of lesbian and gay programmes trawled from the television archives, some dating back to the 1960s, reminds us that this ain't necessarily so.

REFERENCES

Allen, Robert C. (ed.), (1992) *Channels of Discourse Reassembled – Television and Contemporary Criticism*, London: Routledge.
Altman, Dennis *et al.* (1989) *Which Homosexuality?*, London: Gay Men's Press.
Blanchard, Simon and Morley, David (1982) *What's This Channel Fo/ᵘr?*, London: Comedia.
de Lauretis, Teresa (ed.) (1991) *Queer Theory – Lesbian and Gay Sexualities*, vol.3, no.2 of *Differences – A Journal of Feminist Cultural Studies*, Bloomington: Indiana University Press.
Dyer, Richard (1990) *Now You See It*, London: Routledge.
Ellis, John (1992) *Visible Fictions*, London: Routledge.
Finch, Mark (1986) 'Sex and Address in *Dynasty*', *Screen*, vol.27, no.6, November–December 1986, reprinted in Manuel Alvarado and John O. Thompson (eds) (1990) *The Media Reader*, BFI Publishing (page numbers cited in the text refer to the reprint).
Gamman, Lorraine and Marshment, Margaret (eds) (1988) *The Female Gaze*, London: The Women's Press.
Geraghty, Christine (1991) *Women and Soap Opera*, Oxford: Polity Press.
Grosz, Elizabeth (1990) *Jacques Lacan – A Feminist Introduction*, London: Routledge.
Hargreave, Andrea Millwood (1991) *Taste and Decency in Broadcasting* (Annual Review of the Broadcasting Standards Council, 1991), London: John Libbey.
Hargreave, Andrea Millwood (1992) *Sex and Sexuality in Broadcasting* (Annual Review of the Broadcasting Standards Council, 1992), London: John Libbey.
Le Guin, Ursula K. (1979) *A Wizard of Earthsea* in *The Earthsea Trilogy*, Harmondsworth: Penguin Books.
Lewis, Justin (1991) *The Ideological Octopus – An Exploration of Television and its Audience*, London: Routledge.
Merck, Mandy (1993) *Perversions – Deviant Readings*, London: Virago.
Weeks, Jeffrey (1989) *Sexuality and its Discontents*, London: Routledge.
Williams, Raymond (1975) *Television – Technology and Cultural Form*, London: Routledge.

INDEX